THE MARSHALL CAVENDISH ILLUSTRATED ENCYCLOPEDIA OF
WORLD WAR II

Volume 5

An objective, chronological and comprehensive history of the Second World War.

Authoritative text by
Lt. Colonel Eddy Bauer.

Consultant Editor
Brigadier General James L. Collins, Jr., U.S.A., Chief of Military History, Department of the Army.

Editor-in-Chief
Brigadier Peter Young, D.S.O., M.C., M.A., F.S.A. Formerly head of Military History Department at the Royal Military Academy, Sandhurst.

Marshall Cavendish New York & London

Editor-in-Chief Brigadier Peter
Young, D.S.O., M.C., M.A., F.S.A.
Reader's Guide Christopher Chant, M.A.
Index Richard Humble
Consultant Editor Correlli Barnett,
Fellow of Churchill College, Cambridge
Editorial Director Brian Innes
Illustrators Malcolm McGregor
Pierre Turner
Contributors Correlli Barnett, Brigadier Michael Calvert, Richard Humble,
Henry Shaw, Lt.-Col. Alan Shepperd, Martin Blumenson, Stanley L. Falk,
Jaques Nobécourt, Colonel Rémy, Brigadier General E. H. Simmons
U.S.M.C. (ret'd), Captain Donald Macintyre, Jonathan Martin, William
Fowler, Jenny Shaw, Dr. Frank Futrell, Lawson Nagel, Richard Storry,
John Major, Andrew Mollo.
Cover Design Tony Pollicino
Production Consultant Robert Paulley
Production Controller Patrick Holloway
Cover illustration The end of war;
Corporal C. Dunn, U.S.M.C., raises the U.S. Flag over Yokosuka Naval
Base in Japan.

Reference Edition Published 1981

Published by Marshall Cavendish Corporation
147 West Merrick Road, Freeport, N.Y. 11520
©Orbis Publishing Ltd. 1980, 1979, 1978, 1972
©1966 Jaspard Polus, Monaco

Printed in Great Britain by Jarrold and Sons Ltd.

Bound in Great Britain by Cambridge University Press

Cataloguing in Publication Data

Marshall Cavendish Encyclopedia of World War II.
1. World War, 1939-1945—Dictionaries
I. Young, Peter, 1915-
940.53'03'21   D740

ISBN 0-85685-948-6 (set)
ISBN 0-85685-953-2 (volume 5)

Picture Acknowledgements
Page 1121: I.W.M.; 1122: Musée de la Guerre Vincennes/Dorka, *Signal*/Nicole
Marchand; 1123: I.W.M.; 1124: H.M.S.O., H.M.S.O., H.M.S.O., Fox Photos;
1125: I.W.M.; 1126: Orbis; 1127: Popperfoto, I.W.M.; 1128: Fox Photos, Conway
Maritime Press; 1129: Bundesarchiv, Koblenz, Roger Viollet; 1130:
I.W.M./Camera Press, Popperfoto; 1131: Musée de la Guerre Vincennes/Dorka,
B.N. *Signal*/Foliot; 1132/1133: H. Le Masson; 1132: Keystone, I.W.M./Camera
Press, Black Star; 1134: I.W.M./Tweedy; 1135: Popperfoto; 1136: Musée de la
Guerre Vincennes/Dorka, Orbis/Alan Rees; 1137: Conway Maritime Press; 1138:
I.W.M./Camera Press; 1139: Keystone, I.W.M./Camera Press; 1140:
I.W.M./Camera Press, H. Le Masson; 1141: Fox Photos; 1142: Keystone,
I.W.M./Camera Press; 1143: H. Le Masson; 1144: Fox Photos; 1145: Fox Photos,
Conway Maritime Press, I.W.M.; 1146: National Maritime Museum; 1147:
Bulldog, New York, Orbis/Alan Rees; 1148: *Domenica del Corriere*/Dani; 1149:
I.W.M.; 1150: Orbis; 1151: H. Le Masson; 1152: Orbis; 1153: B.N. *Signal*/Dorka;
1154: U.S.I.S.; 1155: I.W.M., Magnum; 1156: Keystone; 1158: Keystone,
Signal/Nicole Marchand; 1159: B.N. *Signal*/Foliot; 1160: I.W.M./Camera Press;
1161: Holmès-Lebel; 1163: H. Le Masson, Aldo Fraccaroli, H. Le Masson; 1164:
Musée de la Guerre Vincennes/Dorka; 1165: I.W.M.; 1166: *Evening Standard*/D.
Low, *Toronto Star*, Toronto, *Punch*, London; 1167: Kukryniksi; 1168:
I.W.M./Camera Press, Popperfoto; 1169: B.N. *Signal*/Dorka, B.N. *Signal*/Foliot;
1170: Ullstein; 1171: Ullstein; 1172: Orbis/Alan Rees; 1173: U.S. Army; 1174:
I.W.M., Keystone; 1175: Keystone; 1176: U.S. Army; 1177: I.W.M.; 1178:
Signal; 1178/1179: Keystone; 1179: I.W.M., Holmès-Lebel/Key, Keystone; 1180:
Bibliothek für Zeitgeschichte, Konrad Adenauer, I.W.M./Tweedy; 1181:
Bundesarchiv, Koblenz, B.N. *Signal*/Foliot; 1182: Ullstein, Novosti, Novosti;
1183: Novosti; 1184: H. Le Masson; 1185: *Signal*/Nicole Marchand, Bundesar-
chiv, Koblenz, *Signal*/Nicole Marchand; 1186: Orbis; 1187: *Signal*/Nicole Mar-
chand; 1188: H. Le Masson, *Signal*/Nicole Marchand; 1189: Novosti; 1190: B.N.
Signal/Foliot, *Signal*; 1191: Novosti, Pictorial Press; 1192: Pictorial Press; 1193:
Pictorial Press, B.N. *Signal*/Foliot; 1194: Novosti, Pictorial Press; 1195: Novosti;
1196: Orbis/Alan Rees; 1197: Staatsbibliothek, Berlin; 1198: Novosti, Novosti,
Keystone, Novosti, Novosti, Novosti, Novosti, Novosti; 1199: Novosti; 1200: Ulls-
tein; 1201: Novosti; 1202: Ullstein; 1203: Novosti; 1204/1205: Orbis; 1206: U.S.
Army, Ullstein/Wolf und Trischler; 1207: Novosti, I.W.M./Tweedy; 1208:
Novosti; 1209: U.S. Army, Bundesarchiv, Koblenz; 1210/1211: Novosti; 1211:
Novosti; 1212: U.S. Army; 1213: U.S.I.S.; 1214: U.S. Army; 1214/1215: U.S. Ar-
my; 1215: Musée de la Guerre, Vincennes/Dorka, New York Public Library; 1216:
H. Le Masson; 1217: H. Le Masson, U.S. Army; 1218: H. Le Masson; 1219: *Daily
Mail*, London, *Simplicissimus*, Munich, *Kladderadatsch*, Berlin; 1220: U.S. Army;
1221: H. Le Masson; 1222: Popperfoto; 1223: Orbis/Alan Rees, H. Le Masson;
1224: Holmès-Lebel; 1225: U.S.I.S.; 1226/1227: U.S. Army; 1227:
I.W.M./Camera Press; 1228: Keystone; 1229: Orbis/Alan Rees, Keystone,
Keystone; 1230: Popperfoto, U.S.I.S.; 1230/1231: Keystone; 1232: U.S. Air Force;
1233: U.S.I.S., Keystone; 1234: U.S.I.S.; 1235: U.S.I.S.; 1236: U.S.I.S.,
Keystone; 1237: Keystone; 1238: Keystone; 1239: Keystone; 1240: Orbis; 1241:
Keystone; 1242: Keystone; 1242/1243: Keystone; 1244: H. Le
Masson, U.S.I.S.; 1245: U.S.I.S.; 1246/1247: U.S. Marine Corps; 1247: U.S.
Marine Corps; 1248: Keystone, Orbis/Alan Rees; 1249: Keystone; 1250: U.S.I.S.,
Keystone; 1251: Popperfoto, I.W.M.; 1252: U.S. Army/Nicole Marchand; 1253:
Keystone; 1254/1255: Orbis; 1255: U.S.I.S., Keystone, H.M.S.O.;
1258: Keystone; 1259: Keystone; 1260: U.S.I.S.; 1261: H.M.S.O., Keystone;
1262: U.S. Marine Corps; 1263: Keystone; 1264: Keystone; 1265: Keystone;
1266/1267: Orbis; 1268: Keystone; 1269: Keystone, U.S. Marine
Corps; 1271: Keystone, U.S. Marine Corps; 1272: Keystone; 1273: Keystone,
Popperfoto, Keystone; 1274: Keystone; 1275: I.W.M.; 1276: Camera Press,
U.S.I.S., Keystone, Associated Press; 1277: U.S.I.S., Keystone; 1278/1279:
I.W.M.; 1280: Robert Hunt Library; 1281: U.S. Army; 1282: Keystone; 1283:
U.S. Army; 1285: I.W.M./Tweedy; 1286: Sikorski Institute; 1287: Bapty; 1288:
Pictorial Press, Novosti; 1289: Pictorial Press, Novosti; 1290: Novosti; 1290/1291:
Novosti; 1291: Keystone, Pictorial Press, Popperfoto; 1292: Bapty; 1292/1293:
Bapty; 1293: Bapty; 1294: Sikorski Institute, Bapty; 1295: Bapty; 1296/1297: Bap-.
ty; 1298: Sikorski Institute, Bapty; 1299: Bapty; 1300: Bundesarchiv, Koblenz,
Mathilde Rieussec/Nicole Marchand; 1301: U.S.I.S.; 1302: Keystone; 1303:
Keystone; 1304: U.S.I.S., Keystone; 1305: Keystone, Keystone, Keystone,
U.S.I.S.; 1306: I.W.M./Tweedy; 1307: Keystone, U.S.I.S.; 1308: Keystone;
1310/1311: Keystone; 1312/1313: Keystone; 1313: Keystone, Keystone, U.S.I.S.;
1314: Keystone; 1315: Staatsbibliothek/Berlin; 1317: Richard Blin; 1318: Camera
Press; 1319: U.S.I.S., Documentation Française; 1320: Camera Press, Keystone;
1321: Novosti; 1322: H. Le Masson; 1323: A.P.N.; 1324: Dr. Paul Wolff und
Tritschler; 1325: A.P.N., H. Le Masson; 1326/1327: Camera Press; 1328/1329:
A.P.N.; 1329: I.W.M./Tweedy; 1330: H. Le Masson; 1331: H. Le Masson; 1332:
I.W.M./Tweedy, U.S.I.S., 1333: A.P.N.; 1334/1335 Dr. Paul Wolff und
Tritschler; 1335: Zec/*Daily Mail*, *Krokodil*, Moscow; 1336: A.P.N. 1337: Orbis;
1338: Keystone; 1339: Roger Viollet, A.P.N.; 1340: Keystone, Popperfoto; 1341:
Bundesarchiv, Koblenz; 1342: U.S.I.S.; 1343: Orbis; 1344: Keystone; 1345:
Keystone; 1346: Camera Press, Keystone, Popperfoto; 1347: Camera Press; 1348:
Musée de la Guerre, Vincennes/Dorka; 1349: Camera Press, Popperfoto, Camera
Press; 1350/1351: Camera Press; 1351: Popperfoto; 1352: Orbis/Alan Rees; 1353:
I.W.M./Tweedy; 1354: Roger Viollet; 1355: Novosti, 1356: Novosti; 1357:
Keystone; 1358/1359: Keystone; 1359: Novosti; 1360: Keystone; 1361: Keystone;
1362: U.S. Army; 1363: Musée de la Guerre, Vincennes /Dorka, I.W.M./Camera
Press; 1364: I.W.M./Camera Press; 1365: Keystone; 1366/1367: I.W.M./Camera
Press; 1368: Orbis/Alan Rees, Keystone; 1369: Keystone; 1370: U.P.I., Keystone;
1371: Keystone; 1372: I.W.M./Camera Press, I.W.M./Camera Press, Keystone;
1373: Keystone; 1374: Keystone; 1375: *Lustige Blätter*, Berlin, U.S. Army;
1376/1377: Imperial War Museum; 1378: Keystone; 1379: Keystone; 1380:
Keystone; 1381: Imperial War Museum; 1382: Imperial War Museum; 1383: Im-
perial War Museum, Keystone; 1384: U.S. Army; 1385: U.S.I.S.; 1386/1387:
Holmès-Lebel; 1387: Documentation Française; 1388: Keystone,
Documentation Française; 1390: Keystone; 1391: I.W.M./Camera Press; 1392:
U.S. Army, Imperial War Museum; 1393: Keystone, U.S.I.S.; 1394/1395: U.S.
Army; 1396: Keystone; 1397: U.S. Army; 1398/1399: I.W.M./Camera Press;
1399: Imperial War Museum; 1400: U.S. Army.

Contents of Volume Five

CONTENTS OF VOLUME FIVE

WORLD WAR II

CHAPTER 84

Dönitz takes over

BITS OF CARELESS TALK ARE PIECED TOGETHER BY THE ENEMY

Convoy sails for tonight — England

△ *The occasional failure to heed such warnings sometimes cost the Allies very dear: Convoy S.C. 118 suffered heavily at the beginning of February because a captive talked.*
▽ *The unmistakable sign of a blazing tanker – a thick, black column of smoke, drawing U-boats to the convoy like ants to honey.*

On the morning of December 31, 1942 an engagement took place in the Barents Sea which had no important strategic consequences, but should be mentioned as it provoked a crisis in the German high command. The occasion was the passage off the North Cape in Norway of convoy J.W. 51B; its 14 merchant ships and tankers were taking 2,040 trucks, 202 tanks, 87 fighters, 43 bombers, 20,120 tons of oil fuel, 12,650 tons of petrol, and 54,321 tons of various products to Murmansk.

This large convoy was escorted by a minesweeper, two trawlers, two corvettes, and six destroyers (shortly reduced to five, as one had to give up after its gyroscopic compass had broken down). The small escort was commanded by Captain Robert St. V. Sherbrooke, a direct descendant of the famous Admiral Jervis who became Lord St. Vincent after his victory in 1797 over the Spanish fleet. Under the command of Rear-Admiral R. L. Burnett, a veteran of the Arctic run, the cruisers *Sheffield* and *Jamaica*,

from Kolos were also sent in to help. Lastly, nine submarines (including the Polish *Sokol* and the Dutch *O 14*) provided a protective screen for the convoy as it passed the Norwegian coast. However, because of the winter ice floes the convoy J.W. 51B was sailing in single file about 240 miles from the German base at Altenfjord and its position had been signalled to Grand-Admiral Raeder by the *U-354* (Lieutenant Herschleb). Raeder acted very quickly on receiving this signal, as Hitler had recently made some extremely unflattering remarks about the Kriegsmarine. Therefore on that same evening of December 30, the pocket battleship *Lützow,* the heavy cruiser *Admiral Hipper,* and six destroyers put out to sea to intercept and destroy the convoy the following dawn. For this purpose, Vice-Admiral Kummetz, who was in command at sea, sent off his two major units in a pincer movement. But as he weighed anchor, he received a message from Admiral Kübler, the commander of the northern sector, which was clearly not

calculated to spur him on:

"Contrary to the operational order regarding contact against the enemy [you are] to use caution even against enemy of equal strength because it is undesirable for the cruisers to take any great risks."

Here Kübler was merely repeating the instructions sent to him by the chief of the *Oberkommando der Kriegsmarine* through Kiel and Admiral Carls. But Raeder was following a standing order promulgated by the Führer after the sinking of the *Bismarck,* and that evening Vice-Admiral Krancke, who had informed Hitler that the two ships and their escort vessels had sailed, wrote:

"The Führer emphasised that he wished to have all reports immediately since, as I well knew, he could not sleep a wink when ships were operating.

"I passed this message subsequently to the Operations Division of the Naval Staff, requesting that any information be telephoned immediately."

Hitler's anxiety was certainly peculiar, since he did not lose any sleep over the terrible fate of the 230,000 Germans encircled in the Stalingrad pocket.

On the next day, at about 0915, Kummetz, who had chosen *Hipper* as his flagship, came into contact with the rear of the convoy. But *Onslow* (Captain Sherbrooke) fearlessly attacked the Germans, followed by three other destroyers. Meanwhile a fifth destroyer, which was under enemy fire, covered the merchant ships withdrawing towards the south-east under a smokescreen. In spite of his impressive superiority in guns, the German admiral did not dare to launch a full-scale attack, as he was afraid that in the prevailing half-light he would not be able to defend himself against the torpedoes which the British would certainly use against him if he came within range. At 1019 the first 8-inch shell hit *Onslow;* three more hits followed, killing 14 men and wounding 33, including Captain Sherbrooke, who lost an eye and had his nose fractured, but continued leading his division.

Lützow appeared a little later and tried to attack the convoy from the rear whilst *Hipper* engaged the escort vessels; however, as visibility was poor and her commander too unenterprising, her six 11- and eight 6-inch guns were hardly fired once. At 1130, the balance of the engagement changed; Rear-Admiral Burnett, who had been alerted by Sherbrooke, appeared on the scene just at the

△ *The British destroyer* Orwell, *sister ship of Sherbrooke's* Onslow *and one of the four "O"-class destroyers involved in the Battle of the Barents Sea. The ships of this class were all launched in 1941 and 1942, and had a displacement of 1,540 tons, an armament of four 4.7-inch guns and eight 21-inch torpedo tubes, and a speed of 36.75 knots. The class was designed with quick conversion into minelayers in mind, and four of the eight eventually underwent the conversion.*

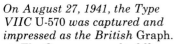

On August 27, 1941, the Type VIIC U-570 was captured and impressed as the British Graph.
△ The German crew huddle on the conning tower under the guns of one of the aircraft that kept them covered until a Royal Navy prize crew arrived.
▷ ▷ Naval officers arrive in a Carley float to take possession.
▷ The prize arrives in Britain.
▽ Graph (far right) alongside the depôt ship Forth in June 1943.

right time; as he was north of *Hipper*, he was able to take advantage of the light to the south while remaining in the darkness himself. Moreover *Sheffield* and *Jamaica*, which both remained unscathed, scored three hits on the German flagship, which retreated with a boiler room flooded with a mixture of sea water and oil fuel.

We shall not describe the game of blind man's buff that followed; during the engagement, the destroyer *Friedrich Eckholdt* was sunk by the British cruisers, which she took for *Lützow* and *Hipper*. *Lützow* fired 86 11-inch and 76 6-inch shells, but none of them scored a direct hit. When the darkness increased, Kummetz broke off contact and the convoy set off again, reaching Murmansk without further mishap. Apart from the damage done to *Onslow*, the convoy had also lost the minesweeper *Bramble* and the destroyer *Achates*, which had heroically sacrificed herself in protecting the front of the convoy.

Hitler's adverse opinion

At Rastenburg, Hitler was awaiting news of the engagement with feverish impatience. At 1145 a message from *U-354* was intercepted and this appeared to indicate a major success; then, a few minutes later, came Kummetz's order to abandon the operation. But on his return journey Kummetz quite properly observed radio silence, and when he had anchored in the Altenfjord a whole series of fortuitous incidents combined to delay the transmission of his report, with the result that at 1700 on January 1 the Führer had nothing but the British communiqué to hand concerning the previous day's engagement. He violently upbraided Admiral Krancke:

"He said that it was an unheard of impudence not to inform him; and that such behaviour and the entire action showed that the ships were utterly useless; that they were nothing but a breeding ground for revolution, idly lying about and lacking any desire to get into action.

"This meant the passing of the High Seas Fleet, he said, adding that it was now his irrevocable decision to do away with these useless ships. He would put the good personnel, the good weapons, and the armour plating to better use."

He received Kummetz's report a few hours later, but it failed to placate him. Far from it, for according to Krancke:

"There was another outburst of anger with special reference to the fact that the action had not been fought to the finish. This, said the Führer, was typical of German ships, just the opposite of the British, who, true to their tradition, fought to the bitter end.

"If an English commander behaved like that he would immediately be relieved of his command. The whole thing spelled the end of the German High Seas Fleet, he declared. I was to inform the Grand-Admiral immediately that he was to come to the Führer at once, so that he could be informed personally of this irrevocable decision."

He added: "I am not an obliging civilian, but the commander-in-chief of all the armed forces."

In this long diatribe, the argument that Vice-Admiral Kummetz had not pursued the engagement to its conclusion was perfectly correct. But it was hardly seemly for Krancke to call Hitler to account for the paralysing effect that his orders had had on the movements of the

▽ *Onslow arrives home after her ordeal. She had been hit by four 8-inch shells from* Hipper, *and these had knocked out her two forward guns, killed 14 of her crew, and severely wounded her commander, Captain Sherbrooke.*

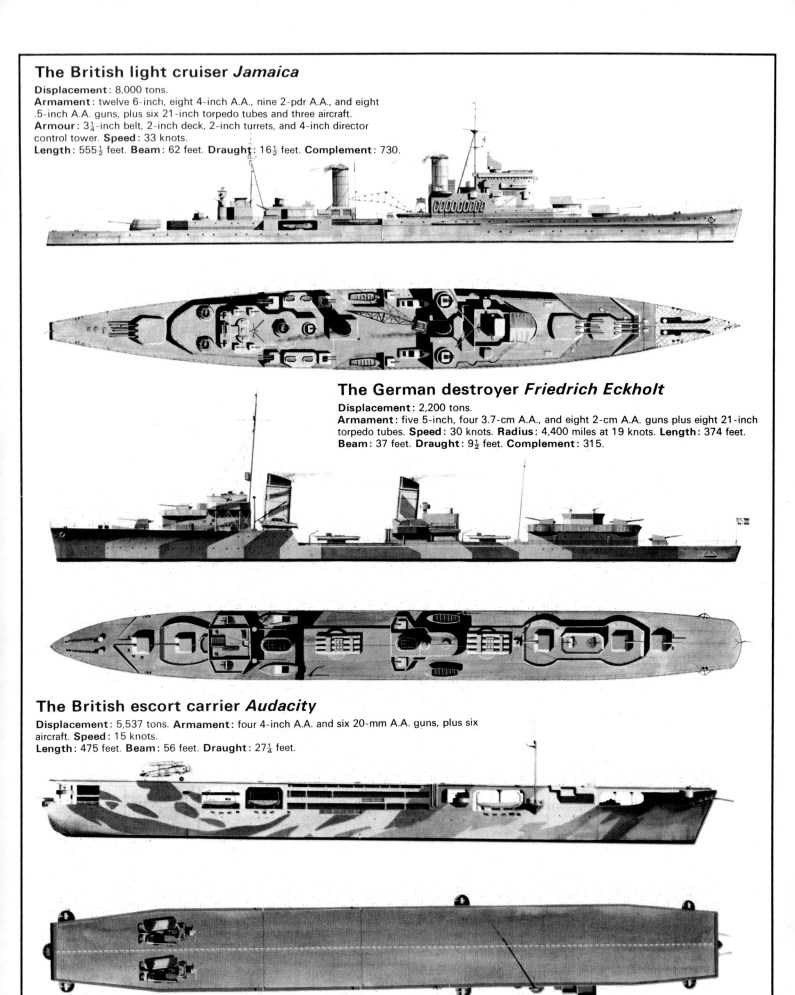

The British light cruiser *Jamaica*

Displacement: 8,000 tons.
Armament: twelve 6-inch, eight 4-inch A.A., nine 2-pdr A.A., and eight
.5-inch A.A. guns, plus six 21-inch torpedo tubes and three aircraft.
Armour: $3\frac{1}{4}$-inch belt, 2-inch deck, 2-inch turrets, and 4-inch director
control tower. **Speed**: 33 knots.
Length: $555\frac{1}{2}$ feet. **Beam**: 62 feet. **Draught**: $16\frac{1}{2}$ feet. **Complement**: 730.

The German destroyer *Friedrich Eckholt*

Displacement: 2,200 tons.
Armament: five 5-inch, four 3.7-cm A.A., and eight 2-cm A.A. guns plus eight 21-inch
torpedo tubes. **Speed**: 30 knots. **Radius**: 4,400 miles at 19 knots. **Length**: 374 feet.
Beam: 37 feet. **Draught**: $9\frac{1}{2}$ feet. **Complement**: 315.

The British escort carrier *Audacity*

Displacement: 5,537 tons. **Armament**: four 4-inch A.A. and six 20-mm A.A. guns, plus six
aircraft. **Speed**: 15 knots.
Length: 475 feet. **Beam**: 56 feet. **Draught**: $27\frac{1}{4}$ feet.

fleet on that occasion. Grand-Admiral Raeder arrived at Rastenburg on January 6, 1943 and was immediately faced with an indictment which began with the part played by the Royal Prussian Navy in the war over the Duchies of Schleswig and Holstein (1864) and went on for over 90 minutes; Hitler's tone was bitterly hostile throughout and he used arguments which, according to Raeder, were so incompetent that they seemed to show the influence of *Reichsmarschall* Hermann Göring.

"Battleships," raged Hitler, "to which he had always devoted his full attention and which had filled him with so much pride were no longer of the slightest use. They required the permanent protection of planes and small ships. In the event of an Allied attack on Norway, these planes would be more usefully employed against the invasion fleet than protecting our own fleet. Large battleships no longer served any purpose and therefore must be taken out of commission, after their guns had been removed. There was an urgent need for their guns on land."

Raeder was, however, authorised to submit to Hitler a memo expressing his objections. Feeling himself offended and discredited by Hitler's manner of address-

ing him, Raeder, who was over 66 years old, asked for and obtained his retirement. On January 30, 1943 he therefore gave up the high command he had held for 15 years and took over an honorary inspectorate-general. But before handing over the command of the German Navy to Admiral Dönitz, he regarded it as his duty to inform the Führer of the disagreeable but inevitable consequences of discarding the Grand Fleet.

The Royal Navy would obtain at no cost to themselves the equivalent of a great naval victory. But even more important, Hitler had overlooked the fact that the application of his "irrevocable decision" would perceptibly affect the balance of forces in the Mediterranean, the Indian Ocean, and the Pacific. In fact, as soon as the potential threat of the German major warships in the North Atlantic disappeared, the Admiralty, recovering full freedom of action, would profit by it and crush Japan.

Events showed that Raeder saw clearly. It is now known that Churchill was impatiently waiting for the time when the elimination of German surface warships would allow the Navy to appear in the Far East again; he was determined to

△ *The end of a tanker.*

Captain F. Walker, Britain's most prolific U-boat killer. He was born in 1896, and at the beginning of the war was head of the experimental department at the Navy's anti-submarine school. Late in 1941 he was given command of the sloop *Stork* and the 36th Group, with which he sank seven U-boats between December 1941 and June 1942. After a spell on shore, he returned to sea in the sloop *Starling* as commander of the famous 2nd Escort Group. He died on board his ship on July 9, 1944, and was buried at sea.

△ The ex-Admiralty yacht Enchantress *takes on supplies at sea. Note the lattice-work H/F D/F mast on the quarterdeck, which allowed German U-boat radio transmissions to be picked up and plotted.*

▽ The depth charge crew of an armed trawler in action. The desperate shortage of inshore escort craft meant that many hundreds of trawlers would be converted to undertake this vital war work.

restore British prestige there, impaired as it had been by the loss of Singapore; and Churchill doubtless had no wish to concede the monopoly of victory over Japan to the Americans, as he was well aware of the fanatical anti-colonialism displayed by Roosevelt. Hitler's whim, if it had been acted upon, would therefore have benefited only the Allies. This is shown by the fact that the Admiralty had to attach a force of battleships and aircraft-carriers to the Home

Fleet, thus giving it a wide margin of superiority in any circumstance. Thus when the powerful *Richelieu* had been refitted and sailed from Brooklyn dockyard, the Admiralty ensured that in November 1943 she joined the other ships at Scapa Flow.

Although he was a U-boat officer, the new Grand-Admiral deferred to the arguments of his predecessor, and Hitler was hardly in a position to thwart him immediately after his appointment.

In these circumstances, by a decision taken on February 18, 1943, the old battleships *Schlesien* and *Schleswig-Holstein,* which had been launched in 1906, the heavy cruiser *Admiral Hipper,* and the light cruisers *Köln* and *Leipzig* were merely declared obsolete, and the radical measures advocated by Hitler were not carried out. In fact, even this decision was only partially carried out; in autumn 1944 some of these units were to appear again in the Baltic to give gunfire support to Army Group "North" in its defence of the Kurland bridgehead.

Captain Sherbrooke had the exceptional distinction of winning the Victoria Cross for his exploit in the Barents Sea.

The *guerre de course*

"The balance sheet of profit and loss in mercantile tonnage was one of the most disturbing issues which confronted the Casablanca Conference when it opened on the 14th of January 1943. Until the U-boats were defeated the offensive strategy to which the Allies were committed could not succeed. Europe could never be invaded until the battle of the Atlantic had been won, and the latter purpose had therefore to be made a first charge on all Allied resources."

Thus Stephen Roskill, the Royal Navy's official historian, begins his chapter describing the decisive phase of this merciless struggle, and one can only confirm his judgement. There is no doubt that even after this battle had been won, the Western Allies would still have gained nothing until the European continent had been invaded, but if this first battle had been lost, all would have been lost with it.

When he took over the command of the German Navy, Karl Dönitz probably made no attempt to disown responsibility for the battle of the Atlantic; he knew what was at stake better than anyone else on the German side. Therefore the new commander-in-chief of U-boats, Rear-Admiral Godt, whom Dönitz himself selected, became even more closely subordinate to the latter's authority than the latter himself had previously been to Raeder. Consequently Dönitz was responsible for all the successes and defeats in this campaign, both before and after his promotion to the command of the Kriegsmarine, though one must make allowances for the fact that he was never free of Hitler's interference.

On January 1, 1943, the German Navy had 212 operational submarines, more than double its strength compared with the same date in 1942, when it had 91. In addition it had another 181 in the Baltic, either training or on trials. Moreover, the Third Reich's shipyards produced 23 or 24 submarines a month in 1943, in spite of Anglo-American bombing. However, as they lacked crews, the U-boats stayed longer and longer in the dockyards when they returned from their cruises; at the end of 1942 they averaged two months in dock to 40 days at sea.

At the beginning of 1943, in this decisive year, the 212 operational submarines

were distributed as follows:
Atlantic: 164
Mediterranean: 24
North Sea: 21
Black Sea: 3, moving down the Danube from Regensburg.

In the main theatre of operations, 98 units were at sea at this time. However, 59 of them were in transit. These were forbidden to attack when they left harbour, unless in exceptional circumstances, and they very often had no torpedoes on the way back. They still used pack tactics, and the strength of their packs had doubled and even tripled since the beginning of 1942. In February and March 1943 there were sometimes 10, 12, or even 16 submarines attacking the same convoy for days on end. Their effectiveness was much strengthened by the fact that German Naval Counter-Intelligence managed continually to decipher Allied communications. "Thus we obtained," Admiral Dönitz wrote at this time, "not only information about the convoys but also, in January and February 1943, the 'U-boat positions', communicated from time to time by the British Admiralty to the commanders of convoys at sea to show them the confirmed or conjectured positions of our warships

△ △ *Impromptu conference in the North Atlantic between two U-boats. With the gradual closing of the "Atlantic gap" and the strengthening of Allied escorts for convoys, it was now becoming very dangerous for U-boats to stay on the surface in daylight and also to communicate with each other or with headquarters by radio.*
△ *The U-boat pens at Lorient. Quite wrongly the R.A.F. had decided to attack these only when they were finished – which proved to be a fruitless task as their concrete construction made them impregnable.*

△ △ *The U-boat pens at Trondheim in Norway, main base for the packs operating against the Arctic convoys. The boat on the left is a Type VIIC (769/871 tons, five 21-inch tubes, 17/7.5 knots) with a Type IXD2 (1,616/1,804, six 21-inch tubes, 19.25/7 knots) on the right.*

△ *A U-boat returns after a successful cruise against Allied shipping.*

in their sector. This was extremely valuable, as we often asked ourselves what the enemy knew about us."

Even today, it is hard to explain the reasons why Dönitz was allowed to read, so to speak, over his enemy's shoulder; the British in fact knew nothing of this for three years and never took the appropriate counter-measures.

When they returned from their cruises,

the U-boats were sheltered in the concrete pens at Lorient and la Pallice from December 1941, and later at Brest, St. Nazaire, and Bordeaux; the pens' 22-foot thick roofs were capable of withstanding the heaviest bombs. As has been mentioned, the R.A.F. did not attack them while they were being built, and when it did so, in accordance with a decision taken at Casablanca, there was no military result. From January to May 1943 English and American bombers dropped about 9,000 tons of bombs and incendiaries on the German Atlantic bases, all to no effect; in vain they destroyed Brest, Lorient, and St. Nazaire without obtaining a single hit on their real targets. The only U-boat sunk at anchor was *U-622,* which was destroyed at Trondheim by a U.S. plane on July 24, 1943. And whilst the French population suffered very severely in these badly directed operations, they cost the Allies 98 planes. One final point: it appears that Raeder's successor was now reduced to using anything that came to hand for sustaining the enormous effort of the submarine war. Unquestionably, his fleets became more and more accident-prone. There were three in 1942 and nine in the following year, seven of them training in the Baltic.

Moreover, the new Grand Admiral had to withstand the weight of this campaign alone. He could not expect any assistance from the Luftwaffe. In fact, during 1943 R.A.F. patrols sank 41 U-boats in the Bay of Biscay without any serious interference from the Germans. It is not surprising that Dönitz, exasperated by the frequent criticisms of the German Navy continually made by Hermann Göring to Hitler, permitted himself a tart reply: "Herr *Reichsmarschall,* kindly spare me your criticisms of the Kriegsmarine. You have got quite enough to do looking after the Luftwaffe!"

Stepped-up production

We shall now consider the Allies' defence against the U-boats.

During 1943 the Western powers' anti-U-boat weapons production was sufficient to meet the extent and urgency of the threat, but the Allied effort was not as one-sided as the German as it placed more importance on the aerial side of naval warfare. However, one must have many reservations about the use the British and Americans made of their air forces in their campaign against the U-boats.

This effort was from now on mainly American. Admittedly, the tactics and technology were mostly British, but the mass production needed to get them into action was predominantly American. The difference in industrial power between the two countries was enormous; the United States, moreover, which had suffered neither Blitz nor black-out, made tremendous innovations in prefabrication.

Escort craft

Amongst escort ships, the British frigate corresponded in its general features to the escort destroyer of the U.S. Navy. But from 1943 till the end of hostilities, Great Britain, with the help of Canadian dockyards, produced 100 frigates, whilst the Americans in the same space of time built 565 escort destroyers; 78 of these were handed over to Britain under Lend-Lease, while eight went to Brazil and six

△ *Admiral Karl Dönitz, who was now promoted to the command of the whole Kriegsmarine with the rank of Grand-Admiral. From here on the desperate struggle against Allied naval and merchant marine strength would be in the hands of this one capable man. He had, however, not only to contend with rapidly increasing Allied strength, but also with Hitler's whimsical idiosyncrasies and Göring's destructive inefficiency.*
◁ *The raw stuff of Germany's naval struggle. Despite the increasingly heavy losses now suffered by the U-boat service, Dönitz was never short of volunteers for his submarine crews.*

It was as if some outside agency had suddenly decided to take a hand on the Allied side—all of a sudden U-boat losses started to climb considerably, while merchant shipping losses declined at an even faster rate. The crisis had been reached and passed, and although the Germans continued their offensive with all the means at their disposal, the Allies had weathered this critical point in their fortunes.
△ A stricken U-boat begins to founder amid a welter of spray.
◁ ◁ A U-boat crew abandons ship just before its vessel is sent to the bottom by one U.S. Navy and two U.S. Coast Guard destroyer escorts. One of the Coast Guard vessels picked up 12 survivors.
◁ △ Another U-boat begins to sink by the stern as its crew scrambles off the conning tower. Note the plumes of water off the U-boat's starboard beam, thrown up by machine gun fire from the Sunderland flying boat responsible for the "kill".
◁ ▽ U-boat survivors in a string of one-man dinghies.

to France. These ships were a little faster than the corvettes of 1940; they had considerable freedom of movement and were profusely armed and equipped for their specialised rôle.

Escort carriers

The story of escort carriers is similar. The British had commissioned their first such carrier, *Audacity,* in November 1941; she was sunk on December 21, 1941, but had performed such signal services that the Admiralty decided to build half a dozen similar ships. The British could not produce as many as the Americans, however, who built 115 between the summer of 1942 and the capitulation of Japan, on new hulls or by converting cargo ships or tankers. But again these 7,000 to 12,000 ton ships were produced quickly and promptly by the prefabrication methods previously referred to. One may take as examples the aircraft carriers *Bogue, Card,* and *Core:*

	Laid down	Launched	Commissioned
Bogue	October 1, 1941	January 15, 1942	September 26, 1942
Card	October 27, 1941	February 21, 1942	November 8, 1942
Core	January 2, 1942	May 15, 1942	December 10, 1942

Considering their escort rôle, a speed of not more than 20 knots was acceptable for carriers of this type. As a result of this feature and the restricted length of their flight decks, catapults had to be installed to launch the planes, of which there were about 20 (fighters and torpedo-bombers). In addition, escort carriers were employed in landing operations as aircraft transports, and as tankers; as they served so many purposes and in such large numbers, they were nicknamed "Woolworth carriers".

By July 1943, the American fleet already had 29 escort carriers in service. Their usefulness soon became evident: by December 31 in the same year they had already destroyed 26 U-boats, and the *Card* alone had accounted for eight of these. Thirty-eight of the 115 escort carriers built by the Americans fought under the British flag.

Operational research

Owing to the increase in the number of escort ships, the convoys were now reinforced; later, "support groups" were also formed as a strategic reserve. The work of the Department of Operational Studies facilitated this development; it was initiated by the Admiralty under the direction of P. M. S. Blackett, professor of physics at Manchester University and Nobel prizewinner in 1948. This organisation also made a most important deduction concerning merchant ship losses; as Captain Macintyre puts it:

"Whereas the number of ships lost in a convoy battle depended, as might be expected, upon the number of U-boats attacking and the size of the escort, it was quite independent of the size of the convoy."

When he demonstrated that the number of escort ships was being built up much more slowly than that of the ships to be escorted, Professor Blackett proved thereby, and in the face of most people's idea of common sense, that large convoys were proportionately less vulnerable than small ones. An important conclusion followed. Macintyre puts it thus:

"Then, as has been said, the economy of force, achieved by reducing the number of convoys to be defended, provided a surplus of warships which could be formed into Support Groups. These themselves resulted in a further economy. For, provided that the convoy escort could be reinforced during the passage of the most dangerous areas, a smaller escort could safely be given for the remainder of the convoy's voyage. Thus Operational Research, too often neglected or ignored, was responsible for a revolution in organisation, which came about in March 1943 with an adjustment of the North Atlantic convoy cycle, whereby fewer and larger convoys were sailed each way."

To the best of our knowledge, this was the first application of what is today called operational research, which is now essential, with the aid of computers, not only in military operations but also in sociology, economics, industry, and commerce.

As regards anti-submarine equipment, we may mention that centimetric wavelength radar equipment was installed on Allied ships and planes; its pulses could not be picked up by the detection apparatus installed by German engineers on all U-boats. In July, however, an R.A.F. bomber carrying this most modern radar equipment was brought down over Rotterdam. Grand-Admiral Dönitz thus learned the secret of the defeat he had suffered, but it was now too late.

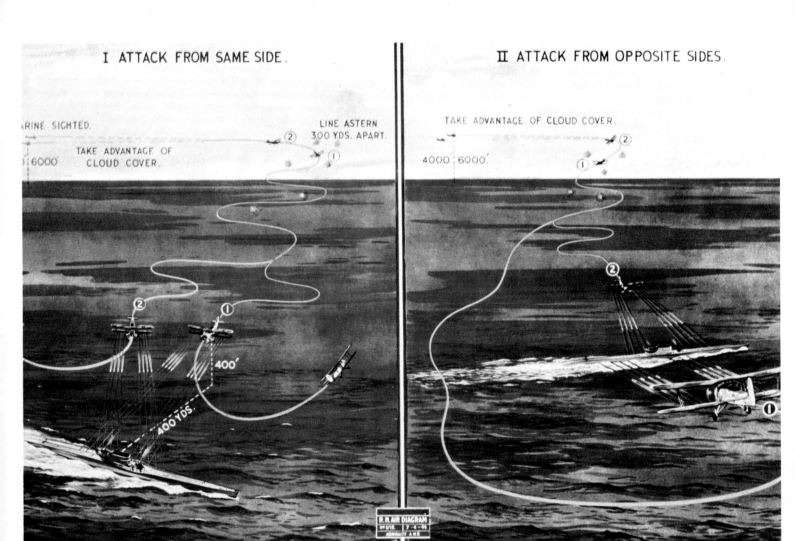

I ATTACK FROM SAME SIDE.

II ATTACK FROM OPPOSITE SIDES.

...RINE SIGHTED.

TAKE ADVANTAGE OF CLOUD COVER.

...6000'

LINE ASTERN 300 YDS. APART.

(2)

(1)

400'

400 YDS.

TAKE ADVANTAGE OF CLOUD COVER.

4000' 6000'

(2)

(1)

(2)

(0)

R.N. AIR DIAGRAM

△ *Yet another rôle for the obsolescent but still versatile Fairey Swordfish: anti-submarine rocket operations. With their docile handling characteristics and low landing speed, these aircraft were ideal for operation from the new escort carriers. From now to the end of the war, large numbers of U-boats were fated to fall to the aircraft of these carriers.*

"Huff Duff" . . .

H/F D/F (High Frequency Direction Finder), goniometric radio equipment, nicknamed "Huff Duff", was undoubtedly another factor in the Allies' success in the Battle of the Atlantic. This had the capacity to detect U-boats whenever they were compelled to transmit. Thus the convoy could be directed away from the area where a pack of submarines was gathering, and a support group of "Hunter-Killers", as the Americans called them, could be launched against them. The U.S. Navy and Army Air Force ordered no less than 3,200 sets of this equipment.

. . . and "Hedgehog"

At the beginning of 1943, the "Hedgehog" was put into general use. This was a projector, fitted in the bows of an escort vessel, which fired a pattern of 24 contact-fused bombs to a range of 250 yards. Thus the pursuer did not have to pass vertically over the top of the submerged target before firing its depth charges.

Finally the rockets which were successfully used by Montgomery's fighter-bombers against the Panzers were also used with the same redoubtable efficiency against the U-boats by the R.A.F.'s, U.S.A.A.F.'s, and U.S.N.'s anti-submarine patrol aircraft.

On May 23, 1943 the new weapon was first used with success by a Swordfish from the British escort carrier *Archer*. In his excellent book on fleet air arm warfare Admiral Barjot gives the following description:

"On the morning of May 23, the convoy was in sight off Newfoundland and the first wave started to attack. The Swordfish B 819 then took off and almost immediately had the good fortune to surprise *U-572*, which had surfaced to keep up with the convoy. The eight rockets lanced off towards the U-boat, holing it so that it had to surface again quickly, as its batteries were flooded. It tried to use its guns, but the fight only lasted a few minutes. A Martlet fighter arrived and machine gunned the U-boat, killing its captain and several men. The rest of the crew lost hope and abandoned ship, the U-boat sinking almost immediately. A few Germans were picked up later by the destroyer *Escapade*."

Bomber Command's part

Following a decision at the Casablanca Conference, the R.A.F.'s Bomber Command and the bomber groups of the American 8th Air Force in England redoubled their attacks against the German shipyards where submarines were under construction. Thus it was hoped to eliminate the danger at its source. In fact, according to Roskill, between May 1 and June 1 the British and American heavy squadrons carried out 3,414 sorties and dropped 5,572 tons of bombs and 4,173 of incendiaries on these targets, now recognised as of prime importance.

But in spite of the loss of 168 planes, the efforts were virtually fruitless. Even worse, this air offensive, which had been so warmly recommended by Churchill and Roosevelt, frustrated the British and American effort in the Atlantic; Bomber Command's requests for reinforcements and replacements could in fact only be satisfied if a parsimonious policy was maintained towards Coastal Command, at least as regards long-range four-engined aircraft for convoy protection.

Professor Blackett realised this perfectly clearly. In 1943 he extended his criticism to all R.A.F. Bomber Command operations:

"From the figures on the effectiveness of air cover, it could be calculated that a long-range Liberator operating from Iceland and escorting the convoys in the middle of the Atlantic *saved* at least half a dozen merchant ships in its service lifetime of some thirty flying sorties. If used for bombing Berlin, the same aircraft in its service life would drop less than 100 tons of bombs and kill not more than a couple of dozen enemy men, women and children and destroy a number of houses.

"No one would dispute that the saving of six merchant ships and their crews and cargoes was of incomparably more value to the Allied war effort than the killing of some two dozen enemy civilians, the destruction of a number of houses and a certain very small effect on production.

"The difficulty was to get the figures believed. But believed they eventually were and more long-range aircraft were made available to Coastal Command."

In fact in February 1943, Air-Marshal Sir John Slessor, who succeeded Sir Philip Joubert de la Ferté as head of Coastal Command, had only ten four-engined B-24 Liberators, whilst the American Navy had only 52. On July 1, however, the figures had risen to 37 and 209 respectively.

▽ *The commander of a German U-boat weighs up the situation before deciding whether or not to make an attack.*
▽▽ *While the captain makes his decision, the torpedo-room crew complete their final preparations on the weapons in the tubes and on the reloads.*

CHAPTER 85

Defeat of the U-boats

a careless word...

A NEEDLESS LOSS

△ *Another poster harping on one of the main themes of Allied propaganda: the need for secrecy where convoys and shipping movements were concerned.*

The graph below gives a precise account of the changing fortunes of the Battle of the Atlantic in 1943, and little more comment is needed. As can be seen, January was relatively favourable to the Allies, as winter storms raged over the North Atlantic; in fact they only lost 37 merchant vessels (261,359 tons) against 106 (419,907 tons) in the same month of the previous year.

West of the Canaries, however, a pack of eight submarines skilfully directed to its rendezvous by Dönitz attacked a convoy of nine tankers heading for North Africa; seven of these were sunk; this was a remarkable feat for which Dönitz duly received General von Arnim's congratulations. In February, Allied losses increased and were slightly over 400,000 tons (56 ships). Nonetheless, between the 4th and 9th of this month, the slow convoy S.C. 118 (63 merchantmen and ten escort vessels) fought off 20 U-boats for four successive nights. A survivor from a previous attack, picked up by *U-632*, had been criminally indiscreet and drawn the attention of his captors to the convoy: the survivor's remarks caused the loss of several hundreds of his comrades' lives. In fact 13 cargo-boats were sunk at dawn on February 9, but as Grand-Admiral

▽ *Evidence that the threat of the U-boat was finally beaten: merchant shipping losses falling, U-boat losses rising.*

Dönitz stated, the defence was keen: "It was", he wrote, "perhaps the worst battle of the whole submarine war. Honour to the crews and commanders who waged it in the harsh winter conditions of the Atlantic! It went on for four successive nights, and the captains were unable to leave their bridges for the whole period. Their ships' safety often depended on the speed of their decisions. It is hard to imagine the self-discipline that is required after a terrible depth-charge attack, to give orders to surface, to approach the convoy, and to bear down on it through its protective screen, bristling with steel, with the alternative of success or destruction. The submarine commanders never performed such a colossal feat in the course of both world wars."

This opinion can be confirmed. The loss of the 13 cargo vessels previously mentioned was countered by that of three U-boats sunk by the escort vessels. They included *U-609* (Lieutenant Rudloff) which was sunk by a depth charge from the French corvette *Lobelia* (Lieutenant de Morsier). In other engagements, a further 16 U-boats were lost during February; on February 28, for the first time since hostilities began, the number of U-boats lost almost equalled the number

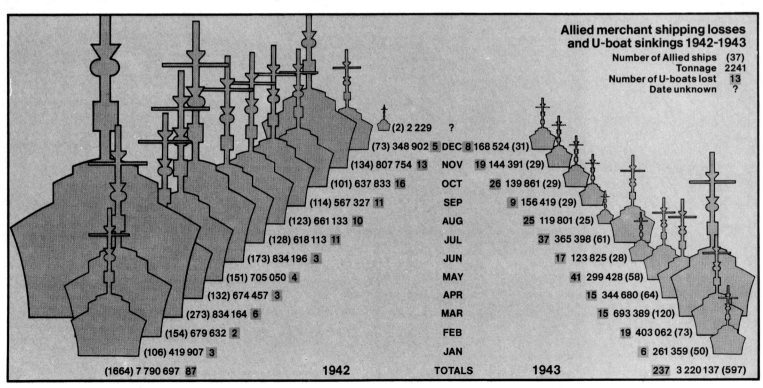

Allied merchant shipping losses and U-boat sinkings 1942-1943

Number of Allied ships	(37)
Tonnage	2241
Number of U-boats lost	13
Date unknown	?

1942			
(2) 2 229	?		
(73) 348 902	5	DEC	8 168 524 (31)
(134) 807 754	13	NOV	19 144 391 (29)
(101) 637 833	16	OCT	26 139 861 (29)
(114) 567 327	11	SEP	9 156 419 (29)
(123) 661 133	10	AUG	25 119 801 (25)
(128) 618 113	11	JUL	37 365 398 (61)
(173) 834 196	3	JUN	17 123 825 (28)
(151) 705 050	4	MAY	41 299 428 (58)
(132) 674 457	3	APR	15 344 680 (64)
(273) 834 164	6	MAR	15 693 389 (120)
(154) 679 632	2	FEB	19 403 062 (73)
(106) 419 907	3	JAN	6 261 359 (50)
(1664) 7 790 697	87	TOTALS	237 3 220 137 (597)

completed by German yards.

In view of this slaughter and the escape, which was often noted, of the convoys from the U-boat onslaught, Dönitz thought for a time that a spy or even a traitor must have penetrated his own staff. The *Abwehr* conducted a search to locate him, but without success. This was not surprising, as, when they changed course to avoid packs, the British and the Americans relied on the contact signals transmitted by their opponents and picked up by their Huff Duff devices. Huff Duff operators had now had so much experience that they were no longer content only to spy out the enemy, but as they were personally involved in operating the device, they also often managed to identify him. In fact the Kriegsmarine only got to the bottom of the mystery in 1945.

In 1956 the official historian of the Royal Navy came to the following conclusion about the sea engagements of March 1943:

"Nor can one yet look back on that month without feeling something approaching horror over the losses we suffered. In the first ten days, in all waters, we lost forty-one ships; in the second ten days fifty-six. More than half a million tons of shipping was sunk in those twenty days; and, what made the losses so much more serious than the bare figures can indicate, was that nearly two-thirds of the ships sunk during the month were in convoy."

Had the system of convoys, begun in September 1939, outlived its usefulness? This was the question which the Admiralty was now anxiously debating. Captain Roskill quotes the following comment from one of its reports, drawn up at the end of 1943:

"The Germans never came so near to disrupting communications between the New World and the Old as in the first

△ *Part of the team that beat Dönitz's U-boats. Seen at Coastal Command's headquarters at Northwood in Middlesex are Air-Marshal Sir John Slessor, Commander-in-Chief of Coastal Command (centre), Air Vice Marshal A. Durston, Slessor's Senior Air Staff Officer (left), and Captain D. V. Peyton-Ward, Slessor's Senior Naval Staff Officer (right). Behind them a W.A.A.F. is plotting movements on a large wall map. According to Slessor, the Bay of Biscay was "the trunk of the Atlantic U-boat menace", and in this area Coastal Command sank 25 U-boats between April and August 1943.*

△ *U-boat eye view of a sinking merchantman. Note the marks of the periscope graticule, which helped the commander gauge the range and speed of the target for incorporation into the calculations made on the plotting table. This gave the captain information as to when and where to fire his torpedoes, plus the best speed and depth to set them to run.*

twenty days of March 1943.''

Between March 7 and 11, the slow convoy S.C. 121 lost 13 of its ships, and these losses remained unavenged. The submarines were not so lucky when they engaged the fast convoy H.X. 228; four merchant ships were destroyed at the cost of two U-boats. During this engagement, according to Captain Macintyre, the commander of the cargo vessel *Kingswood* almost rammed a German U-boat:

"In the darkness and the gale, as he peered anxiously out from his bridge, his eye was caught by what seemed to be a particularly heavy breaking sea on his port bow. Then he saw that the white flurry was travelling with some speed towards him. 'It's a torpedo,' he shouted to the mate standing beside him. But almost at once he realised that he was in fact looking at the wash of a submarine travelling at high speed on the surface. He ran to the telegraph and gave a double ring, calling for the utmost emergency speed and steered to ram. 'I really felt we could not miss,' he recorded.

"'Collision seemed inevitable. About this time I heard the U-boat's engine and a voice in the distance. I was sort of hanging on waiting for the crash when I saw the submarine's wake curling round–the voice I heard must have been the U-boat's commander shouting "Hard a Port" in German. The submarine's wake curled right under my stem–how its tail missed us I still do not know.'"

On March 11, the destroyer *Harvester*

(Commander A. Tait) rammed *U-444* (Sub-Lieutenant Langfeld) which was then sunk by the French corvette *Aconit* (Lieutenant Levasseur). *Harvester,* however, had her propellers badly damaged and became an easy target for *U-432* (Lieutenant Eckhardt). When he saw the column of smoke that indicated *Harvester*'s end, Levasseur returned to the fray and managed to avenge Tait, who had gone down with his ship. From March 16 to 19, the battle reached its high point, pitting 38 submarines against the two convoys H.X. 229 and S.C. 122: in the three nights 21 cargo vessels were sunk whilst the attackers lost only one U-boat.

In all, 102 merchant ships and tankers, a total of 693,389 tons, were sunk by German action during March: a serious situation for the Allies.

The U-boats had much less success during April, however. Less than half the number of merchant ships were destroyed (344,680 tons), for the same number of submarines sunk (15). Moreover, the support groups and escort-carriers began to pursue the enemy more and more closely. The results were clear in May. In that month, at least 47 U-boats were destroyed: 41 were sunk in the North Atlantic, whilst Allied losses fell to below 300,000 tons.

"The situation was changing," wrote Dönitz, acknowledging defeat. "Radar, particularly in aircraft, virtually cancelled out the ability of our submarines to attack on the surface. The previous tactics of our submarines could now no longer be employed in the North Atlantic, a theatre where air reconnaissance was too strong for us. Before using such tactics again, we had to restore our submarines' fighting abilities. I drew my own conclusion and we evacuated the North Atlantic. On May 24 I ordered the submarines to rendezvous in the area south-west of the Azores, taking all the necessary precautions. We had lost the Battle of the Atlantic."

Captain Roskill warmly praises the British captains and crews and summarises the episode as follows:

"In its intensity, and in the certainty that its outcome would decide the issue of the war, the battle may be compared to the Battle of Britain of 1940. Just as Göring then tried with all the forces of the Luftwaffe to gain command of the skies over Britain, so now did Dönitz seek to gain command of the Atlantic with his U-boats. And the men who defeated him–the crews of the little ships, of the air escorts and of our tiny force of long-range aircraft–may justly be immortalised alongside 'the few' who won the 1940 battle of the air."

Amongst these "few", Captain F. J. Walker's name should be mentioned; by March 14, 1944 his 2nd Escort Group had sunk 13 U-boats.

Dönitz shifts theatres

The first five months of 1943 had cost the Allies 365 ships (2,001,918 tons); in the following seven, the losses were reduced to 232 (1,218,219 tons). July was the only month in which the tonnage destroyed (365,398 tons) recalled the position in the first six months, but the Germans paid heavily for this.

Thirty-seven U-boats were lost, one per 10,000 tons sunk, whilst in March the proportion had been one to 46,200 tons.

As the British squadrons were reinforced by Coastal Command and supported by U.S. planes, they went over to the offensive in the Bay of Biscay. Dönitz thought he could ward off this threat by fitting quadruple 2-cm cannon on the conning towers of his U-boats. However, he was underestimating the danger of planes which were kept informed by radar and armed with heavy machine guns, rockets, bombs, and depth-charges. His failure to understand the situation cost him 22 U-boats between June 1 and September 1, 1943: he was therefore compelled to order his captains to submerge by day when they passed through these dangerous waters; thus their cruises took considerably longer. At night, when they recharged their batteries, his raiders still had to reckon with the enemy bombers, which were fitted with powerful radar-aimed Leigh searchlights.

In bringing the submarine war to the south-west of the Azores, the Grand-Admiral came up against the American defences.

At the Pentagon (which had just been built), Admiral Ernest J. King had appointed Rear-Admiral Francis Low as deputy chief-of-staff specially entrusted with anti-submarine problems. On receiving his report, King set up a 10th Fleet on the following May 20, which by his decision on that day "was to exercise (under the direct command of COMINCH [C.-in-C.

U.S. Fleet]) unity of control over U.S. antisubmarine operations in that part of the Atlantic under U.S. strategic control."

Low therefore only acted by King's delegation, whilst King retained command of the organisation. On the other hand, in contrast with what was happening on the other side of the Atlantic, where Sir Max Horton, C.-in-C. Western Approaches, had ships and marine aircraft, the 10th Fleet in Washington controlled neither boats nor planes. In the action it was directing, it therefore had to make use of the aircraft and formations of the Atlantic Fleet, to which it was not allowed to give any orders. This was the reason for what Ladislas Farago, the historian of the 10th Fleet, has called "an impressive flowering of periphrases" in its relations with Admiral Ingersoll, such as "suggest that you...", "it is recommended that you...", "would it be possible for you to...?"

In spite of its paradoxical situation this organisation worked extremely efficiently from the beginning. In July and August the loss of 35 out of the 60 German submarines sunk in all theatres of war was undoubtedly due to the Americans. In the South Atlantic, where the U.S. 4th Fleet was operating, the groups centred on the escort carriers *Core*, *Santee*, *Card*, and *Bogue* (under the command respectively of Captains Greer, Fisk, Isbell, and Short) took a prominent and praiseworthy part in this success. The result was that in his commentary on this period of the merchant navy war, Admiral Dönitz wrote: "Every zone in the South Atlantic was closely watched by long-range four-engined planes or by planes from American aircraft-carriers which were specially deployed to hunt submarines in the central and southern Atlantic. The same strict observation was practised even in the Indian Ocean, although not on such a wide scale. The planes of the two great naval powers therefore took a considerable part in the pursuit of our U-boats, and this continued till the end of hostilities.

"The situation was similar in more distant operational sectors.

"West of the Azores, our ships were still able in mid-June 1943 to refuel from a submarine tanker without interference, before operating in their sectors, which extended from the Straits of Florida to south of Rio de Janeiro and from Dakar to the interior of the Gulf of Guinea. Each

△ △ *A change at the head of the Home Fleet: Admiral Sir John Tovey (left) greets Vice-Admiral Sir Bruce Fraser on board his flagship as the latter takes over from him on May 8, 1943.*
△ *Rear-Admiral R. L. Burnett, who commanded the cruiser force in the action against* Hipper *and* Lützow *on December 31, 1942.*

△△ The German battleship
Tirpitz *at anchor in*
Altenfjord. *On the one side*
she was protected by the shore
and on the other by anti-torpedo
nets, with smoke projectors
capable of covering the whole
area in minutes well deployed all
round this part of the fjord.
△ A British X-craft under way.

commander had a vast area in which to operate as circumstances permitted. We systematically avoided any concentration in order not to provoke a parallel defence concentration. At first the results were favourable, as 16 enemy vessels were sunk initially. But air observation increased rapidly and the boats, particularly those off the American coast, had difficulty in maintaining themselves in their sectors. Similarly, naval refuelling became so dangerous that we had to give it up, thus considerably shortening the length of operations."

Amongst the U-boats destroyed in this sector we may mention some returning from Penang in Malaya, which had valuable cargoes of raw materials.

The episodes of the submarine war are often moving, irrespective of one's sympathies. Ladislas Farago tells one story which may be found amusing. Lieutenant Johannsen's *U-569* had been put out of action by a plane from *Bogue:*

"Johannsen ordered his men to hoist the time-honoured symbol of surrender but the hapless submariners could not find anything white on the boat whose curtains, tablecovers and sheets were all made of some oil resistant drab green cloth. They waved what they had, but those improvised green surrender flags, whose colour blended with that of an angry sea, could not have been made out by Roberts who kept up his fire. However, they were spotted by the Canadian destroyer *St. Laurent* and such evident eagerness to surrender induced her skipper to make preparations for boarding the sub to capture. Johannsen's engineer officer spoiled the scheme. In the last moment he slipped below, opened the flood-valves and went down with the boat, leaving but twenty-four U-boat men for the *St. Laurent* to capture.

"Citing the *U-Johannsen's* fate, we recommended that the U-boats carry something white on board because our pilots could not be expected to distinguish any green cloth waved at them from the level of the green sea. Our suggestion was promptly heeded. A few weeks later the *U-460* was in Johannsen's predicament. Its crew waved that 'something white' we had recommended to keep handy for such emergencies. The 'surrender flag' turned out to be the skipper's dress shirt."

On October 8, 1943 the agreement between the Portuguese and British Governments granting the British naval and air forces the right to establish a base in the Azores was a new blow for German naval strategy; a few months later, moreover, the Americans were granted the same concession. Thus the "Atlantic gap" was finally closed.

The balance of losses

On December 31, 1943, the German submarine flotillas consisted of only 168 operational units; there had been 212 on the preceding January 1. During the year they had lost 237 U-boats and their crews. Eight of these were the result of accident, 75 were sunk by the Americans, five by the French, one by the Russians, and the remainder (148) by the Royal Navy and Coastal Command squadrons. As against these losses, we must put the losses of all kinds of Allied merchant vessels in 1943: they amounted to 3,220,137 tons, made up of 597 ships. These figures may appear very large, but they are nevertheless 4,570,000 tons and 1,067 ships less than the figures in 1942. During the same period merchant ships and tankers of about 13 million tons were launched in British, Canadian, and American shipyards. Here again the predominance of the U.S.A. became apparent. Their Liberty ships, which

were succeeded by their Victory ships, were built with prefabricated parts by methods recommended by the industrialist Henry Kayser, an organiser of genius; they played a distinguished part in the Allied victory of 1945 and the reconstruction of Western Europe, including Germany and Italy, after the close of hostilities. But in spite of this Dönitz did not give up. He believed that new arms would bring victory in 1944, and in the meantime he counted on forcing the enemy to squander his effort within the bounds of the Atlantic; otherwise the Allies would concentrate their resources even more against the industrial might of the Third Reich.

From January 1 to December 31, 1943, more than 680,000 Allied combatants were disembarked in Great Britain and Northern Ireland by 66 convoys as a part of Operation "Bolero", whilst about 127,000 left the British Isles for Africa, Sicily, and Italy. As a general rule the troops crossed the Atlantic without a convoy on fast liners which managed to

△△ *Waist gunners of a Sunderland flying boat. Their duties when on patrol were as much to watch for U-boats as to guard against German air attacks.*
△ *A quadruple 2-pdr "pom-pom" A.A. mounting on board a British warship.*

△ △ *Captain F. J. Walker, commander of the 2nd Escort Group, comes ashore from his sloop* Starling.

△ *Lieutenant-Commander P. W. Gretton, who led the B7 Escort Group with Convoy S.C. 130. On the Atlantic crossing from St. Johns to Londonderry between May 14 and 20, five U-boats were sunk.*

▷△ Scharnhorst *at sea. Visible here is part of the turreted secondary armament of 5.9-inch guns, with four of the 4.1-inch A.A. guns above them and a pair of 3.7-cm A.A. guns in the foreground.*

▷▷ *The British light cruiser* Sheffield.

▷▽ *The* King George V-*class battleship* Duke of York. *Opening fire at long range by radar, she soon slowed* Scharnhorst *with a hit in a boiler room. This long range fire proved to be the decisive factor in the battle –* Duke of York's *14-inch shells, plunging steeply down from the top of their high trajectory, were too much for* Scharnhorst's *deck armour.*

elude U-boat ambushes. Using the "hot berth" system (two berths for three soldiers), the *Queen Elizabeth* and the *Queen Mary* transported 15,000 men per crossing, whilst the French ship *Pasteur* accommodated 4,500.

Nevertheless the rations, fighting equipment, vehicles, fuel, and ammunition for these 680,000 men went via the usual convoy route, and most of the bombers for the U.S. 8th Air Force and all the fighters reached Britain by sea. Even if they had crossed the Atlantic by air, or via Iceland, their fuel supply could only have been secured by the use of tankers. For this reason, we may conclude that if the German submarine raiders had not been defeated in 1943, there would have been no Second Front in Western Europe in 1944.

End of the *Scharnhorst*

At the end of March 1943, the battle-cruiser *Scharnhorst* joined the battleship *Tirpitz* and pocket battleship *Lützow* at Trondheim, and then together the three reached Kåfjord, a small section of the Altenfjord about halfway between Tromsö and the North Cape. From this position they could harass the Allied convoys in the Arctic or even resume the war against the merchant ships in the Atlantic. As the Sicilian operations and the Salerno landing required six British warships in the Mediterranean, the Home Fleet, as whose commander Admiral Tovey had been succeeded by Sir Bruce Fraser in June 1943, had some difficulty in intercepting the German ships.

In addition, the Admiralty in London organised Operation "Source" under the command of Rear-Admiral C. B. Barry, Flag Officer Submarines. The purpose of this operation was to destroy this dangerous German force at anchor by using six 30-ton midget submarines; their armament consisted of two 2-ton charges which could be released to sink under the hull of the target, exploding when set off by a clockwork mechanism. A squadron of reconnaissance planes made Murmansk their base and gave the attackers all possible Intelligence about the obstacles and defences around the anchored German ships.

On September 11, six midget submarines (each manned by four men and towed by conventional submarines), left

an unobtrusive harbour in the north of Scotland and sailed towards Altenfjord. One of them (*X-8*) was to attack *Lützow*, two (*X-9* and *X-10*) *Scharnhorst*, and the remaining three (*X-5*, *X-6*, and *X-7*) *Tirpitz*. But *X-9* was lost with all hands during the crossing, and *X-8* had to be scuttled because it was heavily damaged. The four remaining submarines suffered mishaps of all kinds; even if their compasses managed to work, their periscope tubes filled with water or the electrical engine used for raising them failed.

In spite of all this, at dawn on September 22 Lieutenants Cameron and Place managed to steer *X-6* and *X-7* below *Tirpitz* and release their charges. When *X-6* accidentally surfaced, the huge warship was alerted and had enough time to slew round at her anchorage, thereby managing to escape the worst. But two of her 15-inch gun turrets were immobilised and her engines were badly damaged, and she was out of action for several months. *X-5*, which followed *X-6* and 7, was shelled and sunk. Cameron with his crew of three and Place with only one other survivor were taken prisoner on the ship they had crippled; they were treated in a way that did credit to their heroism. *X-10* was scuttled on its return journey as it was found to have the same defects as its companion submarines. It had missed *Scharnhorst*, its intended victim, because the battle-cruiser was engaged in target practice off the Altenfjord, but it lost nothing by waiting.

On December 22 a Luftwaffe reconnaissance plane spotted an enemy convoy 465 miles west of Tromsö; in fact this was J.W. 55B, which consisted of 19 merchant ships and ten destroyers; it was due to pass R.A. 55A, bringing back 22 empty ships from Murmansk, in the neighbourhood of Bear Island. Vice-Admiral Burnett was responsible for protecting this two-way passage with the heavy cruiser *Norfolk* and the light cruisers *Sheffield* and *Belfast*. In order to provide distant cover, Sir Bruce Fraser, flying his flag on the battleship *Duke of York*, with the light cruiser *Jamaica* and four destroyers, sailed from the Akureyri, the Allied base on the north coast of Iceland, on December 23.

When it received the first signal of an enemy convoy, the German naval group at Kåfjord, as whose commander Rear-Admiral E. Bey had just succeeded Vice-Admiral O. Kummetz, had been put at the alert; on the evening of December 25 it was ordered to attack the convoy. A few hours later, a message from Dönitz arrived to confirm its mission:

"1. By sending the Russians a large consignment of food supplies and *matériel,* the enemy is trying to make our army's heroic struggles on the Eastern Front even more difficult. We must go to the help of our soldiers.

2. Attack the convoy with *Scharnhorst* and destroyers."

Though the mission was clear, the Grand-Admiral followed it with contradictory instructions. Bey should not be satisfied with a "half-success", but should seize the opportunity of "attacking in force". Nevertheless he was allowed the option of breaking off the engagement, and he was reminded that the "essential thing" was always to avoid any "engagement against superior forces".

While Bey was ploughing on and pursuing the enemy, in these bitterly cold northern waters, the Admiralty was able to send a signal to Fraser that *Scharnhorst* was probably at sea. At approximately 0400 on December 26 the Home Fleet commander ordered convoy J.W. 55B to withdraw to the north, with Vice-Admiral Burnett covering its withdrawal. Fraser himself increased to 24 knots to close *Scharnhorst,* which he placed about 250 to 275 miles from *Duke of York.*

At 0840 *Belfast's* radar identified a large enemy warship about 20 miles to the north-west and at 0924, at a distance of eight miles, *Belfast* fired her first star-shell, illuminating *Scharnhorst.* During a brief engagement, *Norfolk,* without being hit, obtained two direct hits with 8-inch shells and destroyed the radar rangefinder in *Scharnhorst's* bows. Bey withdrew, doubtless hoping to circle round the British detachment and attack the convoy which, it will be recalled, was his chief target. This manoeuvre was frustrated by Burnett, who in the meantime had requested the convoy to lend him four destroyers. These moves led to a second engagement at approximately 1230, and this time the light favoured the battle-cruiser; one of her 11-inch shells put *Norfolk's* aft gun-turret out of action, whilst *Sheffield* was covered with shell splinters.

In spite of this success, the German admiral retreated for the second time at a speed of 28 knots. In his memoirs, Dönitz shows moderation in his comments on the movements of his unfortunate sub-

British submarines. Although they had little or no German commerce on which to prey, the Mediterranean offered the possibilities of the Italian merchant marine, and the Pacific such Japanese shipping that the U.S. submarine arm had left. Operations against Germany consisted mostly of patrols to detect and intercept major warships as they left harbour.

△ Alongside a depôt ship. On the right is the "S"-class Stygian, *with another "S" beside her and the "T"-class* Tudor *on the left.*

◁ *Part of another British flotilla. On the left is a "T"-class boat, with inside her the "S"-class* Subtle, *a "V"-class, and another "S".*

▷ △ *A 21-inch torpedo is lowered from a depôt ship to one of her flotilla.*

▷ ▷ *The submarine depôt ship* Forth, *with a torpedo being hoisted from one of her store rooms for a submarine of the 3rd Flotilla.*

▷ *A submarine of the "T"-class.*

△ *"The Sinking of the*
Scharnhorst" *by C. E. Turner.*
The German pocket-battleship
proved a resilient foe–13 14-inch
shells and 11 torpedoes were
needed to sink her.

ordinate, but clearly they do not meet with his approval. However, it is only fair to point out that Bey kept strictly to Dönitz's instruction not to endanger his ship; he would have disobeyed this order had he ventured further with his radar not functioning in the half-light of the Arctic day. On the other hand a message from a plane was signalled to him at 1100: "Five ships north-west of North Cape." As none of *Scharnhorst's* 36 survivors had a hand in the decision which was to lead to its destruction, one must be careful in one's comments.

When he headed for his base at about 1430, the German admiral, who was pursued by Burnett at the limit of radar range, had no idea that he was about to meet the Home Fleet; moreover he did not know that the plane message received at 1100 had an important passage missing: "Including probably one heavy ship." In fact, at 1617 *Scharnhorst* appeared on *Duke of York's* radar screen 25½ miles to the north-north-east, approaching rapidly. At 1650 the English warship, at a range of less than 6½ miles, opened fire on her adversary, who was lit up by *Belfast's* star-shells. Total surprise was achieved. The German battle-cruiser tur-

ned north again, and then meeting Burnett, tried to escape in an easterly direction. During this engagement she had been hit by three 14-inch shells; one of them exploded in a boiler room, and another put the forward 11-inch turret out of action. Although disabled, *Scharnhorst* managed to break contact at 1820 when Bey signalled: "We shall fight to the last shell." By this time the battleship *Duke of York* had ceased fire, but Sir Bruce Fraser's four destroyers attacked *Scharnhorst* on both sides. Although she managed to avoid *Scorpion's* and *Stord's* torpedoes, she laid herself open to the wave of 12 torpedoes launched at her by *Savage* and *Saumarez* at point-blank range. Three hit their mark a little before 1850.

Crushed by *Duke of York's* shells and all the light ships' torpedoes, *Scharnhorst* sank at 1945 on December 26. The victors picked up only 36 out of a crew of just under 1,900 men; both Rear-Admiral Bey and his flag captain, Captain Hintze, were lost. According to Stephen Roskill, 13 14-inch shells and 11 torpedoes were necessary to sink this heroic ship. "Once again the ability of the Germans to build tremendously stout ships had been demonstrated."

CHAPTER 86
Descent on Sicily

If the catastrophe which befell the Axis forces in Tunisia was a defeat of some magnitude and of so far unforeseeable consequences for the Third Reich, for Fascist Italy it was nothing less than a death sentence, without appeal or reprieve.

The mobilisation decree of June 10, 1940 had given *Comando Supremo* an army of 75 divisions. Since that date 20 more had been raised, but these were not enough to make up for the losses sustained since June 10, 1940.

Two divisions had disappeared with the Italian East African empire and 25 more went in the Libyan, Egyptian, and Tunisian campaigns between December 8, 1940 and May 13, 1943. Of the divisions which had fought in the ranks of the Italian Expeditionary Force (later the Italian 8th Army) which Mussolini, overriding all objections, had sent to join the "crusade against Bolshevism", only straggling remnants had returned. The table below bears eloquent witness to these losses. It was drawn up by the Historical Services of the Italian Army and relates to the state of the Italian armed forces at the time of the defensive battle of the Don.

Less than three years of hostilities had therefore cost Italy more than a third of her field army. Even so, on the date in question, no fewer than 36 divisions were immobilised outside Italy and her island dependencies, occupying France or repressing guerrillas in the Balkans.

The situation from Crete to the Italian–Yugoslav frontier as laid down on April 6, 1940 was clearly not improving. Far from it. A communiqué from Rome gave 10,570 killed, wounded, and missing among the Italian occupation troops in the first five months of 1943. The maquis were organising in Savoy and the Dauphiné, whilst in Corsica arms were reaching the resistance fighters via the underwater shuttle-service run by Lieutenant-Commander L'Herminier in the submarine *Casabianca*. No massive recoupment of losses could therefore be made from these 36 divisions.

The defence of the Italian peninsula, Sardinia, and Sicily was thus entrusted to some 30 divisions, but not all these

were immediately available. Two armoured divisions, including the Blackshirt "M" Armoured Division, equipped with German tanks, had not yet finished training. A great effort was therefore made to reconstitute the "Ariete" and the "Centauro" Armoured Divisions, which had escaped from Russia under conditions which we have already described. And so *Comando Supremo* had only about 20 divisions (with equipment no better than it had been in 1940) with which to face the threatened invasion. Its pessimism, in view of the Anglo-American preparations in North Africa, can well be imagined. No reliance could be placed on the so-called "coastal" defences (21 divisions and five brigades) which, as their name indicates, were to offer an initial defence against the enemy landing on the beaches. These units had only local recruits, all in the top age-groups, and they were very poorly officered. Mussolini quoted the case of Sicily, where two battalions were commanded by 2nd Lieutenants retired in 1918 and only recently recalled to the colours. The weapons and equipment of these formations were even more deficient than those of any other divisions. To ease the only too evident shortages, the Duce was counting on the *matériel* coming to him under the Villa Incisa agreement and on what could be pillaged from the now disbanded Vichy French army. But the weapons he did

△ *New York's* Bulldog *derides the ignominious dashing of Mussolini's dream of an African empire.*

▽ *The savage losses of the Italian 8th Army in Russia.*

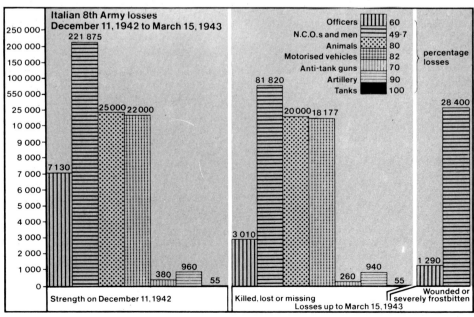

LA DOMENICA DEL CORRIERE

Anno . . . . ITALIA ESTERO	Si pubblica a Milano ogni settimana	Uffici del giornale Via Solferino, 28 - Milano
Semestre . . . . . . L. 22.— L. 36.—	Supplemento illustrato del "Corriere della Sera"	
Per le inserzioni rivolgersi all'Ammi-nistrazione del Corriere della Sera - Via Solfe-rino, 28 - Milano.	Spedizione in abbonamento postale - Gruppo 2	Per tutti gli articoli e illustrazioni è riservata la proprietà letteraria e artistica, secondo le leggi e i trattati internazionali.

Anno 45 — N. 12   21 Marzo 1943 XXI   Centesimi 50 la copia

△ Italy's Domenica del Corriere attempts to inspire faith in the country's defences against Allied invasion: "the guns of a coastal battery point menacingly out to sea."
▷ "Husky" gets under way: the first British troops land in Sicily.

get from these sources often reached him without ammunition or accessories: sometimes they had been astutely sabotaged. Finally, the units were strung out along the coast like a line of customs posts. In Sicily there were 41 men to the mile.

The Italian Air Force impotent

If we remember that the R.A.F.'s defeat of the Luftwaffe in 1940 caused the abandonment of Operation "Sea Lion", it is pertinent to ask what was the state of the Italian Air Force at this time. On June 14, 1943, in the presence of General Ambrosio, Chief of the Italian General Staff, and of the Commanders-in-Chief of the three armed forces, Mussolini had stated unequivocally: "We have neither a powerful bombing force nor the fighters to protect it."

No doubt things would tend to improve in the second half of 1944, but at first it would merely be a drop in the ocean. That is why, Mussolini went on, "it is *absolutely essential* for Germany to supply our needs for A.A. defence in our homeland, that is planes and guns." In calling blithely on the services of his Axis partner, Mussolini was relying on the good will of the Führer, and quite properly. But did he know that the Luftwaffe was then in very dire straits and likely to remain so? On the one hand the Germans had lost all air superiority in the East; on the other they were having to fight off increasing air attacks by Anglo-American bombers on their war industries. There was thus little that could be done to make good the deficiencies in the Italian air strength. Moreover, the aerodromes of Sicily, Sardinia, and southern Italy were regularly being hammered by the Allies.

The Navy hard pressed

By May 13, 1943, 35 months of war had caused the deaths, by killing or drowning, of 35,000 officers and men and the loss of the following ships: one battleship, five heavy cruisers, seven light cruisers, 74 destroyers, and 85 submarines.

It had, of course, proved impossible to build enough new ships to make up for all these losses. Admiral Riccardi, Chief-of-Staff at *Supermarina,* still had, it is true, six battleships, a dozen cruisers, some 60 destroyers and torpedo-boats and the same number of submarines. The smaller surface vessels, however, were worn out after three years' hard escort service. The day after the Battle of Matapan the Duce had decided that until the converted liners *Roma* and *Augustus* came into service as aircraft-carriers, the fleet would not venture outside the radius of action of land-based fighters. No-one had foreseen that the day would come when there was to be no fighter support at all. When the Anglo-Americans set up a powerful bombing force in North Africa, Admiral Riccardi had been compelled to move his squadrons away from their

The German "Lorraine Schlepper" self-propelled heavy howitzer

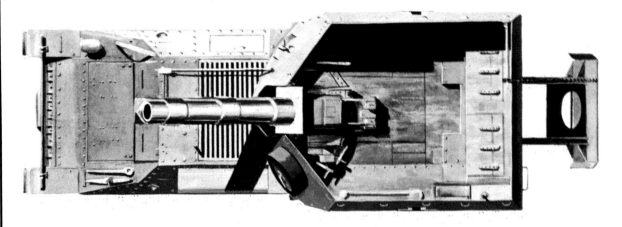

Weight: 8.36 tons.
Crew: 4.
Armament: one 15-cm s.FH 13 heavy howitzer with 8 rounds.
Armour: hull nose 12-mm, front 9.5-mm, sides and rear 9-mm, deck 6-mm, and belly 5-mm; superstructure front and sides 10-mm, mantlet and rear 7-mm.
Engine: one de la Haye 103TT inline, 80-hp.
Speed: 21 mph.
Range: 84 miles.
Length: 17 feet 5 inches.
Width: 6 feet 2 inches.
Height: 7 feet 3¾ inches.

moorings at Taranto, Messina, and Naples. On April 12 the cruiser *Trieste* was sunk by air attack as she lay at anchor in the roads at La Maddalena off the north coast of Sardinia. On June 5 a raid by Flying Fortresses on La Spezia caused varying degrees of damage to the big battleships *Roma, Littorio,* and *Vittorio Veneto.* The fuel crisis had now become critical, and to economise on supplies the cruisers *Duilio, Doria,* and *Cesare* were laid up, the first two at Taranto and the third at Pola.

No way to counter-attack

Faced with this disastrous state of affairs, Mussolini came to the following conclusions on point 2 of the note on which he commented on June 14 to his Chiefs-of-Staff:

"In the present state of the war the Italian forces no longer hold any possibility of initiative. They are forced onto the defensive. The army no longer has any possibility of initiative. It lacks, amongst other things, room to manoeuvre. It can only counter-attack the enemy who lands at one point on our territory and drive him back into the sea." We shall comment no further on Mussolini's remarks on the possibilities open to the Italian Navy and Air Force, as these have been mentioned already. It should be noted, however, that in asking the Army to counter-attack the enemy as he landed and throw him back

△ △ *An Italian mortar crew. The basic equipment of the troops was no better than it had been in 1935.*
△ *Training with an anti-tank gun. Most of them had been lost in Africa.*
◁ *The crew of a coastal battery go through their gun drill.*

The German Sturmpanzer IV *"Brummbar"* (Grizzly Bear) assault howitzer

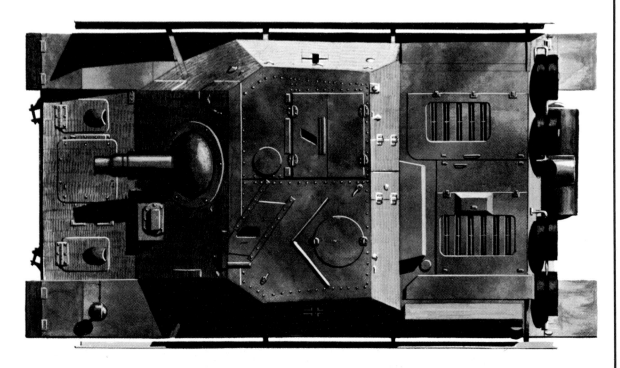

Weight: 28.2 tons.
Crew: 5.
Armament: one 15-cm *Sturmhaubitze* 43 howitzer with 38 rounds.
Armour: nose 80-mm, front 100-mm, sides 30-mm, rear 20- to 60-mm, deck 20-mm, and belly 10-mm.
Engine: one Maybach HL 120 TRM inline, 300-hp.
Speed: 24 mph.
Range: 125 miles.
Length: 19 feet.
Width: 11 feet.
Height: 8 feet 3 inches.

into the sea, Mussolini had overlooked the report made to him on May 8 by the Chief of the General Staff after an inspection in Sardinia.

After noting certain differences of conception in the organisation of defences against landings, General Ambrosio recommended the adoption of what he called the "modern technique". This was to break up the landing on the beaches or, even better, crush the opposing forces whilst they were still at sea. The advanced defensive position therefore had to have guns capable of dealing with ships, landing-craft, personnel, and tanks, not only to stop the mechanised columns which might break through the first defence line, but also to knock out approaching flotillas and all the troops who managed to set foot ashore. "It is all the more necessary to stop the attack on the beach before it can secure a foothold as, not having enough armour, we shall not be able to halt a well-equipped adversary once he has landed and started to make his way inland."

Thus Ambrosio did not believe, any more than Rommel was to in 1944, in a counter-attack from inland against an enemy who had secured an extensive beach-head. His scepticism was backed by a decisive argument: the Italians did not have in their army any powerfully-equipped shock force to carry it out. Had the Duce any more faith in it? Probably not. In his note to his four Chiefs-of-Staff he had sensibly written: "It has been said that the artillery wins the ground and the infantry occupies it." He did not hesitate to apply to Sicily the very recent precedent of Pantelleria. Against Ambrosio it must be remembered that nowhere did the coastal units have the weapons he was recommending and that he was well aware of this. Thus there was no way of driving any invasion force back into the sea or of counter-attacking it as it was striking inland. In other words they had reached the situation covered by the saying quoted by Mussolini on June 14: "He who defends himself dies!"

The peace faction

But was it necessary to die? As we have seen, Mussolini was counting on German aid to drive back the invaders. But even within his own party, a majority of its leaders thought that Hitler's intentions were less to defend Italy than to defend Germany in Italy, and that the final defeat of the Third Reich was written in the stars anyway. The peninsula must therefore not be allowed to become a battlefield. Italy must get out of the war one way or another–and immediately, as she had already lost the war irremediably. We have seen that Ciano, Grandi, and Bottaï, all three former ministers of the Duce, shared this opinion with Marshals Badoglio and Caviglia, with the "young" Generals Castellano and Carboni, with the former Prime Ministers of the liberal era Orlando and Bonomi, and with those close to the King. The Chief of the General Staff accepted the principle of a rupture of the Axis and a cessation of hostilities but, as he continually urged him, preferred Mussolini to take the initiative for this change of tack. Failing this he envisaged arresting the Duce. Finally, General Chierici, Chief of Police, and General Hazon, Commander of the Corps of Carabinieri, also declared themselves in favour of an eventual show of force.

The King, however, hesitated to give the signal. We would impute this not to lack of personal courage but to the fear of provoking indescribable chaos if the elimination of Mussolini, which he thought would be necessary, were to be carried out by other than legal means. In particular the presence in the Lake Bracciano area, some 25 miles from the capital, of the Blackshirt "M" Armoured Division, militated against any ill-considered gesture, and whilst Germany was reinforcing her strength in the peninsula, she could be counted upon to react with some force.

The King's reserve caused Count Grandi to lose patience. On June 3, recalling to Victor Emmanuel III the ups and downs of the House of Savoy, he said: "Your Majesty, there is no choice: either Novara, namely abdication, or a change of front in the style of Victor Amadeus II who, when he realised the mistake of the alliance with the King of France, saved Piedmont and the dynasty at the last moment, by going over to the Imperial camp."

Marshal Badoglio felt the same way on July 17, when he said to Senator Casati: "Either the King accepts the solution which, in agreement with us, he has already anticipated, or he resigns himself to waiting for another moment. In the second case each one of us can choose the way he wishes to follow."

△ Tough, well-armed, and with a superb combat tradition: German paratroopers, who formed the core of the Axis defence of Sicily and went on to add to their laurels on the defensive in Italy.

△ *An Italian marshalling-yard gets a dose of Allied bombs. All key strategic centres were thoroughly bombed before the invasion, as well as the defences along the coast.*

Sardinia or Sicily?

As we have seen in the preceding chapter, Hitler thought that the first objective of the Anglo-American invasion would be Sardinia. General Ambrosio's inspection of the island's defences in early May would seem to indicate that the *Comando Supremo* agreed with the Führer. After the event, Marshal Badoglio gave it as his opinion that the strategists in London and Washington had made a great mistake in preferring the easier way of a landing in Sicily.

This would be correct if the two Western powers had proposed an immediate conquest of Italy, for the occupation of Sardinia means that the peninsula south of a line La Spezia–Ancona cannot be defended and allows, through Corsica and after landings in Liguria, the turning of the Apennine bastion.

But when plans were being drawn up for Operation "Husky", the Anglo-Americans were proposing nothing of the sort. They anticipated, first of all, clearing the

Sicilian Channel, and then securing a bridgehead, including Naples and Foggia, whose great aerodromes would allow bombing raids on the Rumanian oil-fields. But at the "Trident" Conference on May 12-25 in Washington, attended by Roosevelt and Churchill, which was to decide on the follow-up to "Husky", the Americans expressed their conviction that the British had "led them down the garden path by taking them into North Africa". "They also think," continued Alanbrooke in his diary, "that at Casablanca we again misled them by inducing them to attack Sicily. And now they do not intend to be led astray again."

And the American President agreed, apart from a few minor reservations, with the thinking of the Pentagon. According to Alanbrooke, Roosevelt admitted, it is true, "the urgent need to consider where to go from Sicily and how to keep employed the score or more of battle-trained Anglo-American divisions in the Mediterranean. But the continuing drain involved in any attempt to occupy Italy might prejudice the build-up of forces for a cross-Channel invasion, and, though there now seemed no chance of the latter in 1943, it would have to be launched on the largest scale in the spring of 1944."

After long arguments between the British and the Americans, it was agreed that while an invasion of France in late spring 1944 remained the principal Allied operation against Germany, the Allied forces in the Mediterranean after "Husky" were to mount "such operations as are best calculated to eliminate Italy from the war and to contain the maximum number of German divisions".

For "Husky" General Eisenhower kept the same team which had brought him victory in Tunisia. Under his control General Alexander would direct the operations of the 15th Army Group, the number being the sum of its two constituent armies, the American 7th (Lieutenant-General Patton) and the British 8th (Montgomery): an experienced and able high command.

According to the original plan, the British 8th Army was to land between Syracuse and Gela and the American 7th Army on each side of Trapani at the other end of the island. Montgomery, however, objected because, as he wrote to Alexander on April 24: "Planning to date has been on the assumption that resistance will be slight and Sicily will be

captured easily . . . If we work on the assumption of little resistance, and disperse our effort as is being done in all planning to date, we will merely have a disaster. We must plan for fierce resistance, by the Germans at any rate, and for a real dog fight battle to follow the initial assault."

The original plan had therefore to be concentrated so that the two Allied armies could give each other mutual support if either ran into trouble. Credit is due to both Eisenhower and Alexander for having accepted without too much difficulty Montgomery's reasoning. The revised plan set Scoglitti, Gela, and Licata as Patton's first objectives, whilst Montgomery moved his left flank objective over from the Gela area to Cape Passero so as to be able to seize this important promontory at the south-eastern tip of Sicily in a pincer movement.

The British 8th Army comprised the following:

1. XIII Corps (Lieutenant-General Dempsey), made up of the 5th Division (Major-General Bucknall), the 50th Division (Major-General Kirkman), and the 231st Brigade (Brigadier-

General Urquhart); and
2. XXX Corps (Lieutenant-General Leese), made up of the 51st Division (Major-General Wimberley) and the 1st Canadian Division (Major-General Simmonds).

The American 7th Army comprised the II Corps (Lieutenant-General Bradley), made up of the 45th Division (Major-

△ △ *Loading up the landing-craft at Sousse in Tunisia before the descent on Sicily.*
△ *Supply from the air: Douglas C-47 transports are loaded.*

General Middleton), the 1st Division (Major-General Allen), and the 2nd Armoured Division (Major-General Grittenberger), plus also the 3rd Division (Major-General Truscott), unattached to a corps.

Each army had an airborne spearhead of brigade strength, and one division held provisionally in reserve in North Africa.

Admiral Cunningham's armada

An armada of 2,590 ships, large and small, took part in Operation "Husky" under the command of Admiral Cunningham. Under him Admiral Sir Bertram H. Ramsay was in command of the landings.

△ *U.S. soldiers head in to the beaches.*
▽ *Bombs and shells explode around ships of the invasion fleet as it nears the coast of Sicily.*

Ramsay's experience went back to the Dunkirk evacuation, and this time he had 237 merchant vessels and troop transports and 1,742 motorised landing-craft to bring ashore the men, tanks, and supplies. The fighting units had two missions: to neutralise by gun fire all resistance on the shore and to deal with the Italian fleet. They had therefore been given generous support: six battle-ships, two fleet aircraft-carriers (both British), three monitors, 15 cruisers (five American), 128 destroyers (48 American, six Greek, and three Polish), and 26 sub-marines (one Dutch and two Polish).

An enormous concentration, but during the first phase of the operation 115,000 British and Canadians and more than 66,000 Americans had to be put ashore.

As for the Allied air forces, they had 4,000 planes under Air Chief-Marshal Tedder. By D-day they had virtually wiped out the enemy's defences. Over Sicily the opposition was a mere 200 Italian and 320 German planes.

Pantelleria capitulates

On June 12 the *matériel* and morale effect of the air bombardment of Pantelleria was such that Admiral Pavesi surrendered this island fortress of 12,000 men to the Allies after losing only 56 killed and 116 wounded. According to Mussolini, Pavesi had deceived him by giving the reason for his request to surrender as lack of water. According to Admiral Bernotti it was not so much the water which was short as the means of distributing it. There were only four tanker-lorries and three wells for 10,000 civilians and 12,000 troops. Add to this the physical shock of the explosion of 6,550 tons of bombs in six days and it will be seen that the capitulation of June 12 was understandable.

At the same time, the Allied air forces redoubled their attacks on Sicily, particularly on the aerodromes and the harbours. Messina alone received 5,000 tons of bombs. Communications with the main-land were severely affected and feeding the civilian population began to bring enormous problems to the administration. At the end of June there were only 30 days' supplies of flour left.

On June 8, Generals Eisenhower and Alexander and Admiral Cunningham went to Malta. All was going well apart

from the deteriorating weather. The meteorological office reported Force 4 to 5 winds over the sea but there was no going back.

The strength of the Axis forces

Let us now go over to the other side.

On June 1 General Guzzoni succeeded General Roatta in command of the Italian 6th Army, with the task of defending Sicily to the last. According to Mussolini, the enemy was to be wiped out before breaking through inland or "as he took off his bath-robe and before he had had time to get dressed".

As soon as he was informed of the Anglo-American invasion preparations, the Duce, said Marshal Badoglio, "had rushed to make a speech to the nation; the stupidest he ever gave. Later it became known as the 'bath-robe' speech."

The plan adopted for the defence corresponded so closely to the invasion plan abandoned at the request of Montgomery that it can be asked if in fact the Anglo-Americans had not leaked it on purpose. Guzzoni established his headquarters at Enna in the centre of the island and divided his forces into two:

1. west of the line Licata (inclusive)–Cefalú: XII Corps (H.Q. at Corleone) to defend Marsala, Trapani, and Palermo. Commanded by General Arisio it comprised the "Aosta" Division (General Romano) and the "Assietta" Division (General Papini) with the 207th, 202nd, and 208th Coastal Divisions; and

2. east of this line: XVI Corps (H.Q. at Piazza Armerina) to defend Gela, Syracuse, Catania, and Messina. Commanded by General Rossi, it had the "Napoli" Division (General Gotti-Porcinari), the 206th and 213th Coastal Divisions, and the 18th and 19th Coastal Brigades.

The "Livorno" Division (General Chirieleison) was held in army reserve at Mazzarino.

Including the Fascist Militia there were thus 230,000 men and 1,500 guns in the Italian 6th Army which, however, was not very mobile as there were very few motorised units among its formations. The coastal units had tremendous stretches of land to defend: the 206th Division (General d'Havet) had nearly 83 miles between Cassibile and Punte Braccetto, and the 18th Brigade (General Mariscalco) 36 miles between Punte Braccetto to east of Licata. These two units were to take the brunt of the six British and American divisions, while the American attack by 3rd Division was to face only two battalions of the 207th Division (General Schreiber).

The Italian 6th Army was supported by two German divisions, the 15th *Panzergrenadier* (Major-General Rodt) and the "Hermann Göring" Panzer Division (Lieutenant-General Conrath). The first of these was only partially motorised and the second had only two battalions of infantry and fewer than 100 tanks, though these included a company of Tigers. O.K.W. had appointed Major-General von Senger und Etterlin as liaison officer to General Guzzoni.

When Hitler received Senger und Etterlin on June 22 he did not disguise his mistrust of the Italian court, society, and

△ *On the alert as the Allied armada surges onward. The total command of the air which the Allies enjoyed meant that the Axis powers could hardly impede this invasion force.*

▽ *Moment of truth. American tanks hit the beach at Licata.*

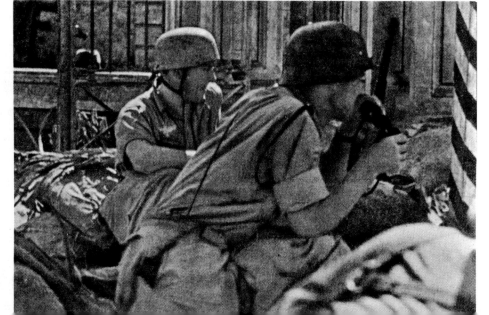

△ *Paratroopers struggle into their harness before a drop. Most of the airborne operations in Sicily went badly awry, and essential lessons were learned the hard way.*
▷ *German soldiers watch a bombardment.*
▽ *German paratroopers on the look-out.*

high command. In spite of this he was optimistic about the outcome of the operations as, he assured Senger und Etterlin, the Allies "by neglecting to attack Sicily immediately after their landings in North Africa had virtually thrown away the war in the Mediterranean!"

General Warlimont, Chief of the Operations Staff at O.K.W., did not share these illusions. "He laid the situation clearly before me" wrote Senger und Etterlin, adding: "the best solution to the mission entrusted to me was to be, in case of heavy enemy attacks, to bring back to the mainland the majority of the troops stationed in Sicily. He recognised that we could not expect to bring back the bulk of our war *matériel*. This appreciation of the situation and the definition of my mission was a corrective to Hitler's viewpoint."

At Enna, where he had gone together with Field-Marshal Kesselring, the question of the intervention of the German units in the battle, now expected any day, gave rise to somewhat confused discussions. In the end the 15th Panzer Division, less one detachment, was relegated to the western tip of the island whilst the "Hermann Göring" Panzer Division was divided between the plain of Catania and the Caltagirone area.

The landing on July 10 came as no surprise. The evening before, Axis aircraft had spotted six Allied convoys leaving Malta and, towards five o'clock in the morning, Enna H.Q. reported that several parachutists had landed. These landings were unfortunate, as the men were widely scattered by the wind; nevertheless they succeeded in harrassing the enemy's movements. Brigadier-General Lathbury, at the head of a hundred or so British troops, seized the bridge at Primosole south of Catania and held out there for five days, preventing its destruction until the arrival of the 8th Army.

Allied success

At dawn, naval guns and tactical aircraft pounded the Italian coastal defences whilst many landing-craft, loaded with men and tanks, advanced on to their objectives in spite of a choppy sea. D.U.K.W.s, American amphibious trucks, were the first vehicles to land. Franz Kurokowski's monograph on the Sicilian campaign tells of numerous acts of heroism by men of the 206th Division and the 18th Brigade, but faced with companies, battalions, and regiments supported by tanks they were overrun and virtually wiped out. In the evening General Guzzoni ordered the 15th Panzer Division to move towards Enna and the "Hermann Göring" Panzer Division, together with the "Livorno" Division, to mop up the American bridgehead at Gela. In the morning of July 11 the Panzers ran into the forward posts of the 1st American Division in the area of Niscemi but when they had got to within 2,000 yards of the beach they were caught by fire from the cruisers *Boise* and *Savannah* and six destroyers, which together loosed off no fewer than 3,194 6- and 5-inch shells at them and wiped out 30 tanks. The "Livorno" Division was also very badly knocked about. On the same day Montgomery occupied, without a shot being fired, the two harbours of Syracuse and Augusta, which had been abandoned by their garrisons in somewhat obscure circumstances.

On July 14 the American 7th Army and the British 8th Army met. This gave them the aerodromes at Ragusa and Comiso, which were put back into shape in record time. Was Montgomery going to race the enemy to Messina and force a surrender, as he had planned? No. Kesselring managed by a great feat to bring over to Sicily two paratroop regiments and the

29th *Panzergrenadier* Division (Major-General Fries). On July 17 General Hube and the staff of XIV Panzer Corps took command of all German fighting troops in Sicily and resistance stiffened on both sides of Mount Etna. The 8th Army was stopped at Catania and so attacked west of Etna, upsetting the advancing Americans.

Patton, by a miracle of improvisation, then threw his army against Palermo, which fell on July 22, having overcome on the way the "Assietta" Division. He then resumed his advance towards Messina, hoping, like Montgomery, to get there before the Germans. Once again, however, Hube parried and on July 23 the forward units of the American 7th Army were stopped in front of the little town of Santo Stefano on the coastal road. Meanwhile the 1st Canadian Division, which formed Montgomery's left flank, after bypassing the important crossroads at Enna, tried to turn the Etna massif from the north-west.

Masters of Sicily

Meanwhile the American 9th Division (Major-General Eddy), which had landed at Palermo, and the British 78th Division (Major-General Keightley), now ashore at Syracuse, brought the number of divisions in the 15th Army Group to 11 and gave the Allies an enormous superiority. Hube therefore began to withdraw, and did it so well that two-thirds of his forces got across to Italy.

Messina and the straits were bristling with A.A., which made life very difficult for Anglo-American aircraft. At 0530 hours on August 17 the commander of XIV Panzer Corps embarked on the last assault-boat leaving for Calabria. Three hours later the Americans and the British were congratulating each other in the ruined streets of Messina.

In his final communiqué, General Alexander announced the capture of 132,000 prisoners, 260 tanks, and 520 guns, and we know from General Faldella, former Chief-of-Staff of the 6th Army, that today there are 4,278 Italian and 4,325 German dead in the war cemeteries in Sicily. On the Allied side, out of 467,000 men in Operation "Husky" the losses were 5,532 killed, 2,869 missing and 14,410 wounded.

▽ *The first supply-dumps begin to build up on the beaches. As Axis resistance to the landings increased, more and more matériel was needed to support the advance to Messina.*

The Italian fleet

Though the battleships *Caio Duilio* and *Andrea Doria* had been brought back into service late in July, the Italian fleet, through lack of sufficient escort and air support, played only a passive rôle in the operation. Furthermore the bulk of the fleet, stationed as it was in La Spezia, was badly placed to intervene in the waters round Cape Passero. Admiral Riccardi thus limited his support to submarines, torpedo planes, and fast patrol boats. At the high cost of nine of their numbers sunk, the Italian submarines torpedoed and damaged the cruisers *Newfoundland* and *Cleopatra*, and sent to the bottom four merchant-vessels and a tanker. The American destroyer *Maddox* was sunk by aerial bombardment on July 10.

CHAPTER 87
The fall of Mussolini

On July 16, after reading the communiqués, Count Grandi was moved to write the following letter to General Puntoni, King Victor-Emmanuel's senior A.D.C.:

"Dear Puntoni:

The news from Sicily has caused deep and poignant grief to my Italian heart. Almost 100 years after the day on which King Charles Albert promulgated the constitution of the kingdom and, with the *Risorgimento,* gave the signal for the struggle for the liberty, unity and independence of Italy, our motherland is now on the road to defeat and dishonour."

As we have said, the King was hesitating over the best way to remove from power not only Mussolini but the whole Fascist Party, a plan which he could not reveal to Grandi. On July 19 there had been a meeting at Feltre, a small town in Venetia, between the Duce, the Führer, Bastianini, the Under-Secretary of State for Foreign Affairs, Ambassadors Alfiere and Mackensen, Field-Marshal Keitel, and Generals Ambrosio, Warlimont, and Rintelen. The outcome of this meeting had convinced the King that he had to cross his Rubicon, and soon, if Italy was to be spared further ruin and misfortune. The Feltre conference opened at 1100 hours and consisted essentially of an interminable monologue by Hitler, exhorting his Italian listeners to stiffen their resistance to the

△ *September 3, 1943: Eisenhower's chief-of-staff, General Walter Bedell Smith, signs the Cassibile armistice. The two Italian emissaries, Castellano and Montenari, in civilian clothes, watch with interest.*

△ Jubilant Romans celebrate the fall of Mussolini. But their joy was to be short-lived: German forces soon moved in to restore the Fascist dictator.
▷ △ The Italian battleship Andrea Doria sails from Taranto for Malta in compliance with the terms of the Italian armistice.
▷ ▷ The battleship Roma, hit by a German glider bomb, begins to settle. More than 1,500 men went down with her.
▷ ▽ Light forces of the Italian Navy in Valletta harbour.

enemy as they were doing in Germany, where boys of 15 were being called up to serve in A.A. batteries. When it came to the support in tanks and planes for which his allies asked he was vague: the most he could offer them was to bring LXXVI Panzer Corps, the 26th Panzer Division, and the 3rd *Panzergrenadier* Division down through the Brenner Pass, and even then he imposed certain conditions. According to Ambassador Alfieri he, Bastianini, and General Ambrosio took advantage of a break in the meeting to urge Mussolini to stop being so passive and to tell Hitler either to take it or leave it. Ambrosio had reported that within a month at most further organised resistance by the army would be out of the question. Hitler had therefore to be given the following alternative: the Third Reich must give Italy all the support she was asking for, or the latter would be compelled to withdraw from the war.

"Mussolini," Alfieri went on, "gave a start, then, pulling himself together, agreed to discuss the matter. He even asked us to sit down, a most unusual courtesy. 'Perhaps you think,' he said with some emotion, 'that this problem has not been troubling me for some long time? To you I may appear calm and collected but underneath I am suffering heart-rending torment. I admit the possible solution: break away from Germany. It looks easy: one fine day, at a given time, a radio message is broadcast to the enemy. But what will happen then? The enemy will rightly ask for capitulation. Are we prepared to wipe out at one go 20 years of government? To destroy the results of labours which have been so long and so bitter? To recognise our first military and political defeat? To disappear off the world stage? It's easy to say, you know... break away from Germany. What will be Hitler's attitude? Do you suppose he will leave us free to act?'"

Regardless of the force of these arguments, the Italian dictator could find no words capable of convincing his German colleague, either because he was ashamed of revealing the state of his military forces or because in his innocence he believed Hitler's hitherto secret reprisal measures: after the end of August new weapons would reduce the British capital to rubble in a matter of weeks and Dönitz would continue his war on Allied shipping with revolutionary submarines. It was true that these new weapons were being built, but it was a downright lie to state that they were ready to be put to use. The Feltre conference, which the interpreter Paul Schmidt called extremely "depressing", finally fizzled out. The two dictators, Deakin relates, said goodbye to each other on the aerodrome at Treviso: "As Hitler's plane took off, the Duce stood with his arm raised at the salute and remained thus until the machine was out of sight. His advisers approached him on the runway. 'I had no need to make that speech to Hitler,' he said, 'because, this time, he has firmly promised to send all the reinforcements which we need.' And turning to Ambrosio, 'Naturally our requests must be reasonable and not astronomic.' Ambrosio and Bastianini travelled in the same car from the airport to Treviso railway station. The former suddenly burst out, 'Did you hear what he said to Hitler after my warning of this morning? He asked him yet again for that war material which they will never send, and he did not take my words seriously. He is mad, I tell you, mad. What I told him is serious, very serious.'"

General Ambrosio, who had only had airy promises from Field-Marshal Keitel, left the conference in a state of high indignation and determined to draw the necessary conclusion from the Duce's culpable debility. As Mussolini had not been able to convince his ally of the tragic dilemma in which Italy was now implicated, this had to be resolved without him and against him. In effect, to defend Italy which, now that Sicily was overrun, would very likely be the enemy's next objective, Army Group "South" had only seven divisions and 12 low-quality coastal divisions, although the 16th Panzer Division, reconstituted, like the 29th *Panzergrenadier* Division, after Stalingrad, had recently arrived in the peninsula: the Italians were nevertheless at the end of their tether.

Mussolini defeated in the Fascist Grand Council

It was in this atmosphere of bitterness and defeat that the meeting of the Fascist Grand Council, called by Mussolini, opened at 1700 hours on Saturday July 24 in the Palazzo Venezia. Strange as it may seem, the dictator does not appear to have got wind of the plot hatched against him or of the fact that a majority of the

Council was now against him. This was borne out by Kesselring, who in his memoirs tells how the Duce had received him on the eve of the meeting and had gaily told him as he stepped into the dictator's office: "Do you know Grandi? He was here a moment ago. We had a clear and frank discussion; we think the same way. He is faithful and devoted to me."

Despite information he was receiving from within the Fascist Party, Ambassador von Mackensen was similarly optimistic and said so to Ribbentrop. The conspirators within the Grand Council were much less reassured than Mussolini as they went in, to such an extent that some had been to confession first. Mussolini's speech restored their spirits. "In a voice without either inspiration or conviction," Alfieri tells us, "the Duce spoke for two hours, disclaiming his responsibilities, blaming Badoglio, accusing the General Staff of 'sabotaging' the war and singing the praises of Germany." Grandi was as brief and penetrating as Mussolini had been irrelevant and long-winded and was supported by Bottaï, Ciano, Federzoni, and old Marshal de Bono, who had been cut to the quick by Mussolini's attacks on his comrades. After a brief adjournment and new exchanges the agenda was voted on and Grandi's motion came out top with 19 votes against eight with one abstention, that of Suardo, the President of the Senate. One of the majority withdrew before dawn; this saved his life at the Verona trial. It was almost three in the morning when Mussolini declared the meeting closed without, it would seem, having himself said one memorable thing during the whole session. The final scene of the Fascist Grand Council is described thus by F. W. Deakin: "Grandi addressed the meeting briefly. He then handed his motion to Mussolini. The names of the nineteen signatories were appended. The Duce put the paper in front of him with 'affected indifference.' And then 'without another word or gesture and in a relaxed and resigned manner' he called on Scorza to put Grandi's motion to a vote.

"Scorza stood up, and starting in order of priority round the table with De Bono, he called the roll of the names of those present. In an oppressive silence he counted. Nineteen in favour; seven against. Suardo abstained; Farinacci supported his own motion, on which no vote was taken. The Duce gathered his papers

and stood up. According to his subsequent account he said: 'You have provoked the crisis of the régime. The session is closed.' Scorza attempted to call for the ritual salute to the Duce who checked him, saying: 'No, you are excused,' and retired to his private study."

Badoglio takes over

Of the rather long text drawn up by Count Grandi we quote the final paragraph, which invited "the Head of the Government to request His Majesty the King, towards whom the heart of all the nation turns with faith and confidence, that he may be pleased, for the honour and salvation of the nation, to assume the effective command of the armed forces on land, on the sea and in the air, according to the article of the Statute of the Realm, and that supreme initiative of decision which our institutions attribute to him and which, in all our national history, have always been the glorious heritage of our august dynasty of Savoy."

As can be seen, this text, in spite of its verbosity, was cleverly drawn up since, without actually opening up a government crisis, it put the onus on the dictator to go to the King and hand over the command of the Italian armed forces. Moreover, the party hierarchy's formal disavowal of its leader by a majority of nearly eight to three authorised the sovereign to remove Mussolini from power.

Mussolini's attitude on the day following his defeat was incomprehensible. The Japanese Ambassador Hidaka, whom he received during the morning of July 26, found him full of confidence, and when the Duce went on to his audience with the King he took with him documents designed to show, as he wrote later, that "The Grand Council's motion committed nobody as this body was purely consultative."

What followed is well known. Mussolini presented himself at the Villa Savoia at 1700 hours and was informed by the King that it was his intention to relieve him of his powers and to appoint Badoglio as head of the government. Twenty minutes later the fallen dictator was requested to leave in an ambulance and was taken to a military police barracks. From here he was put on a boat on the following Tuesday for the island of Ponza.

Marshal Badoglio reported the King's

account to him of this meeting with the Duce: "Mussolini asked for an audience which I arranged to be held here at 1700 hours. At the time in question he presented himself and informed me as follows: the Grand Council had passed a motion against him, but he did not think that this was binding. I then told him that I could not agree because the Grand Council was a body of the State set up by him and ratified by the two houses of the Italian Parliament and that, as a consequence, every act of this Council was binding. 'So then, according to your Majesty, I must resign?' Mussolini said with evident effort. 'Yes,' I replied, 'and I would advise you now that I am accepting without further discussion your resignation as head of the government.'

"His Majesty then added: 'At these words Mussolini bent forwards as if he had received a violent blow in the chest and muttered: 'This is the end then.'"

There was sensation in Rome and throughout Italy, but no reaction in favour of the Duce either among the population in general or within the party. With rare exceptions, such as that of Roberto Farinacci who reached Germany dressed in a Wehrmacht uniform, everyone rallied to the new government. The new Foreign Minister was Baron Guari-

△ *A happy crowd welcomes the arrival of American forces in the Sicilian city of Palermo.*
◁ *Benito Mussolini. His days as the leader of a united Italy were now numbered – all he had to look forward to was a comfortable incarceration by the new authorities, and then rescue by the Germans. But even this latter merely confirmed the ex-dictator's rôle as Hitler's latest lackey.*

glia, formerly Italian Ambassador in Ankara. His was the job of getting Italy out of the war. But as everyone was afraid of Hitler's reaction there was an immediate proclamation: "The war goes on!" As for the Fascist conspirators of July 25, they were kept away from all participation in the new government. Count Ciano thought it wiser to seek refuge in Germany.

Hitler's reaction

When Hitler heard at Rastenburg that his ally Mussolini had been ousted, he realised at once what this meant and Badoglio's proclamation came as no surprise to him. In his evening report on July 25 he had exclaimed, according to his secretary's shorthand notes: "That's just the way people like that would behave. It is treachery. But we too will go on and play the same game: get everything ready to make a lightning grab at the whole clique and put them all away. Tomorrow morning I'll send someone over there to give the commander of the 3rd Motorised Division the order to go into Rome without more ado, arrest the King, the whole bag of tricks, the Crown Prince and seize the scum, especially Badoglio and his gang. You'll see, they'll collapse like pricked balloons and in two or three days there'll be quite a different situation."

Rommel moves in

Whatever may be said about the coarseness and exaggeration of Hitler's words, the fact nevertheless remains that he and his collaborators reacted against this event, which took them by surprise, with all the promptness and the implacable resolution which they had shown in late March 1941 when the coup d'état in Belgrade had taken Yugoslavia out of the Tripartite Pact.

Field-Marshal Kesselring received orders to withdraw XIV Panzer Corps, now up to strength at four divisions, from Sicily and to move over to Corsica from Sardinia the 90th *Panzergrenadier* Division, which had replaced the 90th Light Division, torn to pieces in Tunisia. That same evening, Field-Marshal Rommel, who had just landed in Salonika on a tour of inspection, was ordered to drop everything and to go at once to O.K.W. Here he was given command of Operation *"Alarich"*, a plan which had been ready for some months against an eventual Italian defection. By the 29th he was installed in his Army Group "B" headquarters in Munich, and he moved the lot over to Bologna by about August 15. Within a few days, LI and LXXXVII Corps, amounting to eight divisions, including the 24th Panzer and the *"Leibstandarte Adolf Hitler"*, had come down from France through the Brenner and Tarvis Passes and taken up positions north of the Apennines.

Kesselring, still the commander in the field, was south of this mountain barrier and was reinforced by the 2nd Parachute Division, which had landed unexpectedly in the area of Pratica di Mare some 15 miles south of Rome. All this goes to show that Hitler was not as short of men and *matériel* as he had given out at the Feltre conference. On August 6 Ribbentrop and Field-Marshal Keitel met Guariglia and General Ambrosio at Tarvis. On the 15th Jodl, accompanied by Rommel, met General Roatta, the Italian Army Chief-of-Staff, in Bologna. As can well be imagined, all these conversations went on in an atmosphere of mutual reticence and suspicion. Furthermore, the plan which was to liberate Mussolini and bring him back to power was being hatched in great secrecy under Hitler himself.

Guariglia was the first to admit this duplicity, but excused himself on the grounds of state: "Finally Ribbentrop revealed his hand and asked me solemnly if I could give him my word that the Italian Government was not in the act of treating with the Allies. A single moment's hesitation could have gravely compromised all that I had painstakingly built up during the last two hours. Fortunately this was not to be and I replied at once that I could give him my word, but I confess that for a long time the lie weighed heavily on my conscience even though I tried to excuse it to myself by thinking that at that precise moment negotiations properly speaking had not yet begun in Lisbon and that we were still only at the stage of overtures. Be that as it may, my conscience is still subject to the ancient adage: *Salus Reipublicae suprema lex*. Mine was a situation in which, as Balzac wrote, loyalty ceases to be a force and blind confidence is always a fault."

Rommel, in his notes of the meetings, and Kesselring, in his memoirs, both comment

△ The view from Russia: a despondent Mussolini awaits the worst on the crumbling boot of Italy.

harshly on the behaviour of their ex-ally. In retrospect General von Senger und Etterlin judged the matter more calmly and he probably gave it the right tone when he wrote: "Historically—and not from the point of view of the disappointed ally—Victor Emmanuel III did his people as great a service in pulling out of the war in time as he had done after Caporetto in showing such a spirit of resistance. The fact that he was unable to take this decision openly and in agreement with his National-Socialist ally was a result of the relations of that ally with other powers."

The fact still remains that the armistice signed on September 3 at Cassabile near Syracuse was to plunge Italy into a tragedy, the physical and moral consequences of which were to be remembered for a very long time; indeed they

△ The hotel in which Mussolini was held prior to his rescue by Skorzeny's commandos.
▷ △ Mussolini prepares to board the Fieseler Storch flying him to "liberty".
▷ ▽ The aircraft moves off to the best wishes of Skorzeny's men.

Otto Skorzeny was born in 1908. Invalided out of his regiment in 1942, he was asked to form a commando unit. In 1943 he led the rescue of Mussolini, descending in gliders with 90 men upon a garrison of 250. Later he kidnapped the son of the Regent of Hungary, and in the Ardennes in 1944 he led a group of commandos to create havoc behind the enemy lines.

may even be remembered still.

Could events have taken a different turn? That would have meant that the Italian armed forces would have had to be greater in number and less exhausted than they were on the day when Marshal Badoglio proclaimed the armistice, and that his Anglo-American counterparts would have had to attach greater importance to the complete and total occupation of the peninsula. Remember that at "Trident" both President Roosevelt and General Marshall had shown little inclination to push beyond Naples and Foggia. Finally, the 46 days which elapsed between the fall of Mussolini and the announcement of the armistice allowed the Germans to reinforce their positions in Italy, and this to the extent of 17 divisions.

On August 12 Generals Castellano and Montenari left Rome for Lisbon, where they met General W. Bedell Smith, Eisenhower's chief-of-staff, and General Kenneth Strong, the British head of his Intelligence staff. The Italians were handed the text of an armistice which had been approved at the end of July by London and Washington. On the 27th, Badoglio's delegates returned to the Italian capital with this text, a radio set and a cipher key so that they could communicate directly and secretly with Allied G.H.Q.

During the discussions there had been less disagreement over the conditions asked for by the victors than over quite a different problem: before laying down their arms, Eisenhower reports, the Italians wished to have "the assurance that such a powerful Allied force would land on the mainland simultaneously

with their surrender that the government itself and their cities would enjoy complete protection from the German forces. Consequently they tried to obtain every detail of our plans. These we would not reveal because the possibility of treachery could never be excluded. Moreover, to invade Italy with the strength that the Italians themselves believed necessary was a complete impossibility for the very simple reason that we did not have the troops in the area nor the ships to transport them had they been there. Italian military authorities could not conceive of the Allies undertaking this venture with less than fifteen divisions in the assault waves. We were planning to use only three with some reinforcing units, aside from the two that were to dash across the Messina strait."

Eisenhower's reaction is understandable but so also is Badoglio's anxiety, which was quite legitimate. Expecting a powerful reaction by the Germans, it was important for him to know, as Commander-in-Chief, if the Anglo-American landings would be south or north of Rome and in what strength, and if there would be a diversion in the Adriatic, preferably at Rimini. This was the point of view expressed by Castellano on August 31 when he met General Bedell Smith in the latter's tent at Cassabile. But Bedell Smith maintained an icy silence. It was, however, agreed that on the night of the armistice an airborne division would land on the outskirts of Rome whilst an armoured formation would disembark at the mouth of the Tiber.

Castellano thus returned to Rome with this proposition and on the following day, in accordance with the agreed instructions of the King, Marshal Badoglio, Foreign Minister Guariglia, and General Ambrosio, Castellano sent the following message to Bedell Smith: "Reply affirmative repeat affirmative stop person known will arrive tomorrow Sept 2 at time and place agreed stop confirmation requested."

Thus on September 3, 1943 at 1715 hours the Cassabile armistice was signed in triplicate in the presence of Macmillan and Murphy, the representatives respectively of the British and American Governments. When the signatures had been exchanged, Castellano relates, "Eisenhower came up to me, shook my hand and said that from then on he looked upon me as a colleague who would collaborate with him."

Operation *"Achse"*, the new name for what had formerly been *"Alarich"*.

Though expected, the German reaction caught the Italians off balance. In northern Italy Rommel put into the bag the ten divisions serving alongside his own. In Rome General Carboni's motorised and armoured corps melted away into the dust of the 3rd *Panzergrenadier* and the 2nd Parachute Divisions.

The Royal family, the Badoglio government, and *Comando Supremo* set off for Bari whilst old Marshal Caviglia concluded a cease-fire with Kesselring.

On September 9, at 0300 hours, three battleships, six light cruisers, and nine destroyers left La Spezia for Malta in accordance with the armistice agreement. At 1550 hours, whilst it was off Asinara island, north-west of Sardinia, the convoy was spotted by 15 Dornier Do 217's which had taken off from Istres under the command of Major Jope with orders to intercept. These planes were armed with PC 1400 radio-controlled bombs, weighing a ton and a half with about 770 lb of explosive. One of these hit the forward fuel tanks of the battleship *Roma* (46,000 tons) which went down with 1,523 officers and men, including Admiral Carlo Bergamini. Her sister ship *Italia*, formerly *Littorio*, was also hit. However, on the 10th the La Spezia squadron anchored in the Grand Harbour, where it joined another from Taranto consisting of two battleships, two cruisers, and two destroyers. On the following day the battleship *Giulio Cesare*, which had succeeded in escaping from Pola, announced that it had joined the forces of Admiral Cunningham who was able to telegraph the Admiralty as follows: "Be pleased to inform your Lordships that the Italian Battle fleet now lies at anchor under the guns of the fortress of Malta."

In the Balkans, 19 German divisions surprised and disarmed 29 Italian divisions. The "Acqui" Division (General Gandin) held on the island of Cephalonia until September 22, when it had to lay down its arms through lack of ammunition; it was then almost completely wiped out after capitulating. A similar fate awaited General Cigala-Fulgosi and the officers of the "Bergamo" Division, who were guilty of defending Spalato for 19 days against the *Waffen* S.S. *"Prinz Eugen"* Division. Thousands of survivors of this horrible butchery joined Tito or the Greek resistance in the Pindhos mountains and the Peloponnese. The navy managed

Mussolini escapes his Italian captors on September 12, 1943.
Δ Δ *Walking towards the* Storch *light aircraft that flew him to Rome.*
Δ *With his rescuer Skorzeny just before the take-off.*

Then a serious difficulty arose. Whereas the Italian Government was expecting the landings to take place on September 12, and would put off the declaration of the armistice until this date, D-day for Operation "Avalanche" had been fixed for the 9th. General Maxwell Taylor was sent to Rome on September 8 to arrange the final details for the landing of his airborne division, and it was doubtless from him that Badoglio learned that the newly-signed armistice would be announced that very evening. He tried to gain time, but in vain, for, wrote General Eisenhower, "the matter had proceeded too far for me to temporize further. I replied in a peremptory telegram that regardless of his action I was going to announce the surrender at six-thirty o'clock as previously agreed upon and that if I did so without simultaneous action on his part Italy would have no friend left in the war."

Badoglio had to comply and broadcast a proclamation. This took place an hour later, but within minutes of his leaving the microphone Hitler had launched finally to get 25,000 of them across the Adriatic.

Churchill was quite unable to argue Roosevelt into supporting Italian resistance in the Dodecanese archipelago, though he did get 234th Brigade (Brigadier-General Tinley) put ashore on Cos and Leros. The result was that the Germans counter-attacked with paratroops and on November 18 it was all over.

On September 12, a glider-borne force from the commando led by Otto Skorzeny rescued Mussolini from the remote hotel in which he was being held in the Gran Sasso mountains. In Mussolini's words:

"At dawn on Sunday the summit of the Gran Sasso was covered in heavy clouds. However, some aircraft were heard passing overhead. I had a feeling that this day was going to determine my fate. Towards mid-day the clouds cleared and the sun came through. I was standing with arms folded in front of my open window when—it was precisely two o'clock—an aeroplane suddenly landed a hundred yards away. Four or five men dressed in khaki and carrying two machine guns jumped out of the cockpit and ran towards the villa. A few seconds later, other aircraft landed nearby and their crews all did the same thing. All the carabinieri, brandishing their arms, rushed to the road to cut off the attackers. At the head of the attackers was Skorzeny. The carabinieri were preparing to fire when I spotted amongst the Germans an Italian officer whom I recognised as General Soletti. In the silence just before the shooting began I suddenly shouted: 'What are you doing? Can't you see? You're going to fire on an Italian general! Don't shoot!' As they saw the Italian general approaching they lowered their weapons."

Mussolini was thus able to proclaim the Italian Socialist Republic on September 18. But none of the neutrals, not even Spain, agreed to set up diplomatic relations with it; in Rome Cavallero committed suicide after Kesselring had offered him the command of a new Fascist army; when the snow had made the Alps impassable no fewer than 18,400 Italians in Venetia, Lombardy, and Piedmont had got themselves interned in Switzerland; and in Italy some opposed the new régime by strikes and sabotage, others by armed resistance. Allied operations were soon to benefit from the information fed through by brave and efficient networks of guerrillas.

△ *After his escape from the Gran Sasso by* Storch, *Mussolini transferred to a Ju 52 for the rest of his journey to Germany. Here he is seen alighting at Rastenburg.*

◁ *and* ▽ *Hitler greets his one-time equal. Much to the former's disgust, Mussolini seemed to have lost all his fire, and it was only after much badgering from the Führer that Mussolini declared the new Italian Socialist Republic on September 15.*

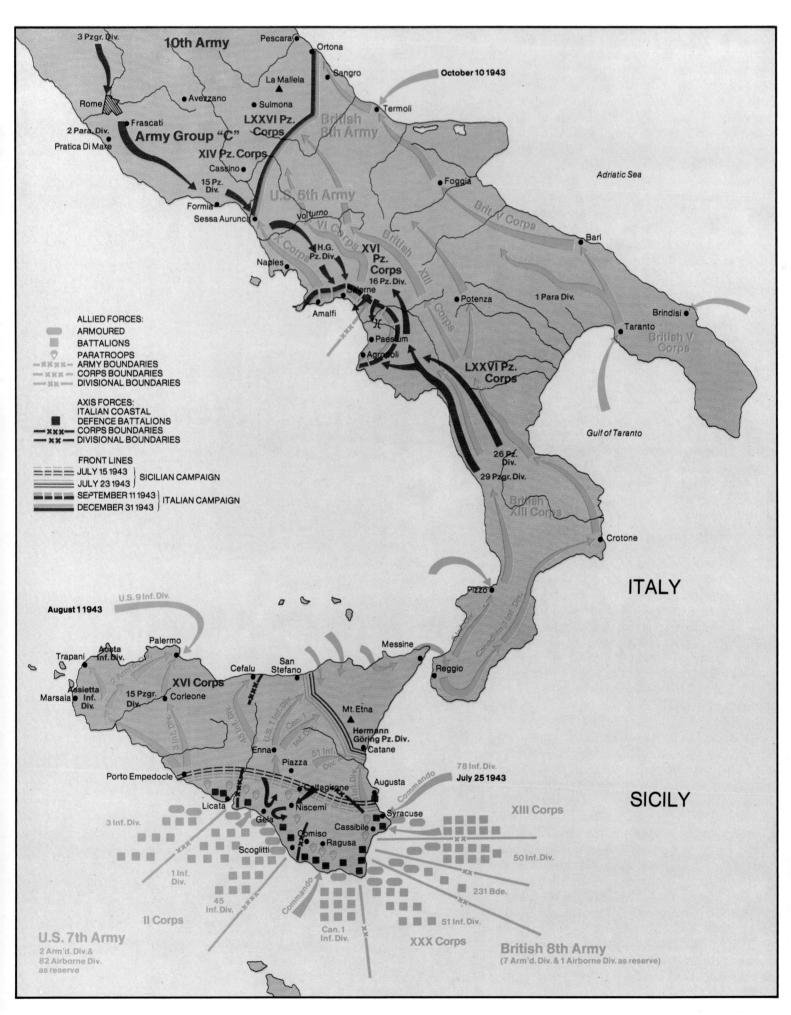

3 Pzgr. Div.

10th Army

Pescara

Ortona

Sangro

La Mallela ▲

Avezzano

Sulmona

October 10 1943

Termoli

British 8th Army

Rome

Frascati

2 Para. Div.

Army Group "C"

Pratica Di Mare

LXXVI Pz. Corps

XIV Pz. Corps

Cassino

15 Pz. Div.

Adriatic Sea

Formia

Sessa Aurunca

Volturno

U.S. 5th Army

VI Corps

X Corps

Foggia

Brit V Corps

Naples

H.G. Pz.Div.

XVI Pz. Corps

16 Pz. Div.

British XIII Corps

Bari

Amalfi

Salerne

Paestum

Potenza

1 Para Div.

Agropoli

LXXVI Pz. Corps

Brindisi

Taranto

British V Corps

Gulf of Taranto

26 Pz. Div.

29 Pzgr. Div.

British XIII Corps

ITALY

Crotone

ALLIED FORCES:
- ARMOURED
- BATTALIONS
- PARATROOPS
- ARMY BOUNDARIES
- CORPS BOUNDARIES
- DIVISIONAL BOUNDARIES

AXIS FORCES:
- ITALIAN COASTAL DEFENCE BATTALIONS
- CORPS BOUNDARIES
- DIVISIONAL BOUNDARIES

FRONT LINES
- JULY 15 1943 } SICILIAN CAMPAIGN
- JULY 23 1943 }
- SEPTEMBER 11 1943 } ITALIAN CAMPAIGN
- DECEMBER 31 1943 }

Pizzo

Canadian 1 Inf. Div.

U.S. 9 Inf. Div.

August 1 1943

Messine

Reggio

Palermo

Trapani

Aosta Inf. Div.

XVI Corps

Cefalu

San Stefano

2 Arm'd Div.

Assietta Inf. Div.

Marsala

15 Pzgr. Div.

Corleone

U.S. 1 Inf. Div.

Mt. Etna ▲

Enna

Hermann Göring Pz. Div.

Catane

Piazza

51 Inf. Div.

Porto Empedocle

Caltagirone

78 Inf. Div.

July 25 1943

Licata

Niscemi

Augusta

Commando

Gela

Syracuse

XIII Corps

3 Inf. Div.

Scoglitti

Comiso

Cassibile

Ragusa

50 Inf. Div.

1 Inf. Div.

231 Bde.

45 Inf. Div.

Commando

Can. 1 Inf. Div.

51 Inf. Div.

SICILY

II Corps

XXX Corps

U.S. 7th Army
2 Arm'd. Div.&
82 Airborne Div.
as reserve

British 8th Army
(7 Arm'd. Div. & 1 Airborne Div. as reserve)

1172

CHAPTER 88
SALERNO: the invasion of Italy

As we have seen, in the case of defection by the Italians, Field-Marshal Kesselring was ordered to withdraw the 90th *Panzergrenadier* Division from Sardinia and send it across the Bonifacio channel to join the forces defending Corsica. To this effect, O.K.W. put the troops stationed on the two islands under the command of General von Senger und Etterlin, who arrived in Ajaccio on board a Dornier Do 17 on September 7.

On Sardinia General Basso, who was in command of the island, had under him XVI and XXX Corps (two infantry and three coastal defence divisions), plus the "Bari" Division and the "Nembo" Parachute Division. This would appear to have been more than enough to deal with the 90th *Panzergrenadier*. It should not be forgotten, however, that the Ger-

man formation, being in reserve, was concentrated in the centre of the island, completely motorised and commanded by a man of high quality, Lieutenant-General Lungershausen. It also had the high morale of all former *Afrika Korps* units.

On the opposing side the Italians had half their forces scattered along the coastline, whilst their "mobile" reserves simply lacked mobility and their anti-tank guns were no use against the Panzers. Under these conditions all General Basso could do was to follow the 90th *Panzergrenadier* as it withdrew. At the end of the day on September 18, the German evacuation of Sardinia was complete. The Germans had left behind them 50 dead, 100 wounded, and 395 prisoners, against the Italians' 120.

△ *American troops during the Salerno landings. The Allies landed on September 9 and soon secured a beach-head, but Kesselring reacted with great skill and energy, nearly managing to cut the Allied position in two.*

▷ *The invasion gets under way. In the foreground are Landing Ships Tank, each capable of transporting some 18 30-ton tanks or 27 3-ton lorries and eight jeeps, with up to 177 troops as well. Until the Allies were able to break out of the bridgehead, it was the tanks that were found more useful.*

▽ *British infantry land from an LST (2) provided by the United States under Lend-Lease.*

On Corsica the Axis forces under General Magli comprised VII Corps ("Cremona" and "Friuli" Divisions), two coastal defence divisions, and an armoured brigade of the *Waffen S.S. Leibstandarte*. On the announcement of the Italian armistice the resistance forces which, since December 1942, had received by submarine or air-drop more than 10,000 automatic weapons, occupied Ajaccio, joined General Magli and appealed for help to Algiers. Meanwhile the Germans were able to drive their former allies out of Bonifacio and Bastia.

General Giraud in Algiers did not turn a deaf ear to the appeal from Corsica. With the help of Rear-Admiral Lemmonier, he improvised a small expeditionary force whose forward units reached Ajaccio on the night of September 12-13. These were 109 men of the famous Shock Battalion, who had crammed themselves aboard the submarine *Casabianca* which was still under the command of L'Herminier. On the following day the large destroyers *Fantasque* and *Terrible* landed over 500 men from the battalion and kept up the shuttle service together with the destroyers *Tempête* and *Alcyon*; then the cruisers *Montcalm* and *Jeanne d'Arc* joined in, despite the Luftwaffe's latest glide bomb.

Italy joins the Allies

But on September 12 O.K.W. had changed its mind and orders were sent to Senger und Etterlin to abandon Corsica and evacuate the 90th *Panzergrenadier* to Piombino. This move was completed by October 4. The 5,000 infantry and *goums* of the 4th Moroccan Mountain Division, with the help of their new Italian allies, had managed to repel the German rearguard but were quite unable to cut off the main force. The British and Americans, busy south of Naples, were too late to get to this miniature Dunkirk, which rescued some 28,000 men for the Wehrmacht.

Only a partial success, in spite of the sacrifice of 222 Frenchmen and 637 Italians, the occupation of Corsica nevertheless gave the Allies a strategic position of the first importance, with 17 aerodromes capable of taking and maintaining 2,000 planes which the American air force moved onto the island within a matter of months. As the armed forces of the Third Reich had by now spilt copious amounts of Italian blood, Marshal Badoglio's government declared war on it on October 13 and received from the "United Nations", as Roosevelt called them, the status of "co-belligerent." This raised the hackles of Harry Hopkins but was fully approved by Stalin.

Near disaster at Salerno

"Salerno: A near disaster" was the title given by General Mark Wayne Clark, commander of the American 5th Army, to the chapter of his memoirs in which he described the landings at Salerno. The whole affair was indeed nearly a disaster and that the Allies did in fact win through

▽ *Bren-gun carriers head inland. Proof against small arms fire, these light carriers provided useful battlefield mobility for tactical infantry units.*

was the result not only of Clark's obstinacy and Montgomery's promptness but also, and perhaps more so, of the bad relationship between Rommel and Kesselring.

The plan drawn up by Generals Eisenhower and Alexander, Air Chief Marshal Tedder, and Admiral Cunningham involved a diversionary action by the 8th Army across the Strait of Messina to pin down the enemy's forces. When this had been done, the 5th Army was to land in the Gulf of Salerno.

On September 3, under cover of fire

from a naval force led by Vice-Admiral Willis, and from some 600 8th Army guns the British XIII Corps made a landing on the coast of Calabria north-west of Reggio di Calabria. It met no serious resistance as the 29th *Panzergrenadier* Division which, with the 26th Panzer Division and the 1st Parachute Division, formed the LXXVI Panzer Corps (General Dostler), had received orders not to get caught up in any engagement. General Dempsey thus had no difficulty in pushing his 5th Division up to Pizzo and his 1st Canadian Division to Crotone. This withdrawal by the enemy had not entered into the plans of the Allied 15th Army Group.

On September 8 Kesselring learned at his H.Q. in Frascati that a powerful Anglo-American fleet was now in the waters of the Tyrrhenian Sea and concluded that a landing must be imminent, though there was nothing to show whether it would be in the Gulf of Salerno, in the Bay of Naples, or on the beaches opposite Rome. To oppose it he had had under his command since August 8 the 10th Army (General von Vietinghoff), the units of which were deployed as follows:

1. XIV Panzer Corps, back from Sicily, had its 15th *Panzergrenadier* at Formia, its "Hermann Göring" Panzer Division in Naples, and its 16th Panzer Division (Major-General Sieckenius) in the Salerno area (by August 22, Hitler had told Vietinghoff to regard Salerno as "the centre of gravity", and this was why 16th Panzer had been moved there);

2. LXXVI Panzer Corps, as we have seen, was engaged in Calabria; and

3. Though earmarked for Operation *"Achse"*, the 2nd Parachute Division and the 3rd *Panzergrenadier* Division were well placed to cover the Italian capital.

The curtain rose at dawn on September 9 when the first elements of the American VI Corps (Major-General Ernest W. Dawley) and the British X Corps (Lieutenant-General Richard L. Mc-Creery) landed between Paestum and Maiori, on either side of Salerno. The naval forces assigned to the operation (codename "Avalanche") were somewhat similar to those used against Sicily: they included seven aircraft-carriers for first-line support and were led by the American Vice-Admiral H. Kent Hewitt.

Attacked on a front of some 25 miles, the 16th Panzer Division had to give ground but did not disintegrate. By the end of the day the American 36th Division had got five miles inland, but

the British X Corps had not reached all its objectives and fighting continued in the streets of Salerno. Sieckenius still controlled the high ground which overlooked the coastal strip from a distance of 600 to 1000 yards. The American 45th Division was landed and this allowed Clark to extend and deepen his bridgehead, which on September 11 was 11 miles inland at its furthest point and stretched from Agropoli to Amalfi with a circumference of over 43 miles.

◁ and ◁▽ Elements of the American VI Corps come ashore in the southern part of the landings at Salerno.
▽ As the forward troops pushed inland, the beach area was organised to feed supplies and reinforcements up to the front as quickly as possible. Here an American amphibious landing vehicle passes a bulldozer at work on the beach.

"Avalanche" was off to a good start. In Frascati, however, Kesselring had remained calm and XIV Panzer Corps was ordered to concentrate and counterattack. LXXVI Corps also came to the rescue, leaving Montgomery facing only its 1st Parachute Division and part of the 26th Panzer Division. The capture of Rome enabled Kesselring to give the 3rd *Panzergrenadier* Division (Lieutenant-General Graeser) to the 10th Army, so that by September 12 Vietinghoff had five and a half divisions, admittedly understrength, against his enemy's four, scattered over a wide front. This led to a crisis that did not end until September 15.

Profiting from the fact that the British right flank (56th Division) had made slower progress than the American left (45th Division), the Germans attempted to get a pincer movement round the latter, cut the British off from the Americans, and destroy both piecemeal. The crux of this battle was at Ponte Bruciato, where Clark threw in everything he had, including two artillery battalions, a regimental band, and his H.Q. orderlies and cooks. The German advance was slowed down and eventually stopped some five miles from the beach, where it

General Mark Wayne Clark was born in 1896 and entered the Army via West Point. He was promoted to major-general in 1942 and served as Eisenhower's deputy in the "Torch" landings. In November of the same year he was promoted to lieutenant-general and appointed to command the 5th Army the following January. Clark commanded at Salerno, first establishing a secure beach-head and then pushing north to take Naples on October 1. The 5th Army now advanced to the Volturno. In December 1944 Clark took over from Alexander as the commander of the 15th Army Group.

was pinned down by the concentrated fire of the fleet which Admiral Hewitt had brought as close inshore as possible. Although the capture of Rome by the Germans had freed the 3rd *Panzergrenadier* Division for Kesselring, it also released the American 82nd Parachute Division (Major-General Ridgway) which was to have landed in support of the Italians; during the night of September 13–14 a first paratroop regiment reached the bridgehead.

Rommel's pessimism

What would have happened if, on the morning of the 9th, Rommel had put at Kesselring's disposal his 24th Panzer Division and the "*Leibstandarte Adolf Hitler*", and Kesselring had then used them at Salerno? The question cannot be answered as the Führer refused to reinforce the 10th Army, having been advised by Rommel that Italy could not be defended south of a line La Spezia–Rimini. In face of the threat to the American 5th Army, Alexander called on Montgomery to come up in haste and catch the forces attacking the bridgehead. Montgomery managed to do this, though in his memoirs he gallantly states that it was more or less all over on September 16 when his 5th Division got to Agropoli. On that day the 5th Army had five divisions or their equivalent engaged in the battle and had lost 5,674 officers, N.C.O.s, and men, including 756 killed and 2,150 missing. In addition, the British battleship *Warspite* and the cruiser *Uganda*, as well as the American cruiser *Savannah*, had been badly damaged by the Luftwaffe's new radio-controlled bombs. After this crisis, Clark got Eisenhower's permission to relieve VI Corps' commander and replaced him by Major-General John P. Lucas. The British Army was assigned the province of Apulia and the Cassibile armistice allowed the uneventful landing of its V Corps (Lieutenant-General Allfrey) in the well-equipped ports of Taranto and Brindisi.

The final defeat of the German 10th Army at Salerno and the threat to his rear forced Kesselring to disengage on September 16, but this brought a renewed conflict with Rommel, who wanted to abandon Rome, whereas Kesselring maintained that the Eternal City could be covered from a line running roughly Formia–Cassino–Pescara, using the Garigliano and the Rapido valleys and the Abruzzi mountains, which reached over 9,000 feet at La Malella. On November 21 Hitler recalled Rommel and moved Kesselring from his position as C.-in-C. South to head a new Army Group "C", thus leaving him in complete command in Italy.

Hitler transferred the 24th Panzer Division and the S.S. *Leibstandarte* Division to the Eastern Front. Kesselring allotted three divisions to the 10th Army and the balance of Army Group "B" in northern Italy went to form a new 14th Army under General von Mackensen.

Careful retreat

Meanwhile Vietinghoff, turning to great advantage the demolition and destruction which had been caused and the heavy autumn rains which, according to Montgomery, covered the roads in "chocolate sauce", did not allow his forces to get caught anywhere, either at Termoli on October 4, in spite of a commando landing behind his left flank, or on the Sangro on November 27 when the three divisions and an armoured brigade of V Corps broke out of the bridgehead and advanced along the line Sulmona–Avezzano to wipe out his 65th Division (Lieutenant-General von Ziehlberg). The rubble left after artillery shelling and aerial bombardment by the British, which their own tanks then had to get through (a sight which was to recur in the Caen campaign) made any exploitation impossible and in a couple of days Vietinghoff was making a stand again and stopping the Allied advance.

Enter the French

In spite of the evacuation of Naples on October 1, it was the same thing along the way to Rome through Cassino and through Formia. When it had got through Venafro and Sessa-Aurunca, the 5th Army came up against the mountains and the deep valley of the Garigliano. The reinforcements which the 5th Army had just received, II Corps and the 1st Armoured Division, were not the most likely formations to cross these obstacles. Invited by General Clark to give his opinion, General Juin stated on October 1

◁ Although uncertain where exactly the Allies intended to land in Italy, Kesselring had a shrewd idea that it was going to be Salerno, and had deployed his forces well. With the aid of large calibre guns he hoped to be able to deal heavy blows to the invasion forces as they approached the beaches, but the first class gunfire support from Allied warships lying off the shore was more than a match for the German artillery shelling the beach-head.
▷ Italian children celebrate the arrival of the Allies, in the form of a Sherman tank and its British crew.
▷ ▽ Sherman tanks of a Canadian armoured regiment, attached to an Indian division. From this railway station they gave close support in the capture of the village of San Donato.

"The whole way along the road from Salerno to Naples we kept running into the British 7th Division in close formation and incapable of getting off the road and deploying in the completely mountainous terrain. I had immediately concluded, along with Carpentier [his chief-of-staff], that the mechanisation of the British and American armies could actually hinder our rapid progress up the Italian peninsula. There is no doubt that the North African divisions would be very welcome . . ."

And indeed from November 22 onwards the French Expeditionary Corps did begin to land in Italy. It consisted of the 2nd Moroccan Division and the 3rd Algerian Division, totalling 65,000 men, 2,500 horses and mules, and 12,000 vehicles. But the corps was not used as such. Its 2nd Moroccan Division (General Dody) was attached to VI Corps which was trying to break out of the Mignano area, and General Lucas used it on his right some seven miles north of Venafro. The fortified position at Pantano was his first objective. This was defended by 305th Division (Lieutenant-General Hauck), a division which, wrote Marshal Juin "could never be caught napping". By December 18 the 2nd Moroccan Division, which had never before been under fire, had got the better of the difficult terrain and the strong enemy resistance. On the 26th it had a further success when it took Mount Mainarde and this enabled General Juin to claim a permanent position for his French Expeditionary Corps. He was successful, and the corps was allocated a position on the right of 5th Army's VI Corps.

All the same, Kesselring's strategy had to a large extent imposed itself on his enemy, so that unless a completely new offensive were to be mounted at once, the victory in Sicily, in spite of the Italian armistice, would now run out of steam. On December 24 Generals Eisenhower, Montgomery, and Spaatz flew to London and the Italian theatre of operations was relegated to the background.

CHAPTER 89
KURSK: greatest land battle

Operation *"Zitadelle"* was launched on July 5 against the Kursk salient and constituted the final attempt by the German Army to recover the operational initiative on the Eastern Front. But before turning our attention to this, it is desirable to examine briefly the events that occurred during the first three months of 1943 along the somewhat circuitous front line running from north of Kursk to Lake Ladoga. These were deliberately omitted from Chapter 83 so as to give full effect to the account of the Battle of Stalingrad and its consequences.

On this front Army Groups "Centre" and "North", still commanded by Field-Marshals von Kluge and von Küchler respectively, were composed of seven armies (23 corps of 117 divisions or their equivalent on January 1, nine of them Panzer and eight motorised). The extremely winding course of the line on which the Germans had stabilised their positions at the end of March 1942 meant that it could not be held in any depth. To make matters worse, the lakes, rivers, and marshy tracts, so characteristic of the region, freeze hard and allow not only infantry and cavalry to pass over them but also lorries, artillery, and even tanks.

On January 4, the 3rd *Panzerarmee* on Kluge's left flank was broken through by troops of the 3rd Shock Army (Kalinin Front) on either side of Velikiye-Luki. A fortnight later, after every attempt to relieve the citadel of the town had failed, its defenders, reduced to 102 in number, managed to find their way back to the German lines, leaving 200 wounded behind them.

Of graver consequence was the defeat inflicted on the German 18th Army (Colonel-General G. Lindemann) to the south of Lake Ladoga. At O.K.H. this sector was known as the "bottleneck" on account of the pronounced salient formed by the front between Mga and the southern shore of the lake. But to evacuate it would have meant abandoning the siege of Leningrad; and for this reason Hitler had always opposed any suggestion that it should be done. XVI Corps (General Wodrig) held the salient and was hence liable to be cut off as soon as the Neva, which covered its left flank, no longer constituted an obstacle to the enemy.

▽ A corporal moves up through a communications trench. He is carrying two Teller 43 anti-tank mines, possibly one of the most efficient mines of World War II.

▽ ▽ A German 8.1-cm mortar troop in action. They are loading the standard H.E. bomb. Note the stack of ammunition boxes, which were made from the same stamped steel pattern as jerricans.

Voroshilov relieves Leningrad

The task of co-ordinating the combined action of the Leningrad Front (Lieutenant-General M. A. Govorov) and the Volkhov Front (General K. A. Meretskov) was entrusted to Marshal K. Voroshilov. Govorov's 67th Army (Lieutenant-General V. P. Sviridov) was ordered to make contact with the 2nd Shock Army (Lieutenant-General I. I. Fedyuninsky) and the 8th Army (Lieutenant-General F. N. Starikov) both under the command of General Meretskov. According to a chart drawn up in Moscow, the operation involved 12 divisions and one infantry brigade taking on four German divisions. And whereas the Soviet divisions in all probability numbered some 10,000 men each, those of the Reich were severely reduced. In particular, the Russians could deploy almost 100 guns and mortars per mile, and each of the two fronts had its own air cover and support.

Hence the Russian attack on January 12, 1943 was backed by massive firepower and followed a sustained artillery bombardment lasting 90 minutes. Nevertheless, XVI Corps held the attack, with Lindemann, then Küchler, soon coming to its aid. Consequently it took a full week for the 2nd Shock Army advancing from the west and the 67th Army from the east to fight their way across the ten miles that divided them. On January 17, General Sviridov's troops entered Petrokrepost'; the following day, the entire population of Leningrad, delirious with joy, learnt that after 17 months' trials and privations borne with fortitude and stoicism, the siege had been broken. On February 6, railway communications between Peter the Great's capital city and the outside world were re-established. But the Russians were halted short of Mga, which meant that Leningrad's lifeline was restricted to a corridor six to seven miles wide. Stalin, however, was so pleased with the result that 19,000 decorations were awarded to the victorious troops who had raised the siege of Russia's second city.

This disaster, in which the 41st and 277th Infantry Divisions were almost entirely destroyed, and still more the rapid and tragic succession of defeats suffered south of Kursk, induced Hitler to

△ △ *A German machine-gunner in the frozen shell-torn soil of the Lake Ladoga sector. With winter the German lines came under greater pressure as the Russians were able to cross the frozen lakes and marshes.*
△ *A Russian officer mans a scissor binocular in an observation post in a ruined village. The assault in January 1943 was preceded by a 90-minute bombardment.*
▷ *A Soviet soldier carries a wounded comrade to the rear. Medical facilities were severely strained during the siege of Leningrad.*

agree to certain adjustments to the front line which he had obstinately refused to allow his generals to make the previous year, on the grounds that enormous quantities of *matériel* might be lost in the course of withdrawal.

Strategic retreat by O.K.H.

With this authorisation, O.K.H., between the 19th and the end of February, effected the evacuation of the "fortress" of Demy'ansk, which was linked to the 16th Army's front line only by a narrow corridor under constant threat. The withdrawal was an orderly one and permitted a front line economy of seven divisions.

Next, starting on March 2, Operation *"Buffle"*, whereby 30 divisions of the German 4th and 9th Armies withdrew 100 miles, was set in motion. Once again, the actual manoeuvre failed to justify the Führer's apprehensions, feigned or real. Rzhev, Gzhatsk, then Vyaz'ma were one after the other evacuated in the course of a manoeuvre which lasted more than three weeks, without the Russians, who in the event were considerably delayed by numerous minefields, showing themselves particularly aggressive. The evacuation of the salient, which had a front of 410 miles, was completed on March 25. Field-Marshal von Kluge was thus able to deploy his armies along a front slightly less than half as long (230 miles), thus releasing 14 divisions.

Two comments seem appropriate here. Firstly, that the 21 divisions pulled back out of salients, in February and March 1943, were more or less equivalent in numbers to the Rumanian 3rd Army and the Italian 8th Army, whose destruction had sealed the fate of the German 6th Army in the Stalingrad pocket. What might the result have been if it had been they who were called on to reinforce Army Group "B" when Paulus reached the Volga? The question is one of pure speculation, however. Secondly, if the Rzhev salient was defended by one division for every 16 miles of front, Operation *"Buffle"*, which left Kluge with 16 divisions in order to hold 240 miles, made no appreciable difference to his own situation (15 miles per division). And proof of this would be given no later than July 13 following, on the occasion of the

Soviet offensive directed against the Orel salient. But how could anything else have been done?

△ Encumbered by greatcoats, Russian infantrymen double through the misty woodland on the Leningrad Front.

The orders go out for Operation *"Zitadelle"*

In any event, this agonising question did not preoccupy Hitler who, on April 15, put his signature to the 13 copies of Operational Order No. 16. The document is

▽ A Russian 152-mm howitzer pounds German positions in the Bryansk area.

△ With a flame-thrower at point, a column of S.S. troopers plod through the rolling steppe. After "Zitadelle" their losses were so severe that they made up with volunteers from occupied countries, though the original units attempted to maintain their Germanic character.

▽ Pzkw IVF2s move through the outskirts of a Russian town. Even with extra armour and a more powerful gun, the Pzkw IV was still a stop-gap weapon when used on the Eastern Front.

a long one, as are all those which Hitler wrote, and the following extract will serve to illuminate the events that subsequently took place:

"I am resolved, as soon as the weather allows, to launch Operation 'Zitadelle', as the first offensive action of this year," were his opening words. "Hence the importance of this offensive. It must lead to a rapid and decisive success. It *must* give us the initiative for the coming spring and summer. In view of this, preparations must be conducted with the utmost precaution and the utmost energy. At the main points of attack the finest units, the finest weapons, the finest commanders will be committed, and plentiful supplies of munitions will be ensured. Every commander, every fighting man must be imbued with the capital significance of this offensive. The victory of Kursk must be as a beacon to the whole world.

"To this effect, I order:

1. Objective of the offensive: by means of a highly concentrated, and savage attack vigorously conducted by two armies, one from the area of Belgorod, the other from south of Orel, to encircle the enemy forces situated in the region of Kursk and annihilate them by concentric attacks.

"In the course of this offensive a new and shorter front line will be established,

permitting economies of means, along the line joining Nejega, Korocha, Skorodnoye, Tim, passing east of Shchigry, and Sosna."

Under Point 2, the Führer went on to define the conditions necessary for the success of the enterprise:

"(a) to ensure to the full the advantage of surprise, and principally to keep the enemy ignorant of the timing of attack;

(b) to concentrate to the utmost the attacking forces on narrow fronts so as to obtain an overwhelming local superiority in all arms (tanks, assault guns, artillery, and rocket launchers) grouped in a single echelon until junction between the two armies in the rear of the enemy is effected, thereby cutting him off from his rear areas;

(c) to bring up as fast as possible, from the rear, the forces necessary to cover the flanks of the offensive thrusts, thus enabling the attacking forces to concentrate solely on their advance;

(d) by driving into the pocket from all sides and with all possible speed, to give the enemy no respite, and to accelerate his destruction;

(e) to execute the attack at a speed so rapid that the enemy can neither prevent encirclement nor bring up reserves from his other fronts; and

(f) by the speedy establishment of the new front line, to allow the disengagement

△ Engineers watch as an 8-ton half-track prime mover tows a gun and limber over a newly completed bridge.

◁ An MG 34 in the sustained fire rôle. The tripod had a mechanism which enabled the firer to remain under cover, while the gun fired on a fixed arc.

▽ A 5-cm mortar crew. The man in the foreground appears to be an officer aspirant: he has the epaulet loops awarded to Unteroffizieranwärter.

The German 10.5-cm Howitzer 18 on Pzkw II chassis *"Wespe"*

Weight: 12.1 tons.
Crew: five.
Armament: one 10.5-cm 1.F.H. 18/2 with 32 rounds and one 7.92-mm MG 34 with 600 rounds.
Armour: nose 20-mm, glacis plate 10-mm, sides 15-mm, upper rear 8-mm, lower rear 15-mm, decking 10-mm, belly 5-mm, superstructure front 12-mm, sides 10-mm, rear 8-mm.
Engine: one Maybach HL 62 TR 6-cylinder inline, 140-hp.
Speed: 24.5 mph on roads, 11.5 mph cross-country.
Range: 90 miles on roads, 60 miles cross-country.
Length: 15 feet 8½ inches.
Width: 7 feet 4½ inches.
Height: 7 feet 8 inches.

of forces, especially the Panzer forces, with all possible despatch, so that they can be used for other purposes."

Then the Führer fixed the parts to be played by Army Groups "Centre" and "South" and the Luftwaffe, apportioned the means at their disposal, and laid down certain requirements for misleading the enemy as to the German intentions, and for the maintenance of secrecy. As from April 28, Kluge and Manstein were to be ready to launch the attack within six days of receiving the order from O.K.H., the earliest date suggested for the offensive being May 3.

Guderian's violent opposition

Hitler's initiative, which in fact stemmed from Colonel-General Kurt Zeitzler, Chief-of-Staff at O.K.H., nevertheless elicited varying reactions amongst the generals. Kluge gave determined support to Operation *"Zitadelle"*, but many others raised objection to it, some categorically, others only provisionally.

On May 2, Hitler had summoned the top commanders concerned in the enterprise, plus Colonel-General Guderian, to Munich. In his capacity as Inspector-General of Armoured Troops, Guderian put forward a whole series of impressive arguments against the projected offensive, which he sums up as follows in his memoirs:

"I asked permission to express my views and declared that the attack was pointless; we had only just completed the reorganisation and re-equipment of our Eastern Front; if we attacked according to the plan of the Chief of the General Staff we were certain to suffer heavy tank casualties, which we would not be in a position to replace in 1943; on the contrary, we ought to be devoting our new tank production to the Western Front so as to have mobile reserves available for use against the Allied landing which could be expected with certainty to take place in 1944. Furthermore, I pointed out that the Panthers, on whose performance the Chief of the Army General Staff was relying so heavily, were still suffering from many teething troubles inherent in all new equipment and it seemed unlikely that these could be put right in time for the launching of the attack."

Manstein expresses his preferences

Manstein had during the previous February and March declared his preference for a plan of operations radically different to that outlined in the order of April 15. He had told Hitler of this on the occasion of the Führer's visit to his H.Q. in Zaporozh'ye. In substance, his idea was to await the offensive that the enemy was bound to launch in order to recover the Donets basin. Once this had got under way, the Germans would conduct an orderly retreat to the Melitopol'–Dniepropetrovsk line, while at the same time a powerful armoured force would be assembled in the Poltava–Khar'kov region. Once the Russians had been led into the trap, this force would counter-attack with lightning speed in the direction of the Sea of Azov, and the superiority which

△ △ A "Marder" *self-propelled anti-tank gun passes a group of S.S. men who have occupied an abandoned Russian trench near Belgorod. Two captured Red soldiers can be seen in the middle of the group.*
△ Hauptmann (*Flight-Lieutenant) Hans-Ulrich Rudel after receiving the Oak Leaves to his Knight's Cross. Rudel destroyed 12 Russian tanks on the first day of "Zitadelle" and by the end of the war he had flown 2,530 operational sorties and destroyed 519 tanks.*

△ "Marder" III tank destroyers, German PaK 40 7.5-cm guns mounted on Czech T-38 chassis, move up through a shell-ravaged Russian village. These Marders were useful, but no real substitute for tanks.

▽ A Pzkw VI Tiger. These heavy tanks first appeared on the Eastern Front in 1942 and in Tunisia in 1943. Their armour, up to 100-mm thick, proved invulnerable to the fire of Allied 75- and 76·2-mm anti-tank guns.

German commanders had always shown over their Russian counterparts in mobile warfare would bring them victory.

"The guiding principle of this operation was radically different from that of the German offensive in 1942. We would attack by a counter-stroke at the moment when the enemy had largely engaged and partially expended his assault forces. Our objective would no longer be the conquest of distant geographical points but the destruction of the Soviet southern wing by trapping it against the coast. To prevent his escape eastwards, as was the case in 1942, we would entice him to the lower Dniepr, as it would be impossible for him to resist this.

"If the operation succeeded, with the consequent heavy losses he would sustain, we could perhaps strike a second blow northwards, towards the centre of the front."

Certainly Manstein was under no illusion that the method he advocated could decide the war in favour of the Third Reich; but at least the situation would again be in Germany's favour and she would obtain what Manstein terms a "putting off" and Mellenthin a "stalemate", enabling her to bide her time. But Hitler did not agree with this line of argument, countering it with his usual economic arguments: Nikopol' manganese, for instance–"to lose Nikopol' would be to lose the war" was his last word, and at the meeting in Munich, Manstein did not raise his plan again.

Red espionage succeeds again

The Soviet authorities still deny the implication of Manstein's criticism of the Red Army high command, yet the counter-offensive which had recently given Khar'kov back to the Germans seems to furnish abundant proof of Manstein's point.

Nonetheless, there is no certainty that Manstein's plan would have been as successful as he claimed it would. Indeed, just as with the offensive directed against the Kursk salient, it had little chance of securing the advantage of surprise. Never before had the direct line linking O.K.W. and O.K.H. with the Soviet agent Rudolf Rössler functioned so surely and swiftly. And it is certain–

insofar as can be discovered—that Stalin had got wind of German intentions within 48 hours of Hitler's issuing an operational order classified "Top Secret" wherein, unknown to Manstein, he took up the suggestion of "attack by counterstrike" with which the commander of Army Group "South" had provided him.

Model and Mellenthin also against Hitler's plan

At all events, when he opened proceedings, Hitler had made reference to a report that had been sent him by Colonel-General Walther Model, whose 9th Army was to supply the north-to-south thrust of the operation. It is beyond question that a commander of Model's dynamic energy approved of the offensive in principle, but he registered concern at making an attempt in May that should have been made in March, for the enemy forces in the Kursk salient had not meanwhile been wasting their time. According to Guderian, "Model had produced information, based largely on air photography, which showed that the Russians were preparing deep and very strong defensive positions in exactly those areas where the attack by the two army groups were

to go in. The Russians had already withdrawn the mass of their mobile formations from the forward area of the salient; in anticipation of a pincer attack, as proposed in this plan of ours, they had strengthened the localities of our possible break-throughs with unusually strong artillery and anti-tank forces. Model drew the correct deduction from this, namely, that the enemy was counting on our launching this attack and that in order to achieve success we must adopt a fresh tactical approach; the alternative was to abandon the whole idea."

Some weeks earlier, Colonel von Mellenthin, in his capacity as chief-of-staff of XLVIII Panzer Corps, which had been given an important part to play in the plans, had voiced the same opinion to General Zeitzler. By holding up the offensive until a first brigade of Panther tanks had been formed, as Hitler intended, the Russians would be given time to recover from the losses inflicted on them. For this they only needed a month or two, and the operation would then be a far more difficult, and hence costly, one. Although Manstein had been lukewarm in his attitude towards the operation at the outset, once it had been decided he pronounced against any procrastination: "Any delay with 'Zitadelle' would increase the risk to Army Group 'South's' defensive front considerably. The enemy

△ *While the fighting for the Kursk salient continued, the Russians completed the plans for their summer offensive. Here General Lyudnikov, commander of the 39th Army, studies a situation map.*

▽ *Soviet infantry counter-attack past a burning German armoured vehicle.*

of the offensive be decided by the state of preparedness of the Panthers. On information that 324 Panthers would be ready on May 31, he settled D-day for June 15, in spite of Manstein's advice. But there were further delays, and Operation *"Zitadelle"* was not begun until July 5, a delay of two months on the original timetable.

As had been pointed out above, the left flank of the offensive was drawn from Army Group "Centre" and the right from Army Group "South". Manstein had concentrated *Gruppe* Kempf, reinforced by one Panzer corps and two infantry corps in the Belgorod sector; its rôle as it moved northwards was to guard the eastward flank of the armoured units of the 4th *Panzerarmee* (Colonel-General Hoth) upon which the main task would devolve; he therefore transferred to it the II *Waffen* S.S. Panzer Corps (General Hausser) with its three *Panzergrenadier* divisions: *"Leibstandarte"*, *"Das Reich"*, and *"Totenkopf"*, as well as XLVIII Panzer Corps, which under the command of General O. von Knobelsdorff included an infantry division, the 3rd and 11th Panzer Divisions, and the *"Grossdeutschland"* *Panzergrenadier* Division, whose 190 tanks and self-propelled guns were supported by a brigade of 200 Panthers. XXIV Panzer Corps (17th Panzer Division and *"Wiking"* *Panzergrenadier* Division) were held in reserve.

In Army Group "Centre", the 9th Army, to the south of Orel, had organised itself as a wedge. In the centre, XLVII Panzer Corps (General Rauss), with five Panzer divisions, constituted its battering ram; it was flanked on the right by XLVI Panzer Corps and XX Corps, on the left by XLI Panzer Corps and XXIII Corps; this flank, which was exposed to counter-attacks from the east, had been reinforced by the 12th Panzer Division and the 10th *Panzergrenadier* Division, under the command of XLI Panzer Corps. General Model's reserve consisted of one Panzer and one *Panzergrenadier* division.

Taken together, *"Zitadelle"* involved 41 divisions, all of them German, including 18 Panzer and *Panzergrenadier* divisions. Manstein had at his own disposal 1,081 tanks and 376 assault guns; air support was given by *Luftflotte* IV, as whose commander Manstein would have liked to see Field-Marshal von Richthofen, who was kicking his heels in Italy. But Hitler was obstinate in his refusal to transfer him. Model, whose

was not yet in a position to launch an attack on the Mius and the Donets. But he certainly would be in June. *'Zitadelle'* was certainly not going to be easy, but I concluded that we must stick by the decision to launch it at the earliest possible moment and, like a cavalryman, 'leaping before you look', a comparison which I quickly realised made no effect on Hitler, who had little appreciation either of cavalrymen or horses."

Model's line of reasoning made its due impression on Hitler, who had total confidence in him. On May 10, Hitler told Guderian: "Whenever I think of this attack my stomach turns over." And he was all the more disposed to let the date

eight Panzer divisions had been brought up to a strength of 100 tanks each, had as many vehicles as he could use. His air support was provided by *Luftflotte* VI.

Massive Russian defence lines

According to a perfectly correct comment in the *Great Patriotic War,* when spring came round again, Stalin had more than sufficient means at hand to take the initiative. But confronted by the German preparations against the Kursk salient reported to him by General N. F. Vatutin, new commander of the Voronezh Front, from April 21 onwards Stalin felt, the same work assures us, that it "was more expedient to oppose the enemy with a defensive system constructed in due time,

Dniepr, and Kerch' Strait, thus liberating the eastern parts of White Russia and the Ukraine, the Donets basin, and what the Germans still held in the Kuban'.

It is true that in adopting these tactics, Stalin had the advantage of detailed information as to the strength and intentions of the adversary and that he followed the *"Zitadelle"* preparations very closely: "Rössler," write Accoce and Quiet, "gave them full and detailed description in his despatches. Once again, *Werther,* his little team inside O.K.W., had achieved a miracle. Nothing was missing. The sectors to be attacked, the men and *matériel* to be used, the position of the supply columns, the chain of command, the positions of reinforcements, D-day, and zero hour. There was nothing more to be desired and the Russians desired nothing more. They simply waited, confident of victory."

And their confidence was all the greater

◁ *The Russians did not have things all their own way, particularly at the beginning of the battle. Here a German soldier prepares to take the crew of a T-34 prisoner.*
◁▽ *German dispatch rider.*
▽ *The Russian counter-offensive gets under way–tanks and infantry of the Voronezh Front move south towards Belgorod.*
▽▽ *One of Russia's tank aces, Akim Lysenko. He destroyed seven German tanks in the great battle for the Kursk salient.*

echeloned in depth, and insuperable. On the basis of propositions made to it by the commanders at the front, Supreme Headquarters resolved to wear the enemy out decisively in the course of his assault, by defensive action, then to smash him by means of a counter-offensive."

Hence, by a curious coincidence, Stalin came round to the idea of "return attack" at the very time that Hitler refused to let Manstein attempt to apply it. With the Panzers smashed in the salient around Kursk, it would be a far easier task to defeat Army Groups "Centre" and "South" and attain the objectives that had been set for the end of autumn 1943: Smolensk, the Sozh, the middle and lower

because first-hand information and reports from partisans confirmed the radio messages of their conscientious informer in Lucerne. Accoce and Quiet make no exaggeration. From a memo of the period it appears that in July 1943 Stalin believed he had 210 enemy divisions, excluding Finns, facing him. The official O.K.W. record for July 7 of that year gives 210 exactly, plus five regiments.

Hitler's delays allowed the Russians to organise the battlefield on which the attack was anticipated and to do so to a depth of between 16 and 25 miles. A cunning combination of minefields was intended to channel the German armoured units onto what the Russians called "anti-

tank fronts", solid defence sectors particularly well provided with anti-tank guns.

The defence of the Kursk salient, which had a front of about 340 miles, was entrusted to the Central and Voronezh Fronts. The Central Front, under the command of General Rokossovsky, had five armies deployed forward, a tank army in second echelon, and two tank corps and a cavalry corps in reserve. The Voronezh Front

▽ *The standard pattern of Soviet attacks – an interwoven line of infantry and tanks.*

△ *Dismounted Russian cavalry put in an assault on a small village. By Western standards they are not only very exposed, but have a long distance to go before they reach the enemy positions. Though the picture may be posed, it still reflects the rudimentary tactics employed by the Red Army, even late in the war.*

(General Vatutin) had four armies forward, two more armies (one of them a tank army) in second echelon, and two tank and one rifle corps in reserve. The Steppe Front (Colonel-General I. S. Konev), positioned east of Kursk, constituted the *Stavka* reserve, and comprised five (including one tank) armies, plus one tank, one mechanised, and three cavalry corps in reserve.

Air support was provided by some 2,500 planes from the 2nd and 16th Air Armies.

Even now, Soviet historians, who are so precise in the case of the German Army, decline to tell us the number of divisions and tanks involved in this battle; nevertheless, if we take a figure of roughly 75 infantry divisions and 3,600 tanks, this would appear to be about right. The *Great Patriotic War,* however, drops its reserve in speaking of the artillery. If we believe what we read, and there is no reason not to do so, Rokossovsky and Vatutin could count on no fewer than 20,000 guns, howitzers, and mortars, including 6,000 anti-tank guns, and 920 rocket launchers. For example, in order to bar the axis along which it was expected that Model's main thrust would be developed, Rokossovsky allocated to Pukhov's 13th Army a whole additional corps of artillery, totalling some 700 guns and mortars. The defensive potential of the Red Army thus surpassed the offensive potential of the Germans, and their complete knowledge of Field-Marshals von Kluge's and von Manstein's dispositions and proposed axes of advance enabled the Russians to concentrate their artillery and armoured units so as to prevent them moving in the direction intended. In the evening of July 4 a pioneer from a Sudeten division deserted to the Russians and revealed the zero hour for Operation *"Zitadelle".*

Failure all the way

Now that most of the pieces on the chessboard are in place we can deal quickly with the actual sequence of events in the Battle of Kursk which, on July 12, ended in an irreversible defeat for the Wehrmacht. Far from taking the enemy by surprise, the German 9th Army, following close on the desertion mentioned above, was itself surprised by a massive artillery counter-barrage, which struck its jump-off points in the final stages of preparation 20 minutes before zero hour. By evening, XLVII and XLI Panzer Corps, consisting of seven armoured divisions, had advanced only six miles across the defences of the Soviet 13th Army, and their 90 "Ferdinands" or *"Elefants",* being without machine guns, were unable to cope with the Russian infantry. More important, XXIII Corps, guarding the left flank, was stopped short of Malo-Arkhangelsk. On July 7, spurred on by the vigorous leadership of General Rauss, XLVII Panzer Corps reached the outskirts of Olkhovatka, less than 12 miles from its start line. There the German 9th Army was finally halted.

Army Group "South's" part of *"Zitadelle"* got off to a better start, thanks largely to impeccable co-ordination between tanks and dive-bombers. In the course of engagements which Manstein in his memoirs describes as extremely tough, *Gruppe* Kempf succeeded in breaking through two defence lines and reaching a point where it could intercept Steppe Front reinforcements coming to the aid of Voronezh Front. On July 11 the situation might be thought to be promising.

For 48 hours the 4th *Panzerarmee* met a solid wall of resistance of which General F. W. von Mellenthin, at that time chief-of-staff to XLVIII Panzer Corps, provides the following description in his book *Panzer Battles:*

"During the second and third days of the offensive we met with our first reverses. In spite of our soldiers' courage and determination, we were unable to find a gap in the enemy's second defence line. The *Panzergrenadier* Division *"Grossdeutschland"* (Lieutenant-General Hoerlein) which had gone into battle in extremely tight formation and had come up against an extremely marshy tract of ground, was stopped by prepared fortifications defended with anti-tank guns, flame-throwers, and T-34 tanks, and was met by violent artillery fire. For some time it remained unable to move in the middle of the battlefield devised by the enemy. It was no easy task for our pioneers to find and fix a passable route through numerous minefields or across the tracts of marshland. A large number of tanks were blown up by mines or destroyed by aerial attacks: the Red Air Force showed little regard for the fact of the Luftwaffe's superiority and fought the battle with remarkable determination and spirit."

On July 7, however, XLVIII Panzer Corps and on its right II *Waffen* S.S. Panzer Corps found themselves unopposed, after repulsing heavy counter-attacks by tanks which developed as pincer movements. Thus on July 11, after establishing a bridgehead on the Psel and getting close to Oboyan, the 4th *Panzerarmee* had advanced 18 to 20 miles through Vatutin's lines, while *Gruppe* Kempf, without having been able to land on the western bank of the Korocha had nevertheless managed to fulfil its primary task of protecting the 4th *Panzerarmee's* right flank. Two days

later, Manstein reported that since D-day he had taken 24,000 prisoners and destroyed or captured 100 tanks and 108 anti-tank guns, and intended to move up his reserve, XXIV Panzer Corps.

These, however, were limited successes and *"Zitadelle"* was a serious reverse for Hitler. Between the spearhead of the 4th *Panzerarmee,* on the edge of Oboyan, and the vanguard of the 9th Army, forced to halt before Olkhovatka, the gap between the two armies remained, and would remain, 75 miles.

Far from feeling discouragement, Vatutin made known to *Stavka* in the evening of July 10 his intention of counter-attacking, and bringing up for this pur-

△ *Soviet infantry and tanks approaching the Kursk area. The Russians were able to keep their reserves undamaged until the Germans had driven themselves to breaking point on the fixed defences in the Kursk salient, and then the Red Army went on to the counter-attack.*

▽ *A Pzkw III emerges from the smoke of a grass fire during the opening stages of "Zitadelle". The operation was to squander the tanks and vehicles that Guderian had built up.*

△ *Lieutenant-General Rotmistrov and Major-General Rodimtsev. Rotmistrov commanded the 5th Guards Tank Army in the Battle of Kursk. He brought it by forced marches over 200 miles and then after a heavy bombardment sent in his force of 850 tanks and assault guns against Hausser's II S.S Panzer Corps, which was fighting in the Prokhorovka area.*

▽ *A Soviet 76-mm gun crew prepares to fire. Before the Germans moved off from their start lines on the first day of Kursk, they were subject to a morale-shattering bombardment.*

pose his 5th Guards Tank Army (Lieutenant-General P. A. Rotmistrov) with its 850 tanks and assault guns, as well as the 1st Tank Army (Lieutenant-General M. E. Katukov).

On the other side of the battlefield, Rokossovsky addressed the following rousing order of the day to his troops on July 12: "The soldiers of the Central Front who met the enemy with a rampart of murderous steel and truly Russian grit and tenacity have exhausted him after a week of unrelenting and unremitting fighting; they have contained the enemy's drive. The first phase of the battle is over."

And indeed, on that same July 12, the Soviet armies of the Bryansk and West Front, following a predetermined plan, proceeded to launch a major offensive against the German-held Orel salient.

Hitler's choice: Sicily or *"Zitadelle"*

With the unexpected development of the situation in the Kursk area, Hitler summoned Kluge and Manstein to his H.Q. at Rastenburg on July 13. Kluge left the Führer with no illusions: the 9th Army, which had lost 20,000 men in a single week, was both incapable of advancing further and at the same time obliged to relinquish part of its remaining strength to bolster the defence of the Orel salient. Manstein was less pessimistic, yet in order for him to be able to compel the Russians to continue to fight, as he proposed, on this altered front in the Kursk region, Kluge had to pin down the maximum Soviet forces in his sector. The argument was thus circular.

Hitler decided matters by simply abandoning the operation. Yet–and this has been insufficiently remarked upon–his decision was motivated not so much by the local situation or by the Russian offensive in the Orel salient as by the fact of the Anglo-American landings in Sicily.

According to Manstein, the Führer took a particularly gloomy view of the immediate outlook in this new theatre of operations: "The situation in Sicily has become extremely serious," he informed the two field-marshals. "The Italians are not resisting and the island will probably be lost. As a result, the Western powers will be able to land in the Balkans or in southern Italy. Hence new armies must be formed in these areas, which means taking troops from the Eastern Front, and hence calling a halt to *'Zitadelle'.*" And there is the proof that the second front in the Mediterranean, derided by President Roosevelt, by Harry Hopkins, and by General Marshall, achieved what none of them expected of it: relief for Russia.

The end of the greatest tank battle

Thus ended the Battle of Kursk which, involving as it did more than 5,400 armoured and tracked vehicles, must be counted the greatest tank battle of World War II.

Some commentators have compared it with the ill-starred offensive launched by General Nivelle which ground to a halt on April 16, 1917 on the steep slopes up to the Chemin des Dames. But it would seem to bear greater similarity to Ludendorff's final attempt to give victory to the German Army. On July 15, 1918, the Quartermaster-General of the Imperial German Army was brought to a standstill in Champagne by Pétain's system of defence in depth, and this failure allowed Foch to detach Mangin and Degoutte in a French offensive against

the Château-Thierry salient. Subsequently the new Marshal of France extended his battle-line to left and to right, and the German retreat lasted until the Armistice on November 11, 1918.

There is one difference between these two sets of circumstances. On August 10, 1918, on receiving the news that Sir Douglas Haig's tanks had scattered the German defence in Picardy, Wilhelm II declared to Hindenburg and to Ludendorff: "This to my mind is the final reckoning", and this flash of common sense spared Germany the horrors of invasion. In July 1943, Hitler, the head of state, was incapable of making a similar observation to Hitler, the war leader, still less of parting company with him as the Kaiser parted company with Ludendorff on October 26, 1918.

The Panzer defeat in the Kursk salient has had its historians in both camps, but it also had its prophet, who in the spring of 1939 mused on the question of what might be the result should an army of tanks collide with a similar army given a defensive function. And in the course of examining this hypothesis which he declared had been neglected, he arrived at the following conclusion and another question: "On land, there does exist a means of halting a tank offensive: a combination of mines and anti-tank guns. What would happen to an offensive by tank divisions which encountered a

defence composed of similar tank divisions, but ones which had been carefully deployed and had had time to work out a considered fire-plan on the chosen battlefield, on which anti-tank firepower was closely co-ordinated with natural obstacles reinforced by minefields?"

Thus, three or four months before the war broke out, Marshal Pétain expressed himself in a preface to General Chauvineau's book *Is an Invasion Still Possible?* that is often quoted and never read. And the event itself would prove him right—but on a scale beyond the wildest imaginings in 1939: to stop 1,800 German tanks it required 3,600 Soviet tanks, 6,000 anti-tank weapons, and 400,000 mines!

△ *A shattered Pzkw III, one of the hundreds of knocked out tanks that the Germans left on the battle field. After Stalingrad they began to fear they could not win the war, but Kursk confirmed that they would lose it.*

▽ *A group of prisoners. German losses during the Battle of Kursk were about 20,000, and by now it was becoming harder for these losses to be replaced. In addition, the Red Army was recovering lost territory and gaining new conscripts.*

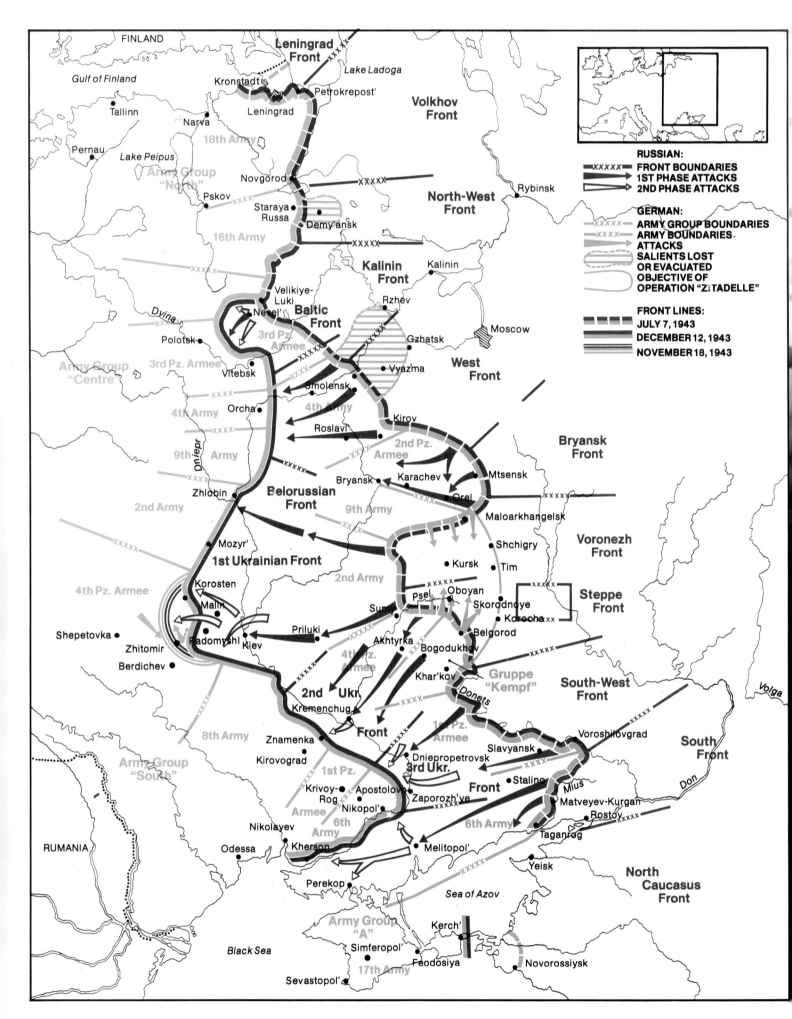

FINLAND

Gulf of Finland

Leningrad Front

Lake Ladoga

Kronstadt
Petrokrepost'
Leningrad

Tallinn

Narva

Pernau

Lake Peipus

Volkhov Front

18th Army

Army Group "North"

Novgorod

Pskov

Rybinsk

North-West Front

Staraya Russa

Demy'ansk

16th Army

Kalinin Front

Kalinin

Velikiye-Luki

Rzhev

Dvina

Nevel'

Baltic Front

Gzhatsk

Moscow

Polotsk

3rd Pz. Armee

3rd Pz. Armee

West Front

Vyazma

Vitebsk

Army Group "Centre"

Smolensk

4th Army

Orcha

4th Army

Kirov

Bryansk Front

Roslavl

9th Army

2nd Pz. Armee

Dniepr

Karachev

Mtsensk

Zhlobin

Belorussian Front

Bryansk

Orel

9th Army

Maloarkhangelsk

2nd Army

Mozyr'

Voronezh Front

Shchigry

1st Ukrainian Front

2nd Army

Kursk

Tim

4th Pz. Armee

Korosten

Psel

Oboyan

Skorodnoye

Steppe Front

Malin

Sumy

Korocha

Shepetovka

Priluki

Akhtyrka

Belgorod

Bogodukhov

Zhitomir

Radomyshl

Kiev

Berdichev

Khar'kov

Gruppe "Kempf"

South-West Front

2nd Ukr.

4th Pz. Armee

Donets

Front

Kremenchug

1st Pz. Armee

Voroshilovgrad

South Front

8th Army

Znamenka

Slavyansk

Kirovograd

Army Group "South"

1st Pz. Armee

Dniepropetrovsk

3rd Ukr.

Staling

Mius

Krivoy-Rog

Apostolovo

Front

Matveyev-Kurgan

Armee

Zaporozh'ye

Rostov

Nikopol'

6th Army

Taganrog

Nikolayev

6th Army

RUMANIA

Kherson

Melitopol'

Yeisk

Odessa

North Caucasus Front

Perekop

Sea of Azov

Don

Army Group "A"

Kerch'

Black Sea

Simferopol'

17th Army

Feodosiya

Novorossiysk

Sevastopol'

RUSSIAN:

═══xxxxx FRONT BOUNDARIES

1ST PHASE ATTACKS

2ND PHASE ATTACKS

GERMAN:

xxxxx ARMY GROUP BOUNDARIES

xxxx ARMY BOUNDARIES-ATTACKS

SALIENTS LOST OR EVACUATED

OBJECTIVE OF OPERATION "ZITADELLE"

FRONT LINES:

JULY 7, 1943

DECEMBER 12, 1943

NOVEMBER 18, 1943

CHAPTER 90
Back to the Dniepr

Just as Foch, once he had reduced the Château-Thierry salient in 1918, never ceased to widen his battle-front, so Stalin was to proceed after taking the bastion of Orel. This meant that nine out of his twelve Fronts or army groups would now be engaged. From July 5 his order of battle was to comprise the following Fronts, stretching from the Gulf of Finland to Novorossiysk on the Black Sea:

Kalinin (A. I. Eremenko)
West (V. D. Sokolovsky)
Bryansk (M. M. Popov)
Central (K. K. Rokossovsky)
Voronezh (N. F. Vatutin)
Steppe (I. S. Konev)
South-West (R. Ya. Malinovsky)
South (F. I. Tolbukhin)
Transcaucasus (I. E. Petrov)

The commanders' names are worth more than a passing glance, as they make up a team which was to remain remarkably stable right through to the end of the war. Others were to be added (those of Bagramyan and Chernyakhovsky for example), but the top echelons of

the Red Army experienced none of that avalanche of disgraces and dismissals which characterised the Wehrmacht after the spring of 1944. Stalin could rightly trust his generals.

On July 12, as we have seen, Generals Sokolovsky and Popov started the Soviet summer offensive by attacking the Orel salient from the north and east along a front of some 190 miles. The line was defended by the 2nd *Panzerarmee* (Colonel-General Rudolf Schmidt) with 12 divisions up and two in reserve, one of which was *Panzergrenadier*. It is true that since the front had stabilised in this sector the Germans had greatly strengthened their positions. So on the West Front the 11th Guards Army (Lieutenant-General I. Kh. Bagramyan), responsible for the main thrust towards Orel, got 3,000 guns and 400 rocket-launchers. It also had 70 regiments of infantry, compared with Rokossovsky's 34 for the final attack on the Stalingrad pocket. It is not to be wondered at, therefore, that Bagramyan's offensive, supported, it is true,

▽ *Cossack cavalrymen serving with the Wehrmacht on the Eastern Front, patrolling near Smolensk in the summer of 1943. The Germans got substantial numbers of volunteers from the Cossacks of the Don, the Terek, and the Kuban'. They served not only in Russia but on anti-partisan operations in Yugoslavia and Italy.*

by 250 tanks, covered over 15 miles in 48 hours. On the Bryansk Front the 61st Army (Lieutenant-General P. A. Belov) attacked Mtsensk, whilst further south the 3rd and 63rd Armies (Lieutenant-Generals A. V. Gorbatov and V. Ya. Kolpakchy) came to grips with the German XXXV Corps (General Rendulic), which was stretched out to the tune of 24 battalions on 75 miles of front, and made a gap in it from seven to ten miles wide. Through the breaches made by artillery and infantry the armour poured in.

"Elastic defence" initiated

Right away a pincer movement began to form, threatening to close in on the defenders of the salient. So Field-Marshal von Kluge relieved Model of the majority of his motorised divisions in order to keep gaps plugged. This sufficed for the immediate danger, but did not halt the Red Army's advance. Furthermore, the armies on the Central Front moved forward and threatened Model's already weakened position. Alexander Werth has left an account of what this gigantic battle was like between not only men determined on victory but also weapons of terrifying power:

"By July 15, after three days' heavy fighting, the Russians had broken through the main lines of the German defences round the Orel salient. There had never been [said General Sobennikov, commander of the garrison of Orel] such a heavy concentration of Russian guns as against these defences; in many places the fire power was ten times heavier than at Verdun. The German minefields were so thick and widespread that as many mines as possible had to be blown up by the super-barrage, in order to reduce Russian casualties in the subsequent breakthrough. By July 20, the Germans tried to stop the Russian advance by throwing in hundreds of planes; and it was a job for the Russian anti-aircraft guns and fighters to deal with them. In the countless air-battles there were very heavy casualties on both sides. Many French airmen were killed, too, during those days."

The partisans, as Werth also relates, played an equally important rôle in these operations: "On July 14, 1943, the Soviet Supreme Command ordered the partisans to start an all-out Rail War. Preparations for this had obviously already been made, for on July 20-21 great co-ordinated blows were struck at the railways in the Bryansk, Orel, and Gomel areas, to coincide with the Russian offensive against Orel and Bryansk following the Kursk victory. During that night alone 5,800 rails were blown up. Altogether, between July 21 and September 27, the Orel and Bryansk partisans blew up over 17,000 rails . . .

"Telpukhovsky's semi-official History claims that in three years (1941-4) the partisans in Belorussia killed 500,000 Germans including forty-seven generals and Hitler's High-Commissioner Wilhelm Kube (who, as we know from German sources–though the Russians for some reason don't mention this–had a partisan time-bomb put under his bed by his lovely Belorussian girl-friend)."

And so on July 29, 1943 there appears for the first time in communiqués from

A. I. Eremenko
Kalinin Front

V. D. Sokolovsky
West Front

M. M. Popov
Bryansk Front

K. K. Rokossovsky
Central Front

N. F. Vatutin
Voronezh Front

I. S. Konev
Steppe Front

R. Ya. Malinovsky
South-West Front

F. I. Tolbukhin
South Front

the Wehrmacht the expression "elastic defence" which might have been thought banned for ever from Hitlerian terminology. This was a delaying tactic which allowed Army Group "Centre" to evacuate the Orel salient, systematically burning the crops behind it, and to regroup along a front line covering Bryansk from the high ground round Karachev. This movement, completed around August 4, provided only temporary respite, as the comparative strengths of the opposing forces remained unchanged.

Continued German reverses

The situation was worse still between the area from north-west of Belgorod to the Sea of Azov, over a front of about 650 miles defended by Manstein:

"On July 17 our 29 infantry and 13 armoured or motorised divisions were facing 109 infantry divisions, nine infantry brigades, ten tank, seven mechanised and seven cavalry corps, plus 20 independent tank brigades, 16 tank regiments and eight anti-tank brigades. Between that date and September 7 these forces were increased by 55 infantry divisions, two tank corps, eight tank brigades, and 12 tank regiments, most of them brought over from the Central and the North Fronts. All in all we must have been outnumbered by seven to one.

"This superiority allowed the Russians not only to go on to the offensive with overwhelming power, often in several places at once, but also to make up their losses, even when very heavy, in an astonishingly short space of time. Thus between July and September, they were able to withdraw from the front 48 divisions and 17 tank corps and reform them, some of the formations even twice, as well as providing reinforcements for all their divisions of up to ten per cent of their fighting strength."

This, according to the Soviet command, was the tally of the Red Army's strength on the South, South-West, Steppe, and Voronezh Fronts: 21 armies facing the one German Army Group "South". Manstein, whose 1st *Panzerarmee* was being driven back at Slavyansk as Tolbukhin was trying to make a breakthrough over the Mius river, was now driven to extremes.

△ *Working cautiously forward through tangled ruins. The German army was now fighting immense odds, and all Wehrmacht units were inferior in numbers and firepower to the forces facing them.*

At Rastenburg, however, Hitler's answer to the strategic problems now arising was to argue economics and politics: the Donets coalfields, the manganese at Nikopol', the indispensable iron ore at Krivoy-Rog, Hungarian morale, the opinion of Bucharest, Bulgarian troop positions, Turkish neutrality, and so on.

This reached such a point that at the end of July Manstein was emboldened to write to Zeitzler: "If the Führer thinks he has at hand a C.-in-C. or an Army Group with nerves stronger than ours were last winter, capable of greater initiative than we showed in the Crimea, on the Donets, or at Khar'kov, able to find better solutions than we did in the Crimea or during the last winter campaign, or to foresee better than we did how the situation will develop, then I am ready to hand over my responsibilities. But whilst these are still mine I reserve the right to use my brains."

Manstein pulls back

In effect, faced with the concentric offensive launched on the South and the South-West Fronts, which threatened to involve the new German 6th Army (Colonel-General Hollidt) in a disaster equal in magnitude to that of Stalingrad, Manstein had decided to evacuate the Donets basin, which would have the additional advantage of shortening his front. Yet Hitler had expressly forbidden such a step, just as he had refused Colonel-General Jaenecke permission to bring his 17th Army back over the Kerch' Strait into the Crimea, even though its 17 German and Rumanian divisions would have been more useful to the defence of the Donets than the Kuban' peninsula. Under the circumstances imposed on him, Field-Marshal von Manstein was forced to make a dangerous move: to weaken his left flank between Belgorod and Sumy so as to strengthen his right in the hope (which was not fulfilled) of being able to make a stand before Konev and Vatutin were able to seize the opportunity offered to them. In fact the transfer of XXIV Panzer Corps (General Nehring) to the 1st *Panzerarmee* allowed the latter to plug the breach at Slavyansk, and the intervention of III Panzer Corps (General Breith) and the S.S. Panzer Corps gave General Hollidt the chance of inflicting a serious defeat on the South Front, which by July 30 had crossed back over the Mius, leaving behind 18,000 prisoners, 700 tanks, and 200 guns.

On August 3, however, more swiftly than Manstein can have supposed, Colonel-Generals Vatutin and Konev, considerably reinforced in artillery and rocket-launchers, made an attempt to drive a wedge between *Gruppe* "Kempf" and the 4th *Panzerarmee*. By the afternoon they were through and had pushed two mechanised armies into the gap. August 5 saw the liberation of Belgorod; on the 7th the Russian 1st Tank Army reached Bogodukhov, nearly 70 miles from its starting point. This breakthrough was now developing in the most dangerous direction for the German forces between the Sea of Azov and Khar'kov: towards Dniepropetrovsk. And so, to keep down his losses Manstein again switched the *Waffen* S.S. Panzer Corps and III Panzer Corps to this front, whilst on the orders of O.K.H. his comrade Kluge gave him back the "Grossdeutschland" Panzergrenadier Division which, on the day after "Zitadelle", had been engaged in the Orel salient. As we can see, the Panzers roamed all over this immense battlefield from one point of conflagration to another, just as the firemen were doing during the same period in German towns.

Red Army tanks reach Khar'kov

The Soviet assaults of the summer of 1943 had almost split open Manstein's Army Group "South". Although a gap in the line 35 miles wide in the Akhtyrka region was closed by the 4th *Panzerarmee*, it was all over at Khar'kov, and the city fell on August 22 under the combined blows of the 5th Tank Army (General Rotmistrov) and the 53rd Army (Major-General I. M. Managarov). On August 30 Khruschev, General Vatutin's political aide, received the ovations of this the second city in the Ukraine. According to the *Great Patriotic War,* which followed him all the way, he cried in tones full of profound Bolshevik fervour: "Let us now get back to work! Let us remain firmly united! Everything for the front; all for victory! Let us further close our ranks under this banner which has brought us victory! Onwards to the West! Onwards for the Ukraine!"

At Army Group "South" H.Q. on that same August 22, General Wöhler and the staff of a new 8th Army started to take over from *Gruppe* "Kempf" south of Khar'kov. Forty-eight hours later, reduced to 25 divisions, including three Panzer, fighting on a front of over 1,300 miles and with ever-shrinking strength, the 6th Army and the 1st *Panzerarmee* reeled under the blows of Tolbukhin's and Malinovsky's 60 infantry divisions and 1,300 tanks. No fire-brigade operation by the Panzers could stop this now and new threats were growing on the left flank of Army Group "South". The German 2nd Army was violently attacked by Rokossovsky who had come back into the battle. By September 7 Manstein's Panzer and *Panzergrenadier* forces had only 257 tanks and 220 assault guns left. There was thus nothing for it but to retreat, even if this meant the loss of the Donets basin and all its industrial wealth, which Hitler was loth to lose.

Retreat over the Dniepr

On September 9 Hitler went to Zaporozh'ye on the Dniepr bend to take stock of the situation with Field-Marshal von Manstein. After eight days of wearying argu-

ment, first one way then the other, permission was given for the army group to be withdrawn behind the deep valley of the Dniepr which, with its right bank overlooking the left, lends itself easily to defence. This meant evacuating the bridgehead in the Kuban' where Field-Marshal von Kleist's Army Group "A" and the 17th Army were being hard pressed by an enemy superior in numbers and *matériel*. On September 10 in particular, a combined amphibious operation by Vice-Admiral L. A. Vladimirsky, commander of the Black Sea Fleet, and Lieutenant-General K. N. Leselidze, commander of the 18th Army, put the Russian troops ashore in the port of Novorossiysk. Amongst the heroes of the day was the army's Chief Political Administrator, Leonide E. Brezhnev, today General Secretary of the Communist Party of the U.S.S.R.

The evacuation of the Taman' peninsula

△ *A Tiger burns. Ponderous and hard to manoeuvre, they were vulnerable to anti-tank fire from the flank and rear.*

was begun in the night of September 15-16 and completed on October 9. The operation was commanded by Vice-Admiral Scheurlen, to the entire satisfaction of his chief, Dönitz, who goes on in his memoirs to give the figures: 202,477 fighting troops, 54,664 horses, 1,200 guns, and 15,000 vehicles ferried across the Kerch' Strait by the German Navy. In a statement which challenges the figures given by General of Mountain Troops R. Konrad, formerly commander of XLIX Mountain Corps, the *Great Patriotic War* claims that the retreat of the 17th Army cost the Germans thousands of men as a result of attacks both by the Red Army land forces and the Soviet Air Force, which sank 70 barges in the Straits. Of these two oppos-

∇ *German machine gunner at his post, commanding the banks of the Dniepr.*

▷ ▷ △ *Russian soldiers come ashore at Novorossiysk during the operation that cleared the eastern Black Sea coast.*
▷ ▷ ▷ *Light flak emplacement at Kerch', held by German and Rumanian forces.*
▷ ▷ ∇ *Russian soldiers and marines in the ruins of Novorossiysk.*

ing versions, that of Dönitz and Konrad is more likely to be true since the Russian version fails to mention any of the equipment captured between September 16 and October 9. Now back in the Ukraine, Field-Marshal von Kleist and H.Q. Army Group "A" received into their command the 6th Army, by which Manstein's burden had been lightened.

To get his troops across the Dniepr, Manstein had six crossing points between Zaporozh'ye downstream and Kiev upstream. The withdrawal was completed in ten days under cover of rearguards whose job it was to create scorched earth areas 15 miles deep on the left bank of the great river. Army Group "South", behind this obstacle, had been brought up to a strength of 54 divisions (17 Panzer and *Panzergrenadier*) but most of them were

worn out. On its right was the 6th Army holding the front Zaporozh'ye–Sea of Azov through Melitopol'. On its left was the 2nd Army (General Weiss), back again under the orders of Kluge. Its right flank came down to the confluence of the Dniepr and the Pripyat'.

In his memoirs Manstein defends the systematic destruction of the land behind him, saying: "We had recourse to the 'scorched earth' policy used by the Russians during their retreat in the previous year. Anything which could be of use to the enemy in an area 12 to 18 miles deep in front of the Dniepr was systematically destroyed or carried away. It was, of course, never a question of plunder. The whole operation was strictly controlled to prevent abuse. Furthermore we only took away goods and chattels belonging to the State, never those privately owned.

"As the Russians, in any land they re-occupied, immediately conscripted any men under 60 capable of carrying arms and forced the remainder of the population to do military work, the German High Command ordered the local inhabitants to be transported over to the other bank of the Dniepr. This in fact was restricted to men who would at once have become soldiers. Yet a great part of the population joined in our retreat voluntarily to escape the Soviet authorities, whom they feared."

Renewed Russian offensives

August and September were months as fatal to Kluge as they were to his colleague Manstein. This is not surprising, since by September 7 he was down to 108 tanks and 191 assault guns.

At the beginning of August Stalin went to H.Q. Kalinin Front. His inspection was recorded thus by the Soviet official historian: "This was the only occasion during the war when Stalin went to visit the troops at the front. At this period it was relatively quiet. This visit had virtually no effect on preparations for the operation against Smolensk." Of greater encouragement no doubt was the visit of N. N. Voronov, delegated to Eremenko by *Stavka* and, after the Stalingrad victory, promoted Marshal and Commander-in-Chief of Artillery.

The battle opened at dawn on August 7, but for four days the German 4th Army, better commanded by General S. Heinrici, beat off the Russian attacks. On August 11 a breach was opened at Kirov and exploited by Eremenko towards Yel'nya and Dorogobuzh, which fell at the end of the month. On September 19 the West Front met the southward advance of the Kalinin Front and on September 25 the armies entered the important city of Smolensk on the border of Belorussia.

Further south still, Colonel-General Popov had defeated Model's attempts to deny his advance to Bryansk. On September 19 this important centre of communications on the Desna had been recaptured by troops from the Front which bore its name.

The Russians cross the Dniepr

The respite gained by Manstein in bringing his troops (the 1st *Panzerarmee,* 8th Army, and 4th *Panzerarmee*) over to the west bank of the Dniepr was shortlived, for Vatutin, Konev, and Malinovsky literally followed at their heels without noticeable hindrance from either the autumn rains or the destruction caused by the retreating Germans. Communications were restored with a speed which aroused everyone's admiration. The engineering and signals commanders, Colonel-Generals Vorobliov and Peresypkin were promoted Marshals of their respective arms of the service by a decision of February 22, 1944.

Hardly had the Russians reached the river than they began to establish bridgeheads on the right bank on either side of Kiev, between Kremenchug and Dniepropetrovsk and up-river from Zaporozh'ye. By October 1 one of these, secured by General Konev, was nearly ten miles deep and over 15 miles wide, thus putting the whole of the river in this area out of range of the German artillery. Magnificent exploits were accomplished by the soldiers, who earned between them 10,000 decorations and 2,000 citations for "Hero of the Soviet Union". On the other side, however, the infantry divisions of Army Group "South" were reduced to a few thousand men each. Manstein's losses had been mounting steadily during the clashes since mid-July but he had only received 33,000 men in replacement, and as usual it was the "poor bloody infantry" who came off worst.

The German *Panzerjäger* Tiger (Porsche) *"Elefant"* tank destroyer

Weight: 66 tons.
Crew: 6.
Armament: one 8.8-cm Sturmkanone 43/2 with 50 rounds.
Armour: hull nose and front plate 100 + 100-mm, sides and rear 80-mm, deck 30-mm, and belly 20 + 30-mm; superstructure front 200-mm, sides and rear 80-mm, and roof 30-mm.
Engine: two Maybach HL 120 TRM inlines, 530-hp together.
Speed: 12½ mph on roads, 6 mph cross-country.
Range: 95 miles on roads, 55 miles cross-country.
Length: 26 feet 8 inches.
Width: 11 feet 1 inch.
Height: 9 feet 10 inches.

The Russian *Samokhodnaya Ustanovka* 76 self-propelled gun

Weight: 12.3 tons.
Crew: 4.
Armament: one 76.2 Model 42/3 gun with 62 rounds.
Armour: hull front 25-mm, superstructure 10- to 15-mm.
Engine: two 6-cylinder inlines, 140-hp together.
Speed: 28 mph.
Range: 280 miles on roads, 185 miles cross-country.
Length: 16 feet 2½ inches.
Width: 8 feet 10¾ inches.
Height: 7 feet 1¼ inches.

△ *Russian prisoners are put to work at bridge-building.*

▽ *Germans plod along a Ukrainian track.*

It took the Russians just about ten days to renew their offensive in this theatre of operations. They threw their armies in simultaneously on the Voronezh, Steppe, South-West, and South Fronts, which for this offensive were renamed the 1st, 2nd, 3rd, and 4th Ukrainian Fronts respectively.

From September 26 the German 6th Army of Army Group "A" found itself under attack from the four armies of the 4th Ukrainian Front. It held out until October 9 then between the 10th and the 20th the battle swayed to and fro for the capture of Melitopol'. The bitterness of the resistance, which did honour to the defence, was also the reason why, after the final collapse, Tolbukhin was able to advance unopposed from Melitopol' to the estuary of the Dniepr. Furthermore, the completely bare and featureless landscape of the Nogayskiye Steppe greatly favoured the headlong advance of the tanks and the cavalry of the Soviet 51st Army (Lieutenant-General V. F. Gerasimenko).

At the beginning of November troops of the 4th Ukrainian Front were outside Kherson. The German 17th Army had failed to force a passage across the Kamenskoye peninsula and was thus trapped in the Crimea. It was now threatened from the rear as Colonel-General Petrov was striving to get his 18th Army across the Kerch' Strait. At the same time, Army Group "South" narrowly escaped disaster twice and only recovered thanks to its commander's powers of manoeuvre. Operating on both sides of the bend in the Dniepr, Colonel-General Malinovsky's intention was to wipe out the Zaporozh'ye bridgehead and at the same time, by breaking the 1st *Panzerarmee's* front above Dniepropetrovsk, exploit the breakthrough along the axis Krivoy-Rog–Apostolovo in the general direction of the river below Dniepropetrovsk. He was not short of men or *matériel:* the 3rd Ukrainian Front had no fewer than eight armies, or a good 50 divisions. Though Hitler had helped the Russians by refusing Manstein permission to withdraw from Dniepropetrovsk, the Soviet manoeuvre did not entirely succeed. On October 14 Zaporozh'ye was taken by a night attack, which brought distinction to General Chuikov, the heroic defender of Stalingrad, and his 8th Army, but after a lightning start under the most favourable of forecasts, General Rotmistrov and his 5th Guards Tank Army, having reached the outskirts of Krivoy-Rog, were held and counter-attacked concentrically by XL Panzer Corps, reinforced by the 24th Panzer Division freshly arrived from Italy. By October 28, their ammunition having failed to follow up in time, they had withdrawn over 15 miles and left behind them 10,000 dead, 5,000 prisoners, 357 tanks, and 378 guns.

Vatutin takes Kiev

This last minute success by the Germans stabilised the situation again, and allowed them to get their troops out of the Dniepropetrovsk salient without much difficulty. They were thus all the more startled to hear, on November 3, the guns of VIII Artillery Corps telling Manstein that Vatutin was preparing to break out of the bridgehead he had won above Kiev. Once more the Russians had managed things well: 2,000 guns at over 500 per mile. Yet contemporary photos show that they were all strung out in a line without the least pretence of camouflage. Where was the Luftwaffe? Nothing more than a memory now.

Under the moral effect of the pulverising attack of 30 infantry divisions and 1,500 tanks, the 4th *Panzerarmee* shattered like glass and during the night of November 5-6, VII Corps hastily evacuated the Ukrainian capital. The sun had not yet

risen on this historic day when Colonel-General Vatutin and his Council of War telegraphed *Stavka:* "Have the joy to inform you that the mission you entrusted to us to liberate our splendid city of Kiev, the capital of the Ukraine, has been carried out by the troops of the 1st Ukrainian Front. The city of Kiev has been completely cleared of its Fascist occupants. The troops of the 1st Ukrainian Front are actively pursuing the task you entrusted to them." The 3rd Guards Tank Army (General Rybalko) dashed in at lightning speed to exploit the situation. By November 12 the bridgehead up-

river from Kiev had widened to 143 miles and at its deepest beyond Zhitomir it was 75 miles beyond the Dniepr. The rapidity of this advance is perhaps less striking when it is realised that the 11 infantry divisions of the 4th Army were about one regiment strong and its 20th *Panzergrenadier* Division was soon wiped out.

Only partial success for Manstein

Perhaps General Vatutin had exaggerated the extent of his victory: as it was, he threw in his columns at all points of the compass between north-west and south-west and this dispersal of the Soviet resources gave Manstein the chance to have another go at him. Refusing to be put off by the Russian manoeuvre, he made a last switch of his armour and brought XLVIII and LVII Panzer Corps into the Berdichev–Shepetovka area, reinforcing them with three armoured divisions and the *"Leibstandarte" Waffen*-S.S. *Panzer-*

△ △ *Kiev, capital of the Ukraine, is recovered, but large parts of the city burn as the Germans pull out.*
△ *Resounding propaganda line: "Those who come against us with the sword shall perish!"*

grenadier Division, putting them under the command of the 4th *Panzerarmee* (General E. Raus, an Austrian officer). General H. Balck, who had again taken up command of XLVIII Panzer Corps, would have liked to see a counter-offensive with Kiev as its objective, thus providing the opportunity for turning the tables on the Russians. Raus spoke up for an attack on Zhitomir first, a cautious move

but one with less potential, and Manstein supported him. Considering the alternating freezing and thawing characteristic of November weather in the Ukraine, the Zhitomir solution admittedly seemed the most likely to succeed immediately, wheareas a move towards Kiev was a long-term gamble which Manstein could not risk.

As it was, the 4th *Panzerarmee* attacked from the south in a northerly direction and on November 15 cut the Kiev-Zhitomir road. During the night of the 17th-18th, XLVIII Panzer Corps took Zhitomir after a neat swing from north to west. The 3rd Guards Tank Army was taken by surprise and, attempting to regain the initiative, had its I Cavalry Corps, and V and VII Tank Corps caught in a pincer. Escape cost it 3,000 killed and the loss of 153 tanks and 70 guns. On December 1, LVII Panzer Corps (General Kirchner), which formed General Raus's left flank, returned to Korosten. Some days later Balck, daringly exploiting his success, recaptured Radomyshl' on the Teterev and Malin on the Irsha. Then, in collaboration with Kirchner, he attempted to encircle three tank corps and a dozen infantry divisions which were

trying to block his advance eastwards. The German pincers, however, were too slow in closing round the enemy, who managed to slip away. On December 23 Manstein was able to draw up a balance-sheet of this operation: he had got back to within 25 miles of Kiev, and had killed 20,000 of the enemy and captured or destroyed 600 tanks, 300 guns, and 1,200 anti-tank weapons, but had only taken 5,000 prisoners. Bad weather and low cloud had, however, helped the operations of the 4th *Panzerarmee,* shielding it from observation and from attack by the Red Air Force. German air support was now so rare that the time was past when the generals hoped for long spells of fine weather.

On the other hand this partial success brought a grievous reversal of fortune. To prevent a collapse on his left flank, Manstein had been compelled to draw on his strength in the centre. Here the 8th Army had been deprived of five divisions, including four Panzer, and was thus forced to give way under the pressure of the 2nd Ukrainian Front. On December 10 the important rail junction of Znamenka fell to Colonel-General Konev. On the 14th he took Cherkassy on the Dniepr in spite of stiff resistance by the German 72nd Division and the *"Wiking"* Waffen-S.S. *Panzergrenadier* Division.

Soviet pressure all along the line

Events on the Central Front were not quite as dramatic, though during the autumn of 1943 they severely tested Field-Marshal von Kluge and his commanders. The enemy was superior in men and *matériel* and kept up his attacks relentlessly.

On October 6 the Kalinin Front, which was to become the 1st Baltic Front on the 20th, opened up an attack on the 3rd *Panzerarmee* at the point where Army Group "Centre" joined Army Group "North". Colonel-General Reinhardt's lines were very thin on the ground and the troops of the 2nd and 3rd Shock Armies were able to break through at Nevel'. The Russians then attempted to drive forwards from the ground they had won north of the Dvina, one arm thrusting towards Polotsk, the other towards Vitebsk. If they won these objectives, the way would then be open to the Baltic coast.

The Germans, however, made a determined stand and counter-attacked, discouraging any further advance by Eremenko's troops, who nevertheless were able to establish a position south of the Vitebsk–Polotsk railway. In the German 4th Army sector General Sokolovsky and his West Front made repeated attempts to force a crossing of the narrow strip of land between the Dvina at Vitebsk and the Dniepr at Orsha. Each attempt was repulsed with heavy losses to the Russians, who advanced on a narrow front and were massacred by General Heinrici's heavy concentrations of artillery, which in places amounted to 70 batteries under unified command. A Polish division, the "Tadeusz Kosciuszko", under Colonel Zygmunt Berling, fought in this battle wearing Red Army uniforms. By the turn of the year the 2nd Baltic Front, formerly the Bryansk Front, under Popov, had reached the Dniepr in the area of Zhlobin and the Belorussian Front, formerly the Central Front (Rokossovsky), was engaged at Mozyr', 56 miles beyond the Dniepr and in contact on its left with the 1st Ukrainian Front.

△ *Soviet troops at one of the Dniepr bridgeheads established in September-October 1943.*

The Russian steamroller gets under way

And so, for the German Army operating on the Eastern Front, 1943 was ending with an outlook as gloomy as that of 1942. There had been no new Stalingrad but between Kursk and Zhitomir the German resistance was on the verge of a breakdown. Since July, they had lost 104,000 men, half of these wounded. A remarkable inconsistency in the figures published at this time was revealed when the Russians claimed 900,000 of the enemy had been killed and 1,700,000 wounded in this same period. More remarkable still was that on November 6, Stalin made a statement to the effect that the Germans had lost four million men in the past year. If this had been remotely true, the war would have been over.

It is undeniable, however, that the remorseless attacks of the Red Army were inexorably flattening the German armies along a 1,250-mile front.

Hence the growing pessimism in the German Army among the generals and chiefs-of-staff. In the preceding spring Field-Marshal von Manstein was able to hope that, if there were a reform of the high command, the Wehrmacht could still draw even. Six months later, when Lieutenant-General von Choltitz, acting commander of XLVIII Panzer Corps, spoke to his chief-of-staff, Mellenthin, it was not about drawing the game, or even of stalemate. According to the latter, Choltitz, as if in a vision, described the situation as waves of Soviet troops pouring over every breakwater Germany could contrive, possibly reaching Germany herself. Mellenthin thought Choltitz unduly pessimistic.

In fact Choltitz was not a congenital or professional pessimist. He merely saw the seriousness of the situation: in the East O.K.H. was throwing in exhausted troops; in the other theatres of war the divisions at the disposal of O.K.W. were

"untouchable", as in Germany no-one doubted that the invasion would come sooner or later. On December 26, 1943, German divisions were deployed as follows:

East	192	(33 Panzer and *Panzergrenadier*)
Norway	10	
Denmark	2	
West	43	(4 Panzer and *Panzergrenadier*)
Italy	16	(5 Panzer and *Panzergrenadier*)
Balkans	15	

Thus on that day 86 of the 278 German divisions deployed between Rhodes and Narvik were unavailable for the Eastern Front and these included nine of the 42 Panzer and *Panzergrenadier* divisions.

That same autumn General Guderian, convinced of the need for a change in the high command, went to G.H.Q.:

"I went to see Jodl, to whom I submitted my proposals for a reorganisation of the Supreme Command: the Chief of the Armed Forces General Staff would con-

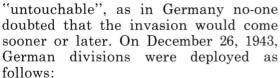

trol the actual conduct of operations, while Hitler would be limited to his proper field of activities, supreme control of the political situation and of the highest war strategy. After I had expounded my ideas at length and in detail Jodl replied laconically: 'Do you know of a better supreme commander than Adolf Hitler?' His expression had remained impassive as he said this, and his whole manner was one of icy disapproval. In view of his attitude I put my papers back in my brief-case and left the room."

△ △ *Tank-borne infantry attack on the Kalinin Front.*
△ *Red Army infantrymen break cover and advance, covered by the tommy-gunners on their right flank.*

In the Pacific the year 1943 was marked, as far as Admiral Nimitz and General MacArthur were concerned, by a series of limited offensives which, whilst gradually wearing down the Japanese forces, were to give the Americans and their Australian allies the necessary bases for the decisive offensive of 1944. The objective of this latter offensive was the complete and final destruction of the Japanese military machine. No more than with the Germans were the Washington political and military leaders prepared to accept, with or without Tojo, anything less than Japan's total and unconditional surrender.

Any change of opinion over these radical aims would have aroused the opposition of the American public. When he held supreme command, Mussolini several times complained that his fellow citizens did not whole-heartedly support him in his war effort. The war against Japan was deeply felt by the American people and, in Churchill's entourage, during the conferences which took him across the Atlantic, it was often noticed that the reconquest of some obscure copra island in the far corner of the Pacific raised as much enthusiasm in New York and Washington as did a whole battle won in Africa or Italy. The White House and the Pentagon had to take these feelings into account.

Along with the concern shown by Roosevelt and Hopkins for the U.S.S.R., a concern which caused them to urge the opening of a second front, there was also the fact that the Americans did not look favourably on their hero MacArthur being kept short of men and *matériel* whilst in Europe U.S. forces stood idle on the wrong side of the Channel. In the Joint Chiefs-of-Staff Committee, that was the sentiment of the rugged Admiral Ernest J. King: instead of giving complete and immediate support to the principle of "Germany first", the centre of gravity of American power should be shifted over to the Pacific. To forestall this reversal of strategy the President and General Marshall were therefore constrained to set in motion Operation "Round-up", which was to become "Overlord".

On the ways to get to Tokyo and the means to be employed there was, to put it mildly, lively discussion between Admirals King and Nimitz on the one side and General MacArthur on the other. This is not surprising, as each of these leaders was a man of strong character

and not given to compromise solutions of which his conscience would not approve.

It fell to General Marshall to pronounce judgement on their arguments and, in the last resort, to impose a solution. We shall see under what circumstances he did this, but let us say at once that it was done with both authority and a sense of opportunity.

American strength

In the last biennial report he presented to the Secretary of War on September 1, 1945, General Marshall had entitled his chapter on the Pacific campaign in 1943 "Relentless Pressure". He introduced it in the following terms:

"It had always been the concept of the United States Chiefs-of-Staff that Japan could be best defeated by a series of amphibious attacks across the far reaches of the Pacific. Oceans are formidable barriers, but for the nation enjoying naval superiority they became highroads of invasion".

We must now consider the means put at the disposal of the commanders to exert this pressure and to crush the "advances" made by the enemy in the Pacific during the first half of 1942.

1. The South-West Pacific Area
At the headquarters of the C.-in-C. South-West Pacific, General MacArthur, they

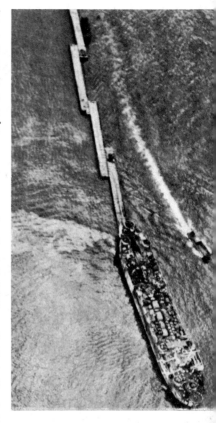

◁ ◁ *Training for the eternal moment of truth in the Pacific war: hitting the beach.*
△ *Landing supplies by artificial jetties – and gaining invaluable experience for the day when the big assault on "Fortress Europe" would be made.*

▽ *Rifles bristle as an amphibious D.U.K.W. comes ashore.*

complained of having to fight a war "stony broke", a "Cinderella War", and being driven to "sling and arrow operations". Even so, on July 1, 1943, MacArthur had the Australian Army (ten divisions), a New Zealand contingent, and four American divisions (to be raised to eight by the end of the year). He was supported by the U.S. 3rd Fleet (Admiral William F. Halsey), although this was not put expressly under his command. Finally he had authority over Major-General George F. Kenney's 5th Air Force, which at the same date of July 1 had 150 four-engined bombers. Some months later the Pentagon allotted him the 13th Air Force (Major-General Nathan F. Twining). From this it will be concluded that the South-West Pacific theatre of operations was less deprived than General MacArthur's entourage might have led one to believe. The opposing forces were no stronger.

However, MacArthur did not complain of the scarcity of his resources and then sit back and do nothing: on the contrary he manoeuvred his divisions, his squadrons, and his warships with considerable determination and skill.

2. The Central Pacific Area

In the Central Pacific theatre, under the command of Admiral Nimitz, Lieutenant-General Robert C. Richardson Junior

had on July 1 nine Army and Marine divisions and was energetically training them for amphibious operations which, during the forthcoming autumn and winter, would give the Americans possession of the enemy's forward defensive posts on the Tarawa, Makin, Majura, and Eniwetok atolls. This offensive, like MacArthur's, evidently depended on the naval or, even better, the naval-air superiority of the United States over Japan.

A gigantic naval effort

We must say something of the Americans' enormous naval effort, just as we have dealt with the development of their land forces.

Programmes completed in 1941 and 1942 had aimed particularly at replacing obsolete battleships and destroyers. In 1943 ships brought into service were:

    2 fast battleships of 45,000 tons
    6 fleet aircraft-carriers of 27,000 tons
    9 light aircraft-carriers of 11,000 tons
    24 escort carriers
    4 heavy cruisers (8-inch guns)
    7 light cruisers (6-inch guns)
    128 destroyers
    200 submarines

and many auxiliary units and supply vessels. Of course, except for specialist anti-submarine vessels, this great effort went as a priority towards building up the Pacific theatre of operations.

Improved Anti-Aircraft defences

The new units which came under Admiral Nimitz's command had all benefited from the experiences of the tough year of 1942. As in France and Britain, American naval architects in the immediate pre-war years had not taken sufficiently into account the threat to the surface vessel of the dive-bomber and the torpedo-carrying aircraft. Battleships, cruisers, and destroyers built under the new programme were to come out of the yards bristling with A.A. weapons of all shapes and sizes. The following table shows how a battleship was equipped before and after Pearl Harbor:

	West Virginia (1923)	New Jersey (1942)
5-inch	8	20
3-inch	4	0
40-mm	0	80
20-mm	0	50
.5-inch	10	0

In addition, the combined work of the Carnegie Institute in Washington, the John Hopkins University, and the National Bureau of Standards had produced a radio-electric fuse for the shells used by the Army and the Marines. This fuse, known as the proximity or V.T. (variable time) fuse, considerably increased the effectiveness of A.A. fire.

The V.T. fuse was first used in open sea in case it failed to go off and fell into enemy hands. On January 5, 1943 it scored its first success in the waters around the Solomon Islands, when two salvoes from the 5-inch guns of the cruiser *Helena* were enough to shoot down a torpedo-bomber. During the V-1 attacks on London the proximity fuse's efficiency against these 435 mph missiles reached 79 per cent under favourable conditions.

Naval-air engagements in 1942 cost Admiral Nimitz no fewer than four aircraft-carriers. Between January 1, 1943 and September 2, 1945 he used a succession of 27 (18 fleet and nine light) and lost only one in 32 months of ceaseless offensives.

△ *and* △△ *Beating the drum on the home front.*
◁△ *and* ◁ *"Train hard, fight easy," was the dictum of the Russian general, Suvorov, in the 18th century. But there was to be no easy fighting in the Pacific theatre.*

Yet these U.S. carriers were the prime target of the famous Kamikaze from October 1944 onwards. During the battle for Okinawa (April 1-June 7, 1945) six carriers were the victims of these suicide attacks, but not one was sunk, thanks to their sturdy construction and to the efficient fire-fighting services on board.

New heavy projectiles

The reconquest of the Pacific and the defeat of Japan after Guadalcanal required many landing operations, supported by naval fire designed to crush the Japanese land defences regardless of the cost in ammunition. But, Admiral King tells us in his second report covering the period March 1, 1944 to March 1, 1945:

"At the time of the attack on Pearl Harbor, the Navy had virtually no high capacity ammunition (so-called because it contains an extremely high amount of explosive). Since then, production of this type of projectile has risen rapidly, and currently accounts for 75 per cent of the output of shells from six to sixteen inches in calibre. Monthly naval production of all types of major calibre ammunition now exceeds the total quantity delivered during World War I."

This supporting fire-power was given by the old battleships which had escaped at Pearl Harbor, suitably refitted and heavily reinforced with A.A. weapons.

An enormous fleet of supply-ships

Because of the huge area of the Pacific, Admiral King gave Nimitz an enormous number of supply-vessels comprising troop transports, ships carrying *matériel,* ammunition, food of all kinds, tankers, hospital ships with homely names such as *Comfort, Mercy, Consolation, Hope,* or *Tranquillity,* aircraft supply-ships, destroyers, submarines, and even floating docks capable of berthing the longest ships in the fleet. This great collection of vessels, known as the Maintenance Fleet, was to allow Halsey, Spruance, and Kinkaid to operate at sea for weeks at a time, relying only on temporary bases in the atolls hastily built for them by the

"Seabee" construction battalions.

As can be seen, in this field as well the American leaders, with no historical precedent to guide them, had seen big, wide, and far, whereas their enemy had relied on time-honoured methods of supply for his troops. The rapid build-up of the American air and sea offensive, resulting from the logistic organisation which we have just described in brief, secured in addition a devastating effect of surprise over the Japanese strategy.

Massive expansion

These material achievements of the U.S. Navy, remarkable though they were, would have been of little avail if they had not been accompanied by a similar build-up in the quality and the quantity of the men who were to benefit from them.

On the day after Pearl Harbor the American Navy had 337,274 officers, petty officers, and other ranks. Twelve months later there were more than a million (1,112,218 to be exact); this figure had increased by nearly 930,000 by the end of December 1943, and had reached about three million on the same date in the following year. This enormous recruiting and training effort required some 947 Instruction Centres which in June 1944 were being attended each day by 303,000 men of all ranks and specialities.

According to Admiral King in the report quoted above, the number of men on active service on the day the Japanese began their aggression was only a tenth of those available. In particular there had to be intensive training of nearly 300,000 officers, 131,000 of whom came straight from civilian life. "Nothing succeeds like success," says an old adage. In the event the methods used by the Navy in selection, basic instruction, specialised training, posting, and promotion for all these men were close to perfection and gave the United States fleets well-manned ships which incurred only a minimum of accidents at sea.

The crews must on the whole have been like those described by J. Fahey, who has left us a fascinating diary of the Pacific campaign, through which he served on board the light cruiser *Montpelier* between February 1943 and August 1945 from Guadalcanal to the Ryukyu Islands. The daily entries made by this young sailor show him to be patriotic, a

△ *Admiral "Bull" Halsey, back in harness after Midway and given the key striking command in the South Pacific Area.*

keen fighter, a skilled and conscientious gunner, cheerfully accepting chores, a good companion and one singularly well aware of the sense and the implications of the actions in which his ship was engaged. Furthermore, Leading Seaman Fahey's snap judgements on Admirals "Tip" Merrill, "Thirty-one knots" Burke, "Bull" Halsey and Mitscher, the "terrific guy" have all been borne out by history. Others have maintained that the Americans overcame their adversaries in Europe and Asia by sheer weight of *matériel*. This is to a large extent true, but the fact remains that this *matériel* was handled by well-trained, well-disciplined personnel.

U.S. production outstrips Japan's

In Japan the year's events bore out Admiral Yamamoto's prediction that his country would not be able to withstand the strains of a prolonged war. In contrast with the United States' steel production of 90 million tons in 1943, Japan made only 7.8 million tons, which in itself was over

two millions short of what the government had planned. Also, in spite of the conquest of Borneo, Sumatra, and Burma, as well as the severe restrictions imposed on civilian consumption, fuel supplies for the Imperial armed forces were by no means fully assured. The British and Dutch refineries had been sabotaged, but the Japanese did not restore them, contenting themselves with shipping the

△ *American P.T. boat in dazzle camouflage. It was in command of one of these craft that the young J. F. Kennedy made his name, saving his crew after shipwreck during the Solomons campaign.*

▽ *Assault teams transfer to inflatable landing-craft from their landing ship.*

△ △ South Dakota, *one of the tough new American battleships rushed into service after Pearl Harbor. It was soon found that the battleship's most important contribution to modern naval warfare was its immense fire-power, both in anti-aircraft defence and in shelling enemy coastal defences.*

△ *The old brigade. Raised after Pearl Harbor and completely overhauled, the veteran battleship* California *participated in every major naval landing made by the Americans in the Pacific theatre.*

crude oil to Japan for refining, then sending the fuel oil and petrol out again to the combat area, thus incurring heavy expense in freight and fuel itself. American submarines were already beginning to take their toll of Japanese shipping and this was not being replaced rapidly enough by the Imperial shipyards.

Let us now have a look at the types and numbers of the warships put into service in the Pacific on both sides during 1943. It will be immediately evident that, without a miracle, the war was already virtually over for Japan:

	U.S.	Japan
Battleships	2	–
Combat aircraft-carriers	15	1
Heavy and light cruisers	11	2
Destroyers	128	11
Submarines	200	58
Totals	356	72

The American naval air forces had got rid of the types of aircraft which had shown up so badly over Midway, in spite of the courage of their crews, but the Japanese had hardly improved their equipment at all. Whereas the Americans were also prepared to go to any lengths in risk and cost to recover a handful of pilots lost at sea, the Japanese cared little for the survival of their flying crews. The American airmen did not, it is true, at this time report any sign of despondency amongst their adversaries, but from now on there was to be evidence of a lessening of their fighting spirit. So little regard was given by the Japanese to what we call "human material" that there was now no time left to retrain the men for their rôle.

The morale of the Japanese fighting man

The morale of the Japanese was unaffected by the fact that they were now on the defensive.

According to Admiral de Belot, whose judgement remains valid today although his book *La guerre aéronavale du Pacifique* appeared in 1948, the fierce fighting in the Solomon Islands, New Guinea, the Aleutians, and the Gilbert Islands brought in only three to four hundred prisoners to the Americans up to the end of 1943, and up to the capitulation of Japan ordered by the Emperor, no Japanese general officer ever fell into the hands of his enemy alive.

There were 2,600 Japanese in the garrison of Attu Island (Aleutians) at the end of May 1943, but the 11,000 Americans of the 7th Division who captured it took only 28 prisoners. When the defenders had used up all their artillery ammunition and most of their cartridges, they assembled by night to the number of about 1,000 and charged, using only their side-arms. The 500 or so who survived were driven off and began all over again the next night. At dawn on May 30 the few who were left committed suicide, some with revolvers, others with grenades, after finishing off the sick and the wounded. This bloody affair cost the Americans 600 killed and 1,200 wounded. On November 10 in the waters south of Bougainville, Leading Seaman Fahey witnessed a chilling and awesome scene which he described as follows in his diary:

"This afternoon, while we were south of Bougainville and just off Treasury Island, we came across a raft with four live Japs in it. Admiral Merrill sent word to one of our destroyers to pick them up. As the destroyer *Spence* came close to the raft, the Japs opened up with a machine gun on the destroyer. The Jap officer put the gun in each man's mouth and fired, blowing out the back of each man's skull. One of the Japs did not want to die for the Emperor and put up a struggle. The others held him down. The officer was the last to die. He also blew his brains out . . . All the bodies had disappeared into the water. There was nothing left but blood and an empty raft. Swarms of sharks were everywhere. The sharks ate well today."

We could quote page after page of macabre examples like this. Those we have chosen may perhaps suffice for us to offer the following remarks: those Japanese fighting men who did not hesitate to finish off their wounded comrades to spare them the inexpiable dishonour of captivity had no consideration either for the enemy prisoners who fell into their hands, even though the Japanese Government had signed the Geneva Convention and had respected it on the whole during the Russo-Japanese War of 1904-1905.

Another observation must be made here concerning the intellectual outlook of the Japanese Army and Navy: they showed unreasonable optimism almost throughout the war about the losses they inflicted on their enemy on land, on sea, and in the air. During 1943, for every action in the waters around the Solomon and Gilbert Islands, G.H.Q. Tokyo's spokesmen blew the victory trumpets and broadcast, as they had done during the previous year, the unlikely lists of battleships, aircraft-carriers, and heavy and light cruisers of the U.S. Navy which they had sunk.

We know from documents which became available after the war that during 1943 the U.S. Navy lost only the cruiser *Helena,* sunk on July 6 in Kula Bay (New Georgia) and the escort-carrier *Liscombe Bay,* sunk on November 24, the day after the successful attack on the Tarawa and Makin atolls in the Gilbert Islands.

Must these clumsy and absurd exaggerations be blamed on General Tojo's Intelligence services alone? Most of them, clearly, but this policy of boasting was continued in even after the loss of the Marianas (July 15-19, 1944). When we see the Imperial G.H.Q. basing its operations on enemy losses reported by its combat forces, as it was still doing after the battle of Leyte (October 1944), we must conclude that there was a peculiar spirit of braggadocio among the staffs at the front or at least a complete inability to see the situation coolly and to weigh up its every feature. The hastily-trained observers of the Japanese naval air force seem to have added confusion at this time by their errors of identification.

At the same time as the American Joint Chiefs-of-Staff Committee was deciding upon a limited offensive in the Pacific, Imperial G.H.Q. in Tokyo, far from taking into account the defeats at Midway and Guadalcanal, adopted a defensive-offensive strategy which Washington had just abandoned. In May 1943 a Plan "Z" was issued. This defined the rôle of the Japanese armed forces as follows:

"a. A defensive front (bounded by the Aleutians, Wake, the Marshall Islands, the Gilbert Islands, Nauru, the Bismarck Islands, New Guinea, and the Malay Barrier) will be established. Local commands will be set up and charged to take defensive measures. The Combined Fleet will be stationed at Truk and on neighbouring islands.

b. In case of attack the enemy will be drawn towards the main force and destroyed by the combined action of land-based and carrier-based aircraft.

c. Enemy aircraft-carriers will be counter-attacked as often as

△ *From London's* Daily Mail. *One Japanese admiral laments to his colleague: "I wish I had followed childhood dream of becoming honourable chauffeur."*
▽ Simplicissimus, *Munich. Wordly wisdom from Uncle Sam: "To build the road to Tokyo you need a lot of American raw materials."*

△ Kladderadatsch *of Berlin. Uncle Sam again: "God, I wish that sun would set on my empire!"*

possible.

d. During engagements the enemy aircraft-carriers are the primary objective, followed by his troop transports.

e. If the enemy attempts to land he must be stopped on the shore. If his landing is successful and he can exploit it, then he must be continuously counter-attacked."

Briefly then, the resistance of forward strategic posts under "a" had to last for some time and cause considerable damage to the enemy so that the Combined Fleet, kept concentrated at the hinge of the fan, could have the time necessary to move in on the enemy and overwhelm him. The atolls or islands on the perimeter of this defensive system were thus so many unsinkable aircraft-carriers. This directive went back to the strategic thinking which had dominated the Imperial Navy between 1920 and 1940. In the situation as

▽ *Troops file ashore down the port and starboard gangways of an assault landing-craft. But only so much could be learned from rehearsals . . .*

it was in 1943, it could still have worked if the Americans had stuck to the means and methods of attack expected to be used about 1930. Then each of the strong-points between the Aleutians and Malaya would have had sufficient aircraft to drive off with losses a battleship squadron protected by one or two aircraft-carriers, giving time for the light surface vessels and the submarines to get the first nibble at the enemy fleet which, thus weakened, would be crushed by the main force of the Combined Fleet.

But it was now 1943. For his attack on the objectives in the Gilbert group, the American 5th Fleet (Vice-Admiral Raymond A. Spruance) had six 27,000-ton aircraft-carriers, five 11,000 ton light carriers and eight escort-carriers with between them some 700 fighters and bombers. This would allow him not only to attack Makin and Tarawa with overwhelming strength, but also to keep up a continuous attack on the Japanese bases in the Marshall Islands to prevent the Japanese from sending help from there to the Gilbert group. The strength of the U.S. force therefore nullified point "b" of the directive above which envisaged the "combined action of land-based and carrier-based aircraft of the Imperial Fleet", for the former were to be destroyed before the latter could intervene.

Such were the disastrous consequences of the dispersion under Plan "Z" of the Imperial forces. Nimitz and MacArthur simply abstained from attacking any enemy positions not immediately on their line of advance towards each other. There was worse still, however: the organisation, then the supply, of this vast chain of support points stretching from the North Pacific to the Indian Ocean demanded a logistic effort by the Japanese command, the cost and the extent of which seem at the time completely to have escaped them. The Japanese were short of ships, fuel, and aviation spirit, and the U.S. submarine fleet, ever expanding, more seasoned, and equipped with better torpedoes, made life very hazardous for transport vessels. At the time of Japan's final capitulation, the Japanese support-points which had been spared by the American strategy were virtually starving and for many months had ceased to have any effect on the outcome of operations in the Pacific, just as the German forces left in Norway or odd pockets on the Atlantic coast had no influence on Eisenhower's offensive.

In our chapter on Kursk we said that Manstein's "return attack" plan, which he had advocated in vain to Hitler, depended on the enemy's not discovering the Germans' intentions. It was the same with Plan "Z" and the success expected of it in Tokyo. The reader will remember that the Japanese naval code had yielded to the efforts of the American code-breakers and that the Japanese G.H.Q. and Admiralty had continued to believe that the transmissions were still secret. This was to provide a final reason for the course events in the Pacific were to take.

CHAPTER 92
Prelude

At the turn of the year General Mac-Arthur, not content with the success he had had in denying the enemy access to Port Moresby in New Guinea, had now assumed the initiative which he was to retain until the end of hostilities.

He put his 32nd and 41st Divisions under the command of Lieutenant-General Robert L. Eichelberger and sent two columns over the Owen Stanley range in the direction of Buna on the north coast of Papua. At the same time there were to be airborne and amphibious landings close to the objective. On December 14, 1942 Buna fell, but it took General Eichelberger until January 2, 1943 to wipe out the last remnants of resistance.

He was then able to write to MacArthur on that day:

"At 4.30 p.m., I crossed the bridge (from the Island) after 'C' Company had passed and I saw American troops with their bellies out of the mud and their eyes in the sun circling unafraid around the bunkers. It was one of the grandest sights I have ever seen . . . the 127th Infantry found its soul."

"Life in the virgin forest was atrocious," explains Marcel Giuglaris. "Every night trees fell; as the earth shook with the bombing their slender roots gave way and the darkness was filled with the thunder of the forest collapsing about you. There were also the poisonous

▽ *Arbiter of sea power in the Pacific War: an American battleship/carrier task force in line-ahead.*

scorpions whose sting sent you mad, the lack of food, malaria, typhoid, snakes, and nervous illnesses. Fighting in the jungle was equally terrifying, merciless, neither side taking prisoner. The Japanese counter-attacked regularly at night, screaming in Banzai charges. The Americans then changed their tactics: they began to lay the ground waste a hundred square yards at a time. The Japanese were astonished that they were still holding out. Every day the number of dead increased, every man fought until he was killed. The end came when Eichelberger's Marines had no more men facing them."

MacArthur's tactics

The reconquest of New Guinea, which was completed in mid-January, cost MacArthur dear and, in view of his losses and the enemy's tenacity, he decided to soften down his methods, as he wrote in his memoirs:

"It was the practical application of this system of warfare–to avoid the frontal attack with its terrible loss of life; to by-pass Japanese strongpoints and neutralise them by cutting their lines of supply; to thus isolate their armies and starve them on the battlefield; to as Willie Keeler used to say, 'hit 'em where they ain't'–that from this time guided my movements and operations.

"This decision enabled me to accomplish the concept of the direct-target approach from Papua to Manila. The system was popularly called 'leap-frogging', and hailed as something new in warfare. But it was actually the adaption of modern instrumentalities of war to a concept as ancient as war itself. Derived from the classic strategy of envelopment, it was given a new name, imposed by modern conditions. Never before had a field of battle embraced land and water in such relative proportions . . . The paucity of resources at my command made me adopt this method of campaign as the only hope of accomplishing my task . . . It has always proved the ideal method for success by inferior but faster-moving forces."

Briefly, MacArthur was applying the "indirect approach" method recommended in the months leading up to the World War II by the British military writer Basil Liddell Hart and practised also by Vice-Admiral Halsey in his advance from Guadalcanal to Bougainville and in the following autumn by Admiral Nimitz in the Central Pacific Area. This also comes out in the following anecdote from Willoughby and Chamberlain's *Conqueror of the Pacific:*

"When staff members presented their glum forecasts to MacArthur at a famous meeting which included Admiral Halsey, the newly arrived General Krueger, and Australia's General Thomas Blamey, MacArthur puffed at his cigarette. Finally, when one of the conferees said, 'I don't see how we can take these strong points with our limited resources,' MacArthur leaned forward.

"'Well,' he said, 'Let's just say that we won't take them. In fact, gentlemen, I don't want them.'

"Then turning to General Kenney, he said, '*You* incapacitate them.'"

The results of this method were strikingly described after the end of the war by Colonel Matsuichi Ino, formerly Chief of Intelligence of the Japanese 8th Army:

"This was the type of strategy we hated most. The Americans, with minimum losses, attacked and seized a relatively weak area, constructed airfields and then proceeded to cut the supply lines to troops in that area. Without engaging in a large scale operation, our strongpoints were gradually starved out. The Japanese Army preferred direct assault, after the German fashion, but the Americans flowed into our weaker points and submerged us, just as water seeks the weakest entry to

△ *Spearhead of the American Expeditionary Force: immaculately turned-out troops of the U.S. Army Air Corps parade in Sydney.*

▽ *American armour for Australian troops: Grant tanks.*

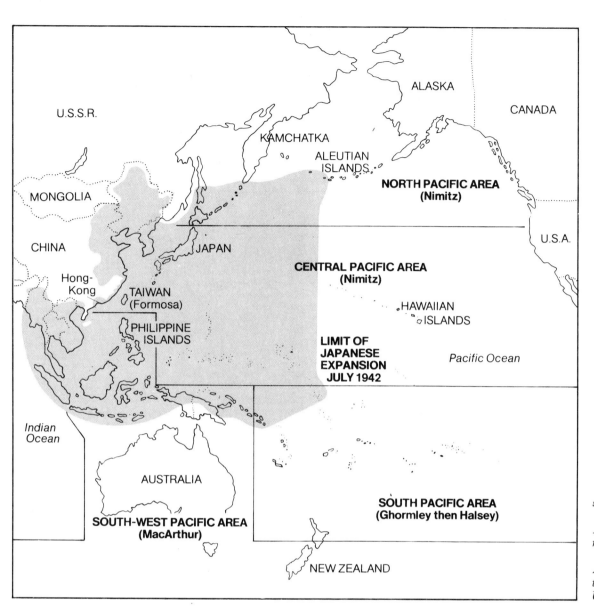

ALASKA

U.S.S.R.

CANADA

KAMCHATKA

ALEUTIAN
ISLANDS

**NORTH PACIFIC AREA
(Nimitz)**

MONGOLIA

U.S.A.

CHINA   JAPAN   **CENTRAL PACIFIC AREA
(Nimitz)**

Hong-
Kong

TAIWAN
(Formosa)   HAWAIIAN
                                        ISLANDS

PHILIPPINE
ISLANDS   **LIMIT OF
JAPANESE
EXPANSION
JULY 1942**   *Pacific Ocean*

*Indian
Ocean*

AUSTRALIA   **SOUTH PACIFIC AREA
(Ghormley then Halsey)**

**SOUTH-WEST PACIFIC AREA
(MacArthur)**

NEW ZEALAND

◁ *The Japanese Empire in 1943,
showing the vast extent of the
"way back" which confronted the
Allies in the Pacific – whichever
route they finally decided to take.*
▽ *Floating medical aid for the
Allies – essential, considering
the distances to be covered: the
U.S. hospital ship* Tranquillity.

sink a ship. We respected this type of
strategy for its brilliance because it
gained the most while losing the least."

This could not be better expressed;
nevertheless, MacArthur's method demanded perfect collaboration of the land,
sea, air, and airborne forces under the
command of the C.-in-C. of the South-
West Pacific theatre of operations. He
handled them like some great orchestral
conductor.

According to the decisions taken at
Casablanca, Nimitz's ultimate objective
was Formosa via the Marshall and Caro-
line Islands. When he reached here he was
to join MacArthur, who would have come
from the Philippines, reinforced in the
vicinity of the Celebes Sea by the British
Pacific Fleet, which meanwhile was to
have forced the Molucca Passage. From
Formosa, the Allies could sever Japanese
communications between the home islands
and the newly-conquered empire, as a
preliminary to invading Japan itself.

A few weeks after Casablanca, the American Joint Chiefs-of-Staff defined as follows the immediate missions that were to be carried out by General MacArthur and Vice-Admiral Halsey:

"South Pacific and Southwest Pacific forces to co-operate in a drive on Rabaul. Southwest Pacific forces then to press on westward along north coast of New Guinea."

General MacArthur was therefore empowered to address strategic directives to Admiral Halsey, but the latter was reduced to the men and *matériel* allotted to him by the C.-in-C. Pacific. This included no aircraft-carriers. In his memoirs MacArthur complains at having been treated from the outset as a poor relation. We would suggest that he had lost sight of the fact that a new generation of aircraft-carriers only reached Pearl Harbor at the beginning of September and that Nimitz, firmly supported by Admiral King, did not intend to engage *Enterprise* and *Saratoga*, which were meanwhile filling the gap, in the narrow waters of the Solomon Islands.

Moreover, the situation was made even more precarious because of the new Japanese air bases at Buin on Bougainville and at Munda on New Georgia. This was very evident to Leading Seaman James J. Fahey, who wrote on June 30:

"We could not afford to send carriers or battleships up the Solomons, because they would be easy targets for the land-based planes, and also subs that would be hiding near the jungle. We don't mind losing light cruisers and destroyers but the larger ships would not be worth the gamble, when we can do the job anyway."

As we can see, all ranks in the Pacific Fleet were of one mind about tactics.

In the meantime, whilst at Port Moresby General MacArthur was setting in motion the plan which was to put a pincer round Rabaul and allow him to eliminate this menace to his operations, the U.S.A.A.F. was inflicting two very heavy blows on the enemy. After the defeat at Buna, the Japanese high command had decided to reinforce the 18th Army which, under General Horii, was responsible for the defence of New Guinea. On February 28 a first echelon of the 51st Division left Rabaul on board eight merchant ships escorted by eight destroyers. But Major-General Kenney unleashed on the convoy all he could collect together of his 5th Air Force. The American bombers attacked the enemy at mast-height, using delayed-action bombs so as to allow the planes to get clear before the explosions. On March 3 the fighting came to an end in the Bismarck Sea with the destruction of the eight troop transports and five destroyers.

MacArthur's biographers write:

"Skip bombing practice had not been wasted. Diving in at low altitudes through heavy flak, General Kenney's planes skimmed over the water to drop their bombs as close to the target as possible.

"The battle of the Bismarck Sea lasted for three days, with Kenney's bombers moving in upon the convoy whenever there was even a momentary break in the clouds.

"'We have achieved a victory of such completeness as to assume the proportions of a major disaster to the enemy. Our decisive success cannot fail to have most important results on the enemy's strategic and tactical plans. His campaign, for the time being at least, is completely dislocated.'"

Rightly alarmed by this catastrophe, Admiral Yamamoto left the fleet at Truk in the Carolines and went in person to Rabaul. He was followed to New Britain by some 300 fighters and bombers from the six aircraft-carriers under his command. Thus strengthened, the Japanese 11th Air Fleet, on which the defence of the sector depended, itself went over to the attack towards Guadalcanal on April 8 and towards Port Moresby on the 14th. But since the Japanese airmen as usual greatly exaggerated their successes, and as we now have the list of losses drawn up by the Americans, it might be useful to see what reports were submitted to Admiral Yamamoto who, of course, could only accept them at their face value. Yet it must have been difficult to lead an army or a fleet to victory when, in addition to the usual uncertainties of war, you had boastful accounts claiming 28 ships and 150 planes. The real losses were five and 25 respectively.

But this was not all, for during this battle the Japanese lost 40 aircraft and brought down only 25 of their enemy's. The results were therefore eight to five against them. Had they known the true figures, Imperial G.H.Q. might have been brought to the conclusion that the tactical and technical superiority of the famous Zero was now a thing of the past. How could they have known this if they were continually being told that for every four Japanese planes shot down the enemy lost 15?

◄ *Scene aboard one of the brand-new* Essex-*class carriers which within months would give the U.S. Pacific Fleet an overwhelming superiority in naval air power.*
△ *"I-will-return" MacArthur, in his characteristic braided cap and dark glasses, visits the front.*

At the beginning of March 1942 Japanese bombs were falling on the eastern half of New Guinea, the great jungle-covered island off the northern coast of Australia. The bombers came from Rabaul on the island of New Britain, to the east.

Rabaul, the capital of territory mandated to Australia at the end of World War I, which included the Bismarcks and a strip along the northern coast of New Guinea, had been captured on January 23 by the Japanese Army's 5,000-man South Seas Detachment (Major-General Tomitaro Horii) supported by the Navy's 4th Fleet (Vice-Admiral Shigeyoshi Inouye). Sailing into its spacious harbour, ringed by smoking volcanoes, the invaders in a few hours forced the small Australian garrison to scatter into the hills.

The Japanese found Rabaul "a nice little town", with wide-eaved bungalows surrounded by red hibiscus. General Horii, the conqueror of Guam, rounded up the white civilians and sent them off to Japan in the transport *Montevideo Maru* (they were all lost *en route* when the ship was sunk by an American submarine). Then he began building an air base. Admiral Inouye helped to make the

▽ *They saved Port Moresby and turned the tide in the Owen Stanleys: Australian troops, fording a river in New Guinea.*
◁ *More muscle from the Americans: a U.S. platoon in the New Guinea jungle.*

base secure by occupying Kavieng on New Ireland to the north. To the south-east, bombing took care of Bougainville, northernmost of the long string of Solomon Islands.

The towns of Lae and Salamaua, in the Huon Gulf in the east of New Guinea, had been heavily bombed in the preliminary attack on Rabaul on January 21. The civilians fled, some on foot to the wild interior, some in native canoes down the Solomon Sea, hugging the New Guinea coast. One party, after a voyage of about two weeks, put in at Gona, an Anglican mission on the coast in Australia's own Territory of Papua, in the south-east of New Guinea.

The arrival of the refugees from the Mandated Territory was long remembered by Father James Benson, the priest at Gona. The big sailing canoes against a flaming sunset sky brought through the surf "thirty-two woefully weatherbeaten refugees whose poor sun- and salt-cracked lips and bearded faces bore evidence of a fortnight's constant exposure." With only the clothes they fled in, "they looked indeed a sorry lot of ragamuffins". Next morning they began the five-day walk to Kokoda, a government station about 50 miles inland. From there planes could take them to Port Moresby, the territorial capital on the Coral Sea, facing Australia.

Planes flying from Kokoda to Port Moresby had to skim the green peaks of the Owen Stanley Range, the towering, jungle-covered mountain chain that runs the length of the Papuan peninsula. After a flight of about 45 minutes they put down at a dusty airstrip in bare brown foothills. From the foothills a road descended to Port Moresby, in peacetime a sleepy copra port with tin-roofed warehouses baking in the tropical sun along the waterfront. A single jetty extended into a big harbour; beyond, a channel led to a second harbour large enough to have sheltered the Australian fleet in World War I.

Because of its fine harbour and its position dominating the populous east coast of Australia, Port Moresby was heavily ringed on military maps in Tokyo. On orders from Imperial General Headquarters the first air raid was launched from Rabaul on February 3. The bombers did a thorough job and returned unscathed. Port Moresby's handful of obsolete planes and small anti-aircraft guns was no match for modern Japanese aircraft.

Star of the Japanese air fleet was the Mitsubishi A6M Zero fighter-bomber, one of the best planes of the war. Armed with two 20-mm cannon and two 7.7-mm machine guns, it could carry 264 pounds of bombs and was fast and agile. Its range of 1,150 miles and ceiling of 32,800 feet also made it invaluable for reconnaissance.

To facilitate the bombing of Port Moresby, some 550 miles from Rabaul,

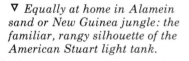
▽ *Equally at home in Alamein sand or New Guinea jungle: the familiar, rangy silhouette of the American Stuart light tank.*

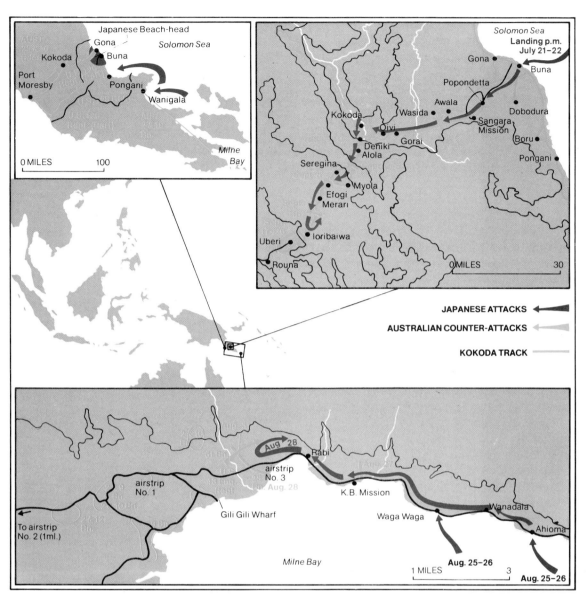

JAPANESE ATTACKS ◄

AUSTRALIAN COUNTER-ATTACKS ◄

KOKODA TRACK

△ *A dense column of smoke marks the grave of an Allied plane, destroyed in a surprise Japanese raid on the air base at Port Moresby.*

▽ *Australian soldiers survey the bodies of four dead Japanese, killed in the destruction of their jungle pillbox.*

Tokyo ordered General Horii to occupy Lae and Salamaua, Lae to be used as an advanced air base, Salamaua to secure Lae. At 0100 hours on the morning of March 8 a battalion of Horii's 144th Regiment made an unopposed landing at Salamaua–the first Japanese landing on New Guinea. An hour later Inouye's Maizuru 2nd Special Naval Landing Force (S.N.L.F.) marines occupied Lae. The naval force, which included engineers and a base unit, then took over at Salamaua. Horii's infantrymen returned to Rabaul to await orders for the next move in the south-west Pacific.

The offensive planned

When Lae and Salamaua were captured, the next move was being hotly debated at Imperial General Headquarters in Tokyo. The Navy, flushed with its easy victories

1229

△ *How to cross rivers in New Guinea without getting wet: an Australian demonstrates a "Flying Fox" ropeway platform.*

▽ *American sappers hack a road through the dense jungle of New Guinea.*

in south-east Asia, wanted to invade Australia. During operations against the Dutch/Portuguese island of Timor, from February 19 carrier aircraft had repeatedly bombed Australia's north-western coast, with little opposition. The east coast was lightly defended, since the bulk of the Australian Army was still in the Middle East. Naval officers believed that the invasion would need only five divisions.

Army officers objected, arguing that to conquer and hold the vast continental area would require 12 divisions and a million tons of shipping–far more than the Army could afford. The Navy warned that the Allies would use bases in Australia for counter-attacks on Japanese bases. This point was reinforced by the news in late March that General Douglas MacArthur had arrived in Australia from the Philippines.

The argument went on for two weeks, at times coming close to blows at the Army and Navy Club. At the end of March a compromise was reached. Australia would not be invaded, but Port Moresby would be captured. This move, with the conquest of Samoa, Fiji, and New Caledonia out in the South Pacific, would isolate Australia by cutting her supply line from the United States.

On April 20 the south Pacific operations were postponed in favour of an ambitious Navy-sponsored plan to take Midway and the Aleutians; but preparations went forward for an amphibious assault on Port Moresby, codenamed Operation "MO". General Horii issued

the orders on April 29, an auspicious date, for it was the Emperor's birthday. The landing was to take place on May 10.

Operation "MO"

On May 2, while the South Seas Detachment was boarding its transports, a force left Rabaul harbour for the small island of Tulagi in the southern Solomons to establish a seaplane base in support of Operation "MO". It landed without opposition the following day, and a few days later put a construction unit ashore on the large island of Guadalcanal to build an airfield.

The Port Moresby invasion force steamed south from Rabaul on May 4 in five transports, well escorted. Off Bou-

gainville the convoy was joined by the light carrier *Shoho,* with six cruisers. Two fleet carriers, *Shokaku* and *Zuikaku,* stood by south of the Solomons. As the invasion convoy was nearing the eastern point of New Guinea on May 7, the carrier *Shoho,* in the lead, was attacked by U.S. carrier planes and sunk, along with a cruiser. Admiral Inouye then ordered the transports back to Rabaul.

The following day the Battle of the Coral Sea was fought between the U.S. carriers *Lexington* and *Yorktown* and the Japanese *Shokaku* and *Zuikaku*–the first carrier battle in history. One Japanese carrier was damaged, the other lost most of her planes. The *Lexington* was sunk. The battle was therefore not a clear-cut victory for either side; but the invasion of Port Moresby had been blocked. For this, credit was due to the U.S. Navy

cryptanalysts in Hawaii who had cracked the Japanese fleet code and thus enabled the Allies to intercept the convoy.

Operation "MO" was not abandoned, only postponed; and the release of Japanese forces from the Philippines after the surrender of Bataan and Corregidor on May 6 made an expanded operation possible, with the Yazawa and Aoba Detachments at Davao and the Kawaguchi Detachment at Palau added to the South Seas Detachment, all to come under the 17th Army (Lieutenant-General Harukichi Hyakutake), which was established on May 18.

In Tokyo, euphoria was at its height. At Army headquarters in late May, Seizo Okada, a war correspondent assigned to the South Seas Detachment, had to fight his way through a crowd of "provincials" (Japanese Army slang for

▽ *Pushing the jungle road across a gulch over a log bridge.*

1231

△ This detail from a Japanese painting vividly expresses the desperate fight put up by the Japanese in their do-or-die attempt to take Port Moresby.

Plans for operations in the southern Pacific had to be revised. Assaults against New Caledonia, Fiji, and Samoa were postponed indefinitely; and, for lack of carriers, Operation "MO" was changed from an amphibious assault to a land attack on Port Moresby over the·Owen Stanley mountains, to be made by the South Seas Detachment with the help of the 15th Independent Engineer Regiment (Colonel Yosuke Yokoyama).

An advance echelon under Colonel Yokoyama, consisting of the engineers, a battalion of Horii's 144th Infantry Regiment, a company of marines of the Sasebo 5th S.N.L.F., and some artillery, anti-aircraft, and service units, in all about 1,800 men, was to land between Gona and Buna, an Australian government station about ten miles down the coast, advance inland to capture Kokoda, and prepare they way for Horii's main force to cross the Owen Stanley Range. Reconnaissance Zeros had spotted a red ribbon of earth winding over the mountains and assumed it to be a road. The engineers were to put it into shape to take trucks, if possible, or at least pack horses.

While the Yokoyama Force was embarking in Rabaul harbour, General Hyakutake on July 18 prepared a plan to assist Horii with a flanking seaplane attack based on Samarai at the entrance to Milne Bay, the 20-mile long, 7-mile wide bay at the eastern end of New Guinea. The Navy was to seize Samarai on August 25 with the help of a battalion of the Kawaguchi Detachment. In this latest version of Operation "MO", the Yazawa Detachment, consisting mainly of the 41st Infantry Regiment (Colonel Kiyomi Yazawa), was allocated to Horii.

civilians) clamouring for permission to go abroad with the Army. After receiving his credentials from a major, Okada asked for a pair of army boots. "Behind a screen that stood by the Major some staff officers were talking and puffing at cigarettes. One of them, as plump as a pig, broke in, 'Hey, what are you talking about? Boots? Don't worry about your boots. You'll get lots of beautiful ones out there–damned beautiful enemy boots'.

"The mocking words drove the other officers into a fit of boisterous laughter. They too, like myself or any other Japanese, were puffed up like toy balloons by the 'brilliant initial success' of the Pacific War."

A week later came news of the first crushing setback. At Midway on June 7 the Japanese Navy was decisively defeated by the U.S. fleet, with a heavy loss of carriers.

Advance to Kokoda

Late on the afternoon of July 21, the Yokoyama Force, in three heavily-escorted transports, began landing on the New Guinea coast just east of Gona. Allied planes arrived and damaged two transports, but only 40 men were lost, and there was no other opposition. At Gona the missionaries had fled, and Buna was found to be deserted when the marines arrived next day to start building an airfield. Colonel Yokoyama concentrated his army troops at a point about half-way between Gona and Buna, where a corduroy road led inland for about 15 miles.

On the evening of the landing the infantry battalion (Lieutenant-Colonel Hatsuo Tsukamoto) and a company of engineers began the march inland, about 900 men with torches, some on bicycles, with orders to "push on night and day to the line of the mountain range".

Half-way to Kokoda they were fired upon by a few Australian and native soldiers, but these were easily dispersed. The natives melted away into the jungle. The Australians, part of a company of raw militiamen, tried to stop the invaders by destroying the bridge that carried the road over the Kumusi river, but when the Japanese threw up a bridge and pressed on, they retreated. On the night of July 28, in a thick mist, Tsukamoto bombarded Kokoda with mortars and a mountain gun and drove the defenders out.

The Japanese were puzzled by the weakness of the opposition. They did not know that the Allies, after recovering from the surprise of the landing, had persuaded themselves that the object of the landing was only to establish airfields in the Buna area. The Australians found it impossible to believe that the Japanese would attempt an overland attack on Port Moresby. The "road" over the mountains was only a native footpath, two or three feet wide.

Known as the Kokoda Track, the path crossed a range of mountains described graphically by an Australian who had made the crossing on foot: "Imagine an area of approximately one hundred miles long. Crumple and fold this into a series of ridges, each rising higher and higher until 7,000 feet is reached, then declining in ridges of 3,000 feet. Cover this thickly with jungle, short trees and tall trees, tangled with great, entwining savage vines." The days were hot and humid, the nights cold; frequent afternoon rains made the track "a treacherous mass of moving mud".

By August 21, when the main Japanese force got ashore under cover of a storm, Horii had landed on the New Guinea coast a total of 8,000 Army troops, 3,000 naval construction troops, and some 450 marines of the Sasebo 5th S.N.L.F. At the head of a formidable body of fighting troops he rode into Kokoda astride his white horse on August 24.

He found that Colonel Tsukamoto's infantry had already pushed up the Kokoda Track for several miles and taken the next village, Deniki, from which the Australian militiamen, evidently reinforced, had been trying to retake Kokoda. Defeated at Deniki, they had withdrawn up a steep slope to Isurava. This was to be Horii's first objective. He began shelling it on August 26.

The Japanese fighting man

Horii's men had two 70-mm howitzers, outranging any Australian weapon on the Kokoda Track, and light enough to be manhandled over the mountains. They

△ G.Is tackle heavy jungle.
▽ Australians peer cautiously at some Japanese killed beside the track. Japanese sick and wounded, left behind by the retreating Japanese, frequently proved a great menace to the advancing Allies by lying in wait and firing at the first sight of an Australian or American soldier.

had an efficient machine gun, the *Juki*, with a rapid rate of fire. They knew how to use their weapons to best advantage, outflanking and encircling prepared positions. They had been taught that they must not be captured, even if wounded. Their manual read, "Bear in mind the fact that to be captured means not only disgracing the Army but that your parents and family will never be able to hold up their heads again. Always save the last round for yourself." They would fight to the death.

They were adept at night operations and preferred to attack in the rain. The manual told them that "Westerners—being very haughty, effeminate, and cowardly—intensely dislike fighting in the rain or mist or in the dark. They cannot conceive night to be a proper time for battle—though it is excellent for dancing. In these weaknesses lie our great opportunity." In night attacks the Japanese smeared their faces with mud; officers wore strips of white cloth criss-

◁◁ *A U.S. Marine reels,
struck by a Japanese bullet.*
◁ *Wading a stream, rifles at
the ready, a patrol pushes
forward.*
▽ *One more river to cross—this
time by means of a more
sophisticated pontoon bridge.*

▷ *Douglas A-26 Invader bombers head out for an air strike.*

▽ *American airmen line the bar at "Sloopy Joe's", a popular canteen on the Port Moresby airfield for a quick cup of tea and a snack.*

▷ ▷ △ *One for the record: a Combat Photography Unit takes pictures on the scene of another jungle battle.*

▷ ▷ ▽ *Australians at rest in a native village. In the background can be seen a line of native recruits, dubbed "Fuzzy-Wuzzy Angels" for their magnificent work in carrying supplies and bringing out the wounded.*

crossed on their backs so their men could follow them in the dark, or doused themselves with perfume and issued orders to "follow your noses".

The Japanese soldier was admirably equipped for jungle warfare. He was camouflaged by a green uniform and green leaves stuck in a net on his helmet; under his helmet he wore a cloth to keep sweat from running into his eyes. He had been instructed to add salt to his tea and salt plums to his rice. He was used to carrying heavy loads–the infantryman about 100 pounds–consisting of rice, powdered bean paste, powdered soy, hand grenades, rifle ammunition, a shovel, a pickaxe, and tenting; the artilleryman and engineer carried some 16 additional pounds.

Seizo Okada, arriving at Kokoda with Horii's headquarters, observed that the soldiers had made "a kind of woodman's carrying rack" for their load and "like pilgrims with portable shrines, carried it on their backs. Now they plodded on, step by step, supported by a stick, through those mountains of New Guinea".

Progress over the mountains

At Isurava, Horii met unexpected resistance. From ground so high that the Japanese referred to it as "Mt. Isurava", the Australians poured down a heavy fire that stopped him for three days. On August 28 his casualties were so heavy that a Japanese officer wrote in his diary, "The outcome of the battle is very difficult to foresee."

That evening, at his command post on a neighbouring hill lit by fires in which his men were cremating their dead, Horii learned the reason for the repulse: the untrained Australian militiamen of the 39th Battalion had been reinforced by experienced regulars of the 21st Brigade, brought home from the Middle East. Horii ordered his reserve forward from Kokoda and on the afternoon of August 29 launched an onslaught that drove the defenders out of Isurava. By the evening of August 30 the Australian forces were in full retreat up the Kokoda Track.

General Horii subjected them to constant pressure, using alternately his 144th (Colonel Masao Kusunose) and his 41st (Colonel Yazawa) Infantry Regiments. Following closely to keep the Australians off balance he gave them no time to prepare counter-attacks, outflanking them from high ground, and bombarding them with his mountain guns at ranges they could not match. His troops crossed mountain after mountain, "an endless serpentine movement of infantry, artillery, transport unit, infantry again, first-aid station, field hospital, signal unit, and engineers".

Between the mountains, swift torrents roared through deep ravines. Beyond Eora Creek the track ascended to the crest of the range, covered with moss forest. "The jungle became thicker and thicker, and even at mid-day we walked in the half-light of dusk." The ground was covered with thick, velvety green moss. "We felt as if we were treading on some living animal." Rain fell almost all day and all night. "The soldiers got wet to the skin through their boots and the undercloth round their bellies."

Coming down from the crest on the morning of September 7, slipping and sliding on the muddy downward track, the Japanese vanguard found the Australians preparing to make a stand on the ridge behind a ravine at Efogi. During the morning Allied planes came over, strafing and bombing, but in the thick jungle did little damage. The following day before dawn the Japanese attacked, and by noon, in bitter hand-to-hand fighting that left about 200 Japanese and Australian bodies scattered in the ravine, they pushed the defenders off the ridge.

In mid-September the Australians, reinforced by a fresh brigade of regulars, the 25th, tried to hold on a ridge at Ioribaiwa, only 30 miles from Port Moresby, so near that when the wind was right the drone of motors from the airfield could be heard. But on September 17 the Japanese, who still outnumbered them, forced them to withdraw across a deep ravine to the last mountain above the port, Imita Ridge.

At Ioribaiwa, Horii halted, his forces weakened by a breakdown in supply and by Allied air attacks. In any case, he had orders not to move on Port Moresby until an advance could be made by sea from Milne Bay.

Disaster in Milne Bay

Bad luck dogged the Milne Bay operation from the start. The second week in August, the battalion of the Kawaguchi Detachment assigned to the 8th Fleet (Vice-Admiral Gunichi Mikawa) for the operation was sent instead to help clear Guadalcanal in the Solomons, where U.S. Marines hand landed on August 7. A replacement battalion could not arrive in time. Admiral Mikawa, who had won a brilliant naval victory at Guadalcanal on August 9, would have no help from the Army at Milne Bay.

At the last minute the target was changed. Reports from reconnaissance planes in mid-August that the Allies were building an airfield at the head of Milne Bay near Gili Gili led planners to change the landing from Samarai, at the mouth of the bay, to Gili Gili.

The Japanese knew little about the Gili Gili area, in peace-time the site of a coconut plantation. Low-lying rain clouds usually protected it from reconnaissance. Estimating that it was held by not more than three infantry companies and 30 aircraft, Mikawa allotted only about 1,500 men to the invasion. Most of them were to come from Kavieng: 612 marines of the Kure 5th S.N.L.F. (Commander Shojiro Hayashi), 362 16th Naval Pioneer Unit troops, and 197 marines of the Sasebo 5th S.N.L.F. The Kavieng convoys were to sail up Milne Bay and land at Rabi, about three miles east of the Gili Gili jetty. At the same time, 353 marines of the Sasebo 5th S.N.L.F. at Buna, carried in seven big, wooden, motor-driven barges, were to land at Taupota on the Solomon Sea side and march over the mountains to Gili Gili.

The overland force was the first casualty of the operation. As it chugged down the coast under cloud cover on August 24 it was sighted and reported by a "coastwatcher"–one of the Australian organisation of planters and officials who had taken to the hills with wireless sets. The following day the marines beached the barges on Goodenough Island and went ashore to eat lunch. At that moment the clouds parted and 12 Australian P-40 fighter planes swooped low and destroyed the barges. The Buna marines were left stranded.

Two cruiser-escorted transports with Commander Hayashi and the first echelon

of the Kavieng marines arrived safely at the head of Milne Bay in a downpour on the night of August 25. Shortly before midnight Hayashi began the landings at a point he believed to be Rabi. But he had no reliable map, and in the darkness and rain he landed about seven miles to the east on a swampy coastal shelf where the mountains came down almost to the water. His only means of advance westward toward Gili Gili was a muddy 12-foot track.

Hayashi was a stickler for night operations. He waited until darkness fell on August 26 to attack his first objective, a plantation astride the track at K. B. Mission, lightly held by Australian militia. Preceded by a flame-thrower, his troops tried to outflank the defenders by wading into the bay on one side and the swamp on the other. By dawn they had almost succeeded; but at first light they retired into the jungle.

The following night the attack was resumed in greater force, the second echelon from Kavieng having arrived. This time the Japanese used two small tanks—the first tanks to be landed on the New Guinea coast. They each had a strong headlight which, shining through the rain, enabled them to illuminate the Australian positions while the attackers remained in darkness. With the help of the tanks, Hayashi's men cleared K. B. Mission, crossed the Gama river beyond, and before dawn on August 28 were attacking an airstrip that U.S. engineers were building between Rabi and Gili Gili. There, lacking the tanks, which had bogged down in mud and had had to be abandoned, they were stopped by heavy fire. At daylight they withdrew into the jungle.

Commander Hayashi had already asked Admiral Mikawa to send him reinforcements. He had been deprived of his overland force and had lost a considerable part of his food and ammunition when Allied aircraft sank the steel barges ferrying it ashore. He had met ground opposition greater than he expected and found the terrain worse than anything he could have imagined. Reinforcements landed on the night of August 29 under cover of a heavy mist. They were 568 marines of the Kure 3rd S.N.L.F. and 200 of the Yokosuka 5th S.N.L.F., all under Commander Minoro Yano who, being senior to Hayashi, took command of operations.

Before one o'clock on the morning of August 31 the combined Japanese forces launched a furious assault on the airstrip. They were beaten back by intense fire from anti-tank guns, heavy machine guns, and mortars, expertly sited with a clear field of fire and backed by heavy artillery positioned in the rear. Before day broke, three Japanese bugle calls rang out, the signal for retreat.

The Australians pursued. By nightfall on September 1 they had retaken K. B. Mission. Commander Yano, setting up defences on the track to block the pursuit, cabled Admiral Mikawa on September 3 for permission to withdraw from Milne Bay. He himself had been wounded; Hayashi had been killed; he had lost 600 men and had more than 300 wounded on his hands. The rest of the men, most of

them suffering from trench foot, jungle rot, and tropical fevers, could not hold out.

Mikawa sanctioned the evacuation. By dawn of September 6, Japanese ships, carrying the 1,300 men remaining of the 1,900-man invasion force, were on their way to Rabaul.

The crowning misfortune of the Milne Bay invasion was the miscalculation of the strength of the defenders. Unknown to the Japanese, the Allies had landed at the head of Milne Bay between June 25 and August 20 some 4,500 Australian infantrymen, supported by about 3,000 Australian and 1,300 American engineer, artillery, and service units.

Japanese fanaticism had met its match; but it had been a close run thing.

◁ ◁ *A smashed Japanese transport. Allied air supremacy made it impossible for the Japanese to send sufficient seaborne reinforcements either to New Guinea or to the Solomons.*
◁ ◁▽ *The advance continues, past the wreckage caused by a recent bombardment.*

△ *Japanese dead, huddled in the trench where they fell.*
◁ ◁ *A keen look at a knocked-out Japanese light tank.*

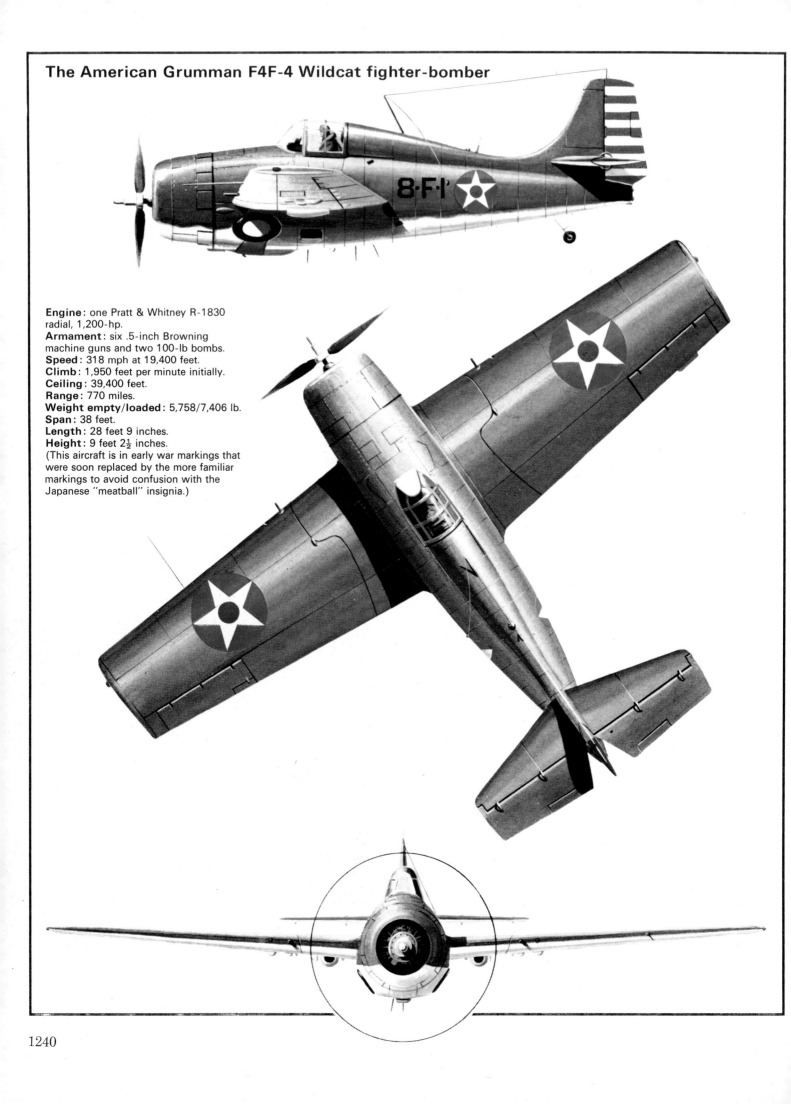

The American Grumman F4F-4 Wildcat fighter-bomber

Engine: one Pratt & Whitney R-1830 radial, 1,200-hp.
Armament: six .5-inch Browning machine guns and two 100-lb bombs.
Speed: 318 mph at 19,400 feet.
Climb: 1,950 feet per minute initially.
Ceiling: 39,400 feet.
Range: 770 miles.
Weight empty/loaded: 5,758/7,406 lb.
Span: 38 feet.
Length: 28 feet 9 inches.
Height: 9 feet 2½ inches.
(This aircraft is in early war markings that were soon replaced by the more familiar markings to avoid confusion with the Japanese "meatball" insignia.)

The Japanese retreat

On September 20 General Horii called together his commanders and praised them for their success in crossing "the so-called impregnable Stanley Range". At the proper time they were "to strike a crushing blow at the enemy's positions at Port Moresby". The halt at Ioribaiwa would give the tired troops, many of them wounded and ill, a chance to regain their fighting strength. Most were hungry; little or no rice remained in the dumps. Horii had already ordered detachments to dig up native gardens in the area and sent parties over the mountains to bring up provisions from the rear. To block an Australian attack, he ordered his engineers to build a stockade of tree trunks.

The Australians did not attack; but no supplies came from the rear, no Zeros flew over. "An atmosphere of uneasiness," noted Okada, "stole over the mountain, a feeling that things were not going well at Guadalcanal. On September 24 in a night of drizzling rain the blow fell. A signal commander came into Horii's tent with a message from Imperial General Headquarters ordering Horii to withdraw his force from the Owen Stanleys to the coast at Buna."

The reason for the order was a major defeat at Guadalcanal on September 15, in which the Kawaguchi Detachment had been virtually wiped out. Imperial General Headquarters decided to subordinate everything to the retaking of Guadalcanal. Once that had been accomplished, it would be possible to resume Operation "MO". In the meantime, Horii's mission was to defend the Buna beach-head.

For Horii, the order "to abandon this position after all the blood the soldiers have shed and the hardships they have endured" was agonising. He sent his chief-of-staff, Lieutenant-Colonel Toyanari Tanaka, to break the news to the battalion commanders. Some of them almost rebelled, urging a desperate, single-handed thrust into Port Moresby.

On September 25 the movement back over the mountains began. The order to withdraw had crushed the spirit of the soldiers, which, Okada reported, "had been kept up through sheer pride". For a time they remained stupefied. "Then they began to move, and once in retreat they fled for dear life. None of them had ever thought that a Japanese soldier would turn his back on the enemy. But they were actually beating a retreat!"

As soon as they accepted this bitter fact, "they were seized by an instinctive desire to live". Each tried to flee faster than his comrades. Passing by bodies of men killed in the fighting of early September, already rotting and covered with maggots, the soldiers stopped only to dig for taroes or yams. They found little; the fields had been dug up almost inch by inch. By the time they reached the crest of the Range, they were fleeing from starvation, a greater menace than the Allied planes roaring overhead or enemy guns rumbling in the rear.

To delay the Australian pursuit, which began on September 27, Horii ordered a rearguard battalion to make a stand on the heights above Eora Creek. There it was attacked by troops of the Australian 16th Brigade on October 21. Reinforced from Kokoda and Buna, it held out for seven days, long enough for Horii to evacuate Kokoda and set up his last defences, at Oivi and Gorari in the foot-hills between Kokoda and the Kumusi river.

At Oivi, strongly fortified by Colonel Yazawa, the Australians attacking on November 5 could make no headway; but at Gorari, where Colonel Tsukamoto was in command (Colonel Kusunose having been evacuated because of sickness and wounds), an Australian assault on November 10 succeeded, after heavy fighting. Yazawa's position was now untenable. He withdrew his 900-man force after dark that evening over a little-known track leading north-east to the mouth of the Kumusi. With him was General Horii, who had been on an inspec-

△ Moving out a stretcher case from an advanced dressing station. Without facilities such as this, the Japanese losses rose even higher than the figure of those killed or wounded in combat.

▽ The luckier ones: Australian "walking wounded".

tion trip to Oivi.

The rest of the South Seas Detachment, about 1,200 men, began crossing the Kumusi river on the night of November 12, guided by the light of a bonfire. They had no bridge. Incendiary bombs dropped from Allied planes had burned the wooden bridge built in August by the Yokoyama Force and defeated all attempts to replace it. The soldiers crossed in six-man folding boats, then pushed on in the darkness toward Buna.

Seizo Okada crossed with the vanguard. Stopping at a newsmen's hut about half-way to Buna, he watched the "men of the mountains" as they moved along the road, day and night, toward the coast. "They had shaggy hair and beards. Their uniforms were soiled with blood and mud and sweat, and torn to pieces. There were infantrymen without rifles, men walking on bare feet, men wearing blankets or straw rice-bags instead of uniforms, men reduced to skin and bone plodding along with the help of a stick, men gasping and crawling on the ground."

The stretcher-bearers, themselves too weak to carry stretchers, dragged the sick and wounded to the overcrowded field hospital near Buna and laid them on straw mats in the jungle. "The soldiers had eaten anything to appease hunger – young shoots of trees, roots of grass, even cakes of earth. These things had injured their stomachs so badly that when they were brought back to the field hospital they could no longer digest any food. Many of them vomited blood and died."

Later, Okada learned that General Horii had drowned while on the march northwards with Yazawa. Horii, anxious to rejoin his men at Buna, tried to cross the lower Kumusi river on a log raft. In the swift current the raft carrying him and Colonel Tanaka overturned.

So ended, in tragedy, the overland march on Port Moresby. Misgivings about it had been felt by at least one officer at Imperial General Headquarters, Colonel Masanobu Tsuji, who warned, "Cross the mountains and you will get the worst of it." At the end his verdict was, "a blunder".

Though the Buna beach-head was reinforced from Rabaul and held out for several months, Operation "MO" was never resumed. Beginning early in October, the attention of Imperial General Headquarters was diverted from New Guinea and focused on Guadalcanal.

◁ ◁ △ *Another American casualty on the Buna front.*
◁ ◁ ▽ *The confidence of victory. An Australian platoon advances.*
△ *Fitting out a paratrooper.*
▽ *The first hot soup after eleven days of combat for the victors of Buna.*

CHAPTER 94
GUADALCANAL: ordeal
by Henry I. Shaw

Allied resources in the Pacific were stretched to the limit in the summer of 1942, and the greater part of the American war effort was directed toward the European theatre and the defeat of Germany. The Japanese, checked only by the crucial naval Battle of Midway in June 1942, were riding a tide of victory and easy conquests. Tulagi Island, site of the headquarters of the British Solomon Islands Protectorate, was not on the original

▽ America hits back: in the landing-craft, heading for the beaches.
▽ ▽ Moment of truth: the Marines storm ashore on Guadalcanal.

schedule of targets the Japanese had projected for the South Pacific, but it too was taken as the victory tide swept onward. The seaplane base and radio station that the Japanese had established on Tulagi did not particularly worry the Allies, but reports in June 1942 that Japanese troops had begun levelling an aircraft runway on the kunai grass plains of the Lunga river on the large island of Guadalcanal, 20 miles south across Sealark Channel from Tulagi, were a different story. Here was a clear threat to the shipping lifeline stretched across the South Pacific from the U.S. to New Zealand and Australia.

At the time the Japanese moved to Tulagi, the nearest American troops were on the outposts of Espiritu Santo in the New Hebrides, 550 miles away. An airfield was rushed to completion there, to be ready by the end of July to support operations against the Japanese. The American Joint Chiefs-of-Staff, urged on by the Navy's leader, Admiral Ernest

J. King, had decided to mount a ground offensive to halt the enemy drive to the south and to provide a base for offensive operations against Rabaul, the Japanese area headquarters and nerve centre on New Britain in the Bismarcks.

Guadalcanal and Tulagi were the objectives, and the assault force was the only amphibious trained division readily available, the 1st Marine Division. It was, in fact, the only unit of its size that was available. Commanded by Major-General Alexander A. Vandegrift, a veteran of the jungle fighting of the Banana Wars in the Caribbean, the 1st Division had been formed in 1940 and included many veteran Marines in its ranks as well as a number of men without combat or expeditionary experience. Its forward echelon had just arrived in Wellington, New Zealand, for six months of intensive combat training when the word was passed that it would go into battle instead. Some troops were still at sea; one of its regiments, the 7th Marines, was committed to the defence of Samoa and the 2nd Marines of the 2nd Marine Division had to be sent out from San Diego to replace it. Other major elements to be attached to the 1st Division were located on New Caledonia and in the Hawaiian Islands. All had to be alerted, equipped, and assembled in less than a month's time to meet a D-day of August 7, 1942.

Working around the clock and pushing aside New Zealand dock workers who wanted to invoke union labour rules, the Marines in Wellington unloaded transports as fast as they arrived, sorted and repacked equipment and supplies for combat, and loaded ship again. There was not enough room for all the division's motor transport and most of the heavier trucks had to be left behind. Only 60 days of supplies and rations, ammunition for 10 days' heavy fighting (units of fire), and the bare minimum of individual equipment were taken.

The expedition sails

The amphibious task force which would transport, land, and support the Marines was commanded by Rear-Admiral Richmond K. Turner; overall commander of the naval expeditionary force, including carriers and their escorts, was Rear-Admiral Frank J. Fletcher. Since this

was to be a naval campaign and the landing force was to be of Marines, Admiral King had insisted that it be conducted under naval leadership. Accordingly, the Joint Chiefs-of-Staff shifted the boundary of Vice-Admiral Richard H. Ghormley's South Pacific Theatre northward to include all of the 90-mile-long island of Guadalcanal, which precluded the possibility that General Douglas MacArthur, the South-West Pacific Area commander, would control operations.

The plan for the seizure of the objective, codenamed "Watchtower", called for two separate landings, one by the division's main body near Lunga Point on Guadalcanal and the other at Tulagi by an assault force made up of the 2nd Battalion, 5th Marines and the 1st Raider and 1st Parachute Battalions. In all, General Vandegrift had about 19,000 men under his command when the transports and escorts moved into position on D-day. They had come from a rehearsal at Koro, in the Fiji Islands, where the inexperienced ships'

△ *A Marine patrol probes the jungle on the outskirts of the American beach-head on Guadalcanal.*

▽ *Shattered and half buried by American bombardment: Japanese bodies on the beach at Guadalcanal, killed before they even had the chance to close with the Marines.*

△ *A dusk patrol sent out by Vandegrift's Marines sets out, tramping through the Matanikau river.*

crews and the polyglot Marine units reinforcing the 1st Division had combined to take part in a run-through that General Vandegrift called a "complete bust".

Behind a thunderous preparation by cruisers and destroyers and under an overhead cover of Admiral Fletcher's carrier aircraft, the landing craft streaked ashore at both targets. Surprise had been achieved; there was no opposition on the beaches at either objective. True to preliminary Intelligence estimates, however, the Japanese soon fought back savagely from prepared positions on Tulagi.

It took three days of heavy fighting to wrest the headquarters island and two small neighbouring islets, Gavutu and Tanambogo, from the Japanese naval troops who defended them. All three battalions of the 2nd Marines were needed to lend their weight to the American attacks against Japanese hidden in pill-boxes and caves and ready to fight to the death. The garrison commander had radioed to Rabaul on the morning of August 7: "Enemy troop strength is overwhelming. We will defend to the last man." There were 27 prisoners, mostly labourers. A few men escaped by swimming to near-by Florida Island, but the rest of the 750 to 800-man garrison went down fighting.

On Guadalcanal, the labour troops working on the airfield fled when naval gunfire crashed into their bivouac areas. Consequently, there was no opposition as the lead regiment, the 1st Marines, overran the partially completed field on August 8. Japanese engineering equipment, six workable road rollers, some 50 handcarts, about 75 shovels, and two tiny petrol locomotives with hopper cars, were left behind. It was a good thing that this gear was abandoned, for the American engineering equipment that came to Guadalcanal on Turner's ships also left on Turner's ships, which departed from the area on August 9. Unwilling to risk his precious carriers any longer against the superior Japanese air power which threatened from Rabaul, Admiral Fletcher was withdrawing. Without air cover, Turner's force was naked. Japanese cruisers and destroyers and flights of medium bombers from Rabaul had made the amphibious task force commander's position untenable.

Constant air attack

Almost constant Japanese air attacks, which began on the afternoon of August 7, thoroughly disrupted unloading as the transports and escorts manoeuvred to escape the rain of bombs. The Marines

did not have enough shore party troops to handle the supplies that did reach the beach. Ships' captains in a hurry to empty their holds and inexperienced coxswains combined forces to dump an unprogrammed jumble of ammunition, rations, tentage, vehicles, and assorted supplies on the shoreline, offering another tempting target for the Japanese planes. When Turner reluctantly sailed south to Espiritu Santo and New Caledonia, only 37 days' supply of rations and four units of fire had been landed. Vandegrift had 16,000 men ashore, 6,000 on Tulagi, with the rest still on board ship when the task force departed.

After this event, the commanding general of Army forces in the South Pacific, Major-General Millard F. Harmon, was far from optimistic about the chances of success for the Guadalcanal venture. On August 11 he wrote to the Army's Chief-of-Staff in Washington, General George C. Marshall:

"The thing that impresses me more than anything else in connection with the Solomon action is that we are not prepared to follow up . . . We have seized a strategic position from which future operations in the Bismarcks can be strongly supported. Can the Marines hold it? There is considerable room for doubt."

Cast loose, or at least promised only a

tenuous lifeline to Allied support bases, the 1st Marine Division made do with what it had. The completion of the airfield that the Japanese had begun was crucial; without it there was little ground for hope that the Marines could stay on Guadalcanal. Japanese engineering equipment was used to the fullest extent; captured Japanese weapons were included in defensive positions; Japanese rations were added to the Marines' meagre stocks; and Japanese trucks were used to supplement the small American motor pool. The airfield was ready for use on August 18; it was named Henderson Field after a Marine pilot killed in the Battle of Midway. On the day that the runway was finished, the Japanese took their first step toward wresting control of the island back from the Americans, landing a battalion of the 28th Regiment to the east of Vandegrift's perimeter. This was to be the first of many runs by the "Tokyo Express," a cruiser–destroyer transport force commanded by Rear-Admiral Raizo Tanaka, which was largely responsible for the reinforcement and resupply of the Japanese on Guadalcanal.

The red letter day for the Marines was August 20. Two squadrons flew in to Henderson Field from the escort carrier *Long Island,* 19 Grumman F4F Wildcat fighters from Marine Fighting Squadron 223 and 12 Douglas SBD-3 Dauntless dive-bombers from Marine Scout-Bomber Squadron 232. The planes came just

△ *For the honour of the Emperor.*

▽ *Two Marines discover for themselves what they are up against: resistance to the death.*

in time to help with the destruction of the Japanese battalion that had landed two days before. Making a night attack headlong against the positions of the 1st Marines' battalion holding the west bank of the Ilu River, which marked the eastern edge of Vandegrift's perimeter, the Japanese were ground up in a fury of artillery, machine gun, and 37-mm canister fire. When daylight came, a Marine battalion mopped up the remnants of the attacking force, helped by strafing attacks by the newly arrived Wildcats. The Japanese commander, Colonel Kiyono Ichiki, disheartened by his failure, committed suicide; 800 of his men had died in the fighting.

Colonel Ichiki, like his superior in Rabaul, Lieutenant-General Harukichi Hyakutake, commanding the 17th Army, had underestimated both the strength and the determination to hold of the Marines. Time and again, the Japanese were to repeat Ichiki's error, sending thousands of men from Rabaul but never enough at one time so that Vandegrift could not handle them. The troops available to Hyakutake in August and September was more than enough to overwhelm the Marine defences, but these troops were never committed in sufficient force to sustain a determined attack.

△ *As in New Guinea, the Allies battling their way down the chain of the Solomons found that the natives were eager to join up and fight against the hated "Japani".*
▷ *The ordeal of Vandegrift's Marines, penned for months in the narrow beach-head near the original landing-ground on Guadalcanal.*

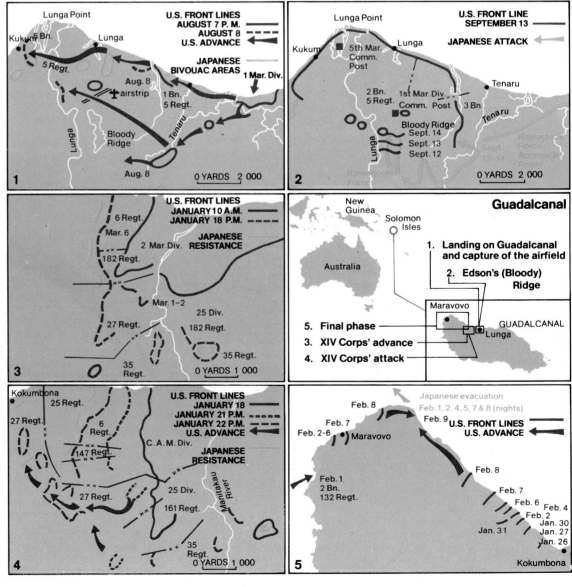

CHAPTER 95
GUADALCANAL: triumph
by Henry I. Shaw

General Vandegrift never lost sight of his primary mission of defending Henderson Field. He was aggressive and mounted a number of limited objective offensives; he kept strong combat and reconnaissance patrols forward of his lines constantly. But he always kept his perimeter intact, always maintained a reserve, and showed a marvellous ability for meeting strength with strength. The Japanese pattern of reinforcing Guadalcanal, and the impetuosity of Japanese leaders once they reached the island, played right into the American general's hands. Typically, a few thousand Japanese troops would be landed at night by Tanaka's Tokyo Express a few miles to either side of the Marine perimeter and they would attack almost without delay. The action would be furious at the point of contact, sometimes the Marine lines would be penetrated, but then the fire-brigade would arrive–a fresh infantry battalion, a platoon of tanks, the fire of an additional reinforcing artillery battalion, a flight of dive-bombers, perhaps all of these at once, and the Japanese would be thrown back, decimated by their own relentless courage in the face of killing fire.

The same fate that befell the Ichiki battalion was met by a 6,000-man brigade under Major-General Kiyotaki Kawaguchi, which landed on both sides of the 9,000-yard-wide perimeter in early September. The main body, about 4,000 men, mostly of the 124th Infantry, pressed inland under cover of the jungle to attack from the south against the inland perimeter toward the airfield. That portion of the Marine line was thinly held, as the greatest danger was expected from attacks along the coast or from the sea.

Fortunately, Vandegrift had moved the original assault force at Tulagi across Sealark Channel to bolster the Marine defences. Combining the raider and parachute battalions under one commander, Colonel Merritt A. Edson, he placed this unit astride an open, grassy ridge that led directly to the division command post and the airfield. The 2nd Battalion, 5th Marines was one mile away in reserve and a battalion of 105-mm howitzers from the division's artillery regiment, the 11th Marines, was in direct support. The Kawaguchi Force lightly probed Edson's position on September 12, while a Japanese cruiser and several destroyers shelled Henderson Field, a frequent accompaniment to Japanese ground attacks. On the 13th, Edson tried a counter-attack but was forced back to his original positions; the Japanese were too strong. That night, in a driving rain that severely limited visibility, the Japanese poured out of the jungle, smashing into the ridge position and forcing the American flanking companies back on the centre of the ridge. There the Marines held, the artillery smothered the attacking columns and troop assembly areas, and reinforcements from the 5th Marines joined the raiders and paratroopers in their fox-

▽ *A Marine struggles with the murderous jungle on Guadalcanal. The battle lasted six months. Not once did the intensity of the combat slacken. It was, quite literally, "the Stalingrad of the Pacific".*

Major-General Alexander A. Vandegrift, commander of the Marine forces on Guadalcanal.

holes. In the morning there was little left to do but mop up. Only about 500 of Kawaguchi's men struggled back alive through the jungle. A pair of diversionary attacks, mounted against the coastal perimeters while Kawaguchi struck, died in the face of stubborn Marine fire.

Japanese misinterpretation

Another much needed respite had been gained by the Japanese failure to appreciate the Marines' strength. The 1st Marine Division had received no reinforcements or ammunition since the landing in August, the troops were eating only two meals a day and part of those were Japanese rations, and tropical diseases, particularly malaria, were beginning to fell large numbers of men. The "Cactus Air Force", so named by its pilots after the island's codename, was now

The all-important objective on Guadalcanal: "Henderson Field" airstrip, begun by the Japanese, captured and retained by the U.S. Marines.

Unglamorous war trophy: a Japanese steamroller, used to level the airstrip at "Henderson Field" before falling into American hands.

a battered collection of Army P-40's, Navy fighters and dive-bombers from damaged carriers, and Marine Corps aircraft. Plane availability was often less than 50 and all types were woefully short of fuel and parts. The forward echelon of the 1st Marine Aircraft Wing under Brigadier-General Roy S. Geiger controlled the motley air force, but its attrition rate was heavy from its constant clashes with the Japanese and operational accidents caused by the primitive condition of the runways, and Geiger was hard put to it to provide replacement aircraft.

For both the ground and air elements of Vandegrift's force, then, September 18 was a day for celebration. The 7th Marines arrived from Samoa to rejoin the division; with its reinforcing artillery battalion of 75-mm pack howitzers, the regiment stood at 4,262 very welcome men. Moreover, the ships that Admiral Turner sent forward with the regiment also carried over 3,000 drums of aviation spirit, 147 vehicles, engineering equipment, 1,000 tons of rations, and about ten units of fire for all weapons. Things were looking less bleak for Vandegrift's men.

The newly arrived regiment soon got a chance to test its mettle in combat. The Japanese were building up their forces west of the Marine perimeter and on the 23rd Vandegrift sent the 1st Battalion, 7th Marines inland toward Mt. Austen, which overlooks the Lunga plain, with the mission of crossing the jungle-covered foothills and turning north to patrol to the mouth of the Matanikau River. It was a hotly contested advance and the 2nd Battalion, 5th Marines came up to reinforce and help evacuate casualties. The Raider battalion moved along the coast to probe across the Matanikau. The Japanese made a stand at the river mouth and the action escalated. Colonel Edson, who now commanded the combined force, decided on a landing behind the Japanese position and chose the 7th Marines battalion for the job. Using the landing craft that had been left at Guadalcanal by damaged and sunken transports, the Marines made a shore-to-shore movement and drove inland to a ridge about 500 yards from the beach. The Japanese closed in behind them and cut them off from their boats. The battalion's radio was inoperative, but an SBD pilot overhead saw its predicament and repeatedly attacked the encroaching Japanese troops. Offshore, the destroyer *Ballard* used her 5-inch guns to blast a path to the beach and cover the landing craft. The battalion fought its way out of the trap, taking 60 dead and 100 wounded Marines with it. The coxswains of the landing craft made the evacuation despite a constant hail of enemy fire and considerable casualties.

This fight was just the first of a series of violent clashes, as Vandegrift sought to drive the Japanese away from the perimeter. Heavy artillery, 150-mm howitzers, had been landed near Kokumbona, the Japanese headquarters, and these guns could now shell Henderson Field and a fighter strip which had been completed nearby. If the Cactus Air Force could be kept from flying, the Japanese transports and bombardment ships could have an unmolested run-in with reinforcements. As long as the mixed bag of American fighters and bombers could stay aloft, Sealark Channel was virtually shut off to the Japanese during daylight hours.

The Marines advance

On October 7, the Marines set out again in force with two battalions of the 5th Marines to engage the Japanese at the mouth of the Matanikau. Inland, two battalions of the 7th Marines, the 3rd Battalion, 2nd Marines, and the division's scout-sniper detachment were to drive west and then south after crossing the Matanikau upstream to pin the Japanese against the coast. Three battalions of artillery were in direct support of the attack. The advancing Marines ran into the Japanese 4th Infantry Regiment, which was also moving forward to the attack. The resulting action spread over two days in the rain-swept jungle. The Americans trapped one sizable pocket of Japanese near the coast; only a few escaped death. Another force of 1,500 men was isolated in a deep ravine inland.

△ *A rapid cash-in on the souvenir market; the "novelty shop" set up by Corporal Robert E. Weeks of Illinois. His stock-in-trade consisted of painted-up Japanese trophies.*

▽ *Normal conditions during the rainy season on Guadalcanal.*

There, while Marine riflemen on the high ground picked off the hapless enemy soldiers as they struggled up the steep slopes, artillery shells methodically blasted the floor of the ravine. Vandegrift broke off the action on October 9 when Intelligence indicated that a strong Japanese attack would be mounted from the Kokumbona area. When the Marine battalions retired to the perimeter, they took with them 65 dead and 125 wounded, but they left behind 700 Japanese dead.

The Intelligence was correct. General Hyakutake himself had landed on Guadal-

△ A dramatic piece of propaganda by the American war artist Lea. A dogged U.S. pilot on a mission over the Solomons heads back into combat, with a suitably-punctured aircraft, victory tallies marking past kills, and a Japanese plane plunging into the sea behind him.

canal on October 9 to take personal charge of the Japanese effort. He brought with him heavy reinforcements, the rest of the 2nd Division to join those elements already on the island, two battalions of the 38th Division, and more artillery. By mid-October, Hyakutake's strength was about 20,000 men, but Vandegrift had 23,000, for on October 13, the first American Army troops arrived on Guadalcanal, the 164th Infantry of the Americal Division from New Caledonia. The night after the 164th arrived, Japanese battleships fired a 90-minute bombardment against Henderson Field, partly to cover a daylight run of Tanaka's transports carrying Hyakutake's reinforcements. Although only 42 of Geiger's 90 planes were operational when the bombardment ended and Henderson Field was a shambles, the pilots used the fighter strip as soon as the sun rose and made the muddy runway firm enough to take off from.

Any plane that could carry a bomb or torpedo, including General Vandegrift's lumbering PBY flying boat, attacked the transports. Three were left burning and beached and the other two fled, but some 4,000 men of the 2nd Division were able to get ashore.

The jungle spoils Japanese plans

Hyakutake's plan was to attack the inland perimeter as Kawaguchi had done with some 6,000 men of Lieutenant-General Masao Maruyama's 2nd Division, while another 3,000 men simultaneously struck along the Matanikau, where the Marines now maintained a strong forward position. On October 16, Maruyama's column began cutting its way through the jungle, using the impenetrable cover of the giant trees to escape American observation planes. The march inland was a nightmare for the Japanese: all heavy equipment, including artillery, had to be abandoned and the time schedule kept slipping backwards. On the 19th, when the two-pronged attack was to have been launched, the serpentine column had not even reached the upper reaches of the Lunga river. Hyakutake set the date back to October 22, but even that was not enough, and further days were added.

But the Japanese commander at the Matanikau got his signals crossed and attacked one day early, launching a tank-led thrust across the mouth of the Matanikau on the 23rd. Marine 37-mm guns stopped the tanks dead in their tracks and artillery massacred the following infantry. One result of this abortive attack, however, was that a battalion of the 7th Marines was pulled out of the inland defensive perimeter to reinforce along the Matanikau.

The battle for Bloody Ridge

On October 24, therefore, the 1st Battalion, 7th Marines held 2,500 yards of jungle front anchored on the ridge, now generally known as Edson's Ridge or Bloody Ridge, which the raiders and parachute troops had defended so gallantly in September. To the Marine battalion's left, the 2nd Battalion of the

continued on page 1258

GUADALCANAL: The Sea Battles

Guadalcanal stands out as the one battle of World War II in which the troops in the line were utterly dependent on their naval and air forces controlling the sealanes and the sky at all times. The same would hold true of later campaigns, but only at Guadalcanal was the issue constantly in doubt. And the vicious sea battles which occurred never achieved more than tactical stalemate. The Japanese proved themselves masters of night combat; the overwhelming American reserves meant that another battle was always necessary. So it was that the naval campaign of Guadalcanal developed into the one thing the Japanese could not afford: a battle of attrition.

Within 24 hours of the news of the landings on Guadalcanal a Japanese cruiser force was speeding down "The Slot" to counterattack the landing force while it lay off the beaches. Mikawa's deftly-timed attack in the Battle of Savo Island, resulted in the loss of several Allied warships, but the Japanese cruisers withdrew before the invasion fleet itself was threatened. It was a chastening start to the sea battle for Guadalcanal.

Next came the first carrier battle, a confused encounter known as the "Battle of the Eastern Solomons". This took place on August 24 and it was an inconclusive affair. The Americans sank the light carrier *Ryujo*, a destroyer, and a cruiser; the Japanese badly damaged the U.S. carrier *Enterprise,* and she had to retire. Although honours were about even between the opposing fleets, the Japanese attempt to

◁ △ △ △ *Japanese heavy cruiser* Chokai, *Mikawa's flagship at Savo Island.*
◁ △ △ *U.S. light cruiser* Honolulu, *a survivor of Tassafaronga.*
◁ △ *U.S. battleship* South Dakota, *badly damaged at "Second Guadalcanal".*
◁ *Japanese battleship* Hiei, *sunk at "First Guadalcanal"— the first, but not the last, Japanese battleship lost in World War II.*

land a substantial number of reinforcements was abandoned when their fleet withdrew.

However, on September 15 the Japanese submarine patrols off Guadalcanal struck home with a vengeance. They badly damaged the battleship *South Dakota* and set the carrier *Wasp* ablaze; she had to be sunk by a destroyer.

The night battle of Cape Esperance (October 11-12) was a classic example of how American modern technology failed to match up to Japanese professional skill. The cruiser/destroyer force under Admiral Scott, with all the benefits of radar, caught a Japanese squadron in a perfect position, steaming right across its bows in the classic "crossing the T" manoeuvre. But the American tactics were so inept that the Japanese escaped with the loss of a destroyer and a cruiser. Scott lost one destroyer. This battle, which should have resulted in the annihilation of the Japanese force, was therefore an indecisive affair with the balance slightly in favour of the Americans.

The battle for Guadalcanal rose to a climax on October 25-26. Massive attacks on Henderson Field coincided with the naval battle of Santa Cruz, in which American and Japanese carrier forces clashed again. As before it was an indecisive battle; the Japanese lost heavily in aircraft and had two carriers badly damaged while the Americans lost the *Hornet* and, for the moment, *Enterprise,* which once more suffered heavy damage. But both the American and Japanese carrier fleets were neutralised for the moment.

The result was two tremendous night battles in which American and Japanese battleships fought it out practically at point-blank range. The Japanese plan was to neutralise Henderson Field by bombardment from the battleships while other forces landed more troop reinforcments. But U.S. Intelligence got wind of the Japanese naval build-up in time and Admiral Halsey was able to send a strong task force to intercept. On the night of November

12-13 "First Guadalcanal" was fought in the area of the Savo Island battle back in August. It saw the American cruisers and destroyers concentrate their fire on the battleship *Hiei* and give her such a battering that she withdrew, and after suffering more bomb damage the following morning her crew scuttled her. But American losses were heavy: four destroyers and a cruiser were sunk, and eight others badly damaged. Apart from *Hiei* the Japanese lost two destroyers, *Yudachi* and *Akatsuki*.

"First Guadalcanal" had been a setback for the Japanese but it did not halt their all-out effort to retake the island. On the night of the 13th three Japanese cruisers and four destroyers plastered Henderson Field with shell-fire for 45 minutes. And on the night of November 14-15 another huge battle was fought off the island. This time the Americans had battleship superiority: *South Dakota* and *Washington* versus *Kirishima*. The Americans lost two destroyers but they sank *Kirishima* and the destroyer *Ayanami*. Admiral Kondo, the Japanese commander, broke off and retired (to the disgust of many of his subordinates). Of equal importance was the smashing of the relief attempt. The Japanese transports beached themselves but came under heavy attack, and only 2,000 troops managed to escape into the jungle.

Halsey put it in a nutshell when he stated that if the Americans had lost "Second Guadal-canal" their land forces would have been trapped like the Bataan garrison. But the battle was by no means over. The Japanese made repeated efforts to supply their troops by night runs by the "Tokyo Express", and one of these attempts led to the last sea battle of the Guadalcanal campaign.

On the night of November 30 Admiral Tanaka and eight destroyers were heading in to land supplies off Tassafaronga when they were intercepted by a cruiser force under Admiral Wright. Once again the Americans picked up the Japanese on their radar before being sighted themselves, but Wright's ships gave away their position by opening up with gun-fire. Tanaka replied with a devastating torpedo attack which crippled four of the American cruisers, one of which, *Northampton*, sank. Tanaka's losses were limited to the destroyer *Takanami*.

But the Japanese tactical victory at Tassafaronga was a hollow one. The initiative on shore had passed to the Americans for good. In a way Tassafaronga was typical of the whole campaign, in which no amount of tactical victories won by the Japanese managed to compensate for the completeness of their eventual strategic defeat by American numbers.

▷ *The blazing end of the U.S. carrier* Wasp, *torpedoed by the Japanese submarine* I-19 *on September 15.*

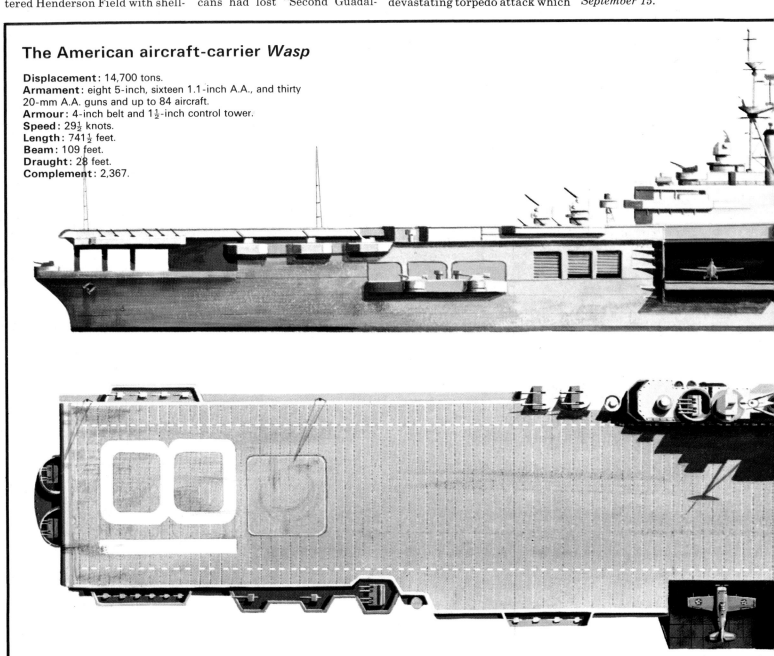

The American aircraft-carrier *Wasp*

Displacement: 14,700 tons.
Armament: eight 5-inch, sixteen 1.1-inch A.A., and thirty 20-mm A.A. guns and up to 84 aircraft.
Armour: 4-inch belt and 1½-inch control tower.
Speed: 29½ knots.
Length: 741½ feet.
Beam: 109 feet.
Draught: 28 feet.
Complement: 2,367.

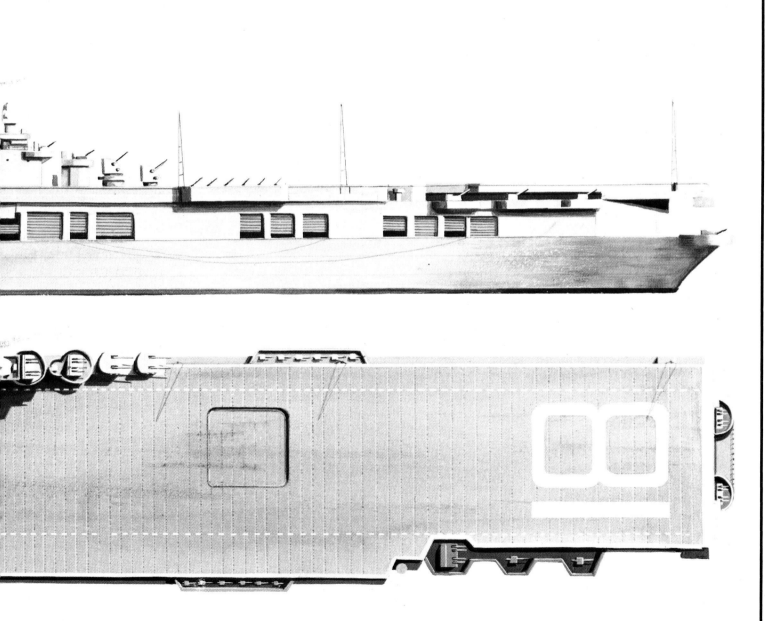

Aleutian Sideshow

In the summer of 1943 the U.S. North Pacific Command turned its attention to the recovery of the islands of Attu and Kiska in the western Aleutians, which the Japanese had occupied the previous year at the time of Midway. It was not a costly operation; the Japanese on Kiska pulled out without firing a shot. So it was that the north-eastern outpost of the Japanese Empire returned to American control, and the entire Aleutian chain was cleared as a supply-line to Russia via Siberia.

△ △ An American landing-party returns Japanese fire at "Massacre Beach" on Attu, May 6, 1943.

◁ △ A crashed Japanese plane.

◁ ◁ Laying an airstrip on the island of Amchitka for the preliminary bombardment.

◁ Build-up of supplies for the Aleutian operation, with the jaunty signpost indicating "2,640 miles to Tokyo."

▷ △ Raising the flag on Attu after the brief but fierce struggle with the Japanese. With Attu back in American hands, Kiska could be menaced from the west—but the Japanese decided to cut their losses in the Aleutians and evacuate Kiska.

▷ ▷ △ A mud-invested supply dump on Kiska.

▷ American troops go ashore on Kiska. Only one other front in World War II was as depressing as the Aleutian theatre: the Russo-German front in the Arctic west of Murmansk.

continued from page 1252

164th Infantry held the portion of the line that curved back toward the coast. The two American battalions held the area that was to be the focal point of Japanese attacks. When Maruyama's soldiers surged forward from the jungle after nightfall on the 24th, they were met by a solid wall of Marine and Army small arms fire, canister shells from 37's, and a deadly rain of artillery and mortar fire. As soon as it became apparent that the main thrust of the attack was aimed at Edson's Ridge, the 3rd Battalion, 164th Infantry, in reserve, was started forward to reinforce the Marines. Slipping and stumbling through the rainy darkness, the soldiers were fed into the Marine positions as they arrived and wherever they were needed. The lines held and they held again the next night as Maruyama made another attempt with his dwindling forces. Then it was over, and all Japanese attempts to penetrate the 1st Division's lines had failed; 3,500 of the enemy lay dead in, around, and in front of the American positions, including the 2nd Division's infantry group commander and two regimental commanders. One of these, Colonel Sejiro Furumiya of the 29th Infantry, had made a pledge to his men when they landed on Guadalcanal, that if they were unsuccessful in capturing the island "not even one man should expect to return alive".

Things were looking up for Vandegrift's troops. Despite the horrendous losses that the Allies had suffered in sea battles in the waters off Guadalcanal, a steady stream of supplies and men continued to be landed on the island under the protective cover of the "Cactus" pilots. And on October 18, the vibrant and aggressive Vice-Admiral William F. Halsey relieved Admiral Ghormley as Commander, South Pacific Area and brought with him a resolve that Guadalcanal would be held and the Japanese driven off. In that determination he was supported by President Roosevelt, who personally ordered the tempo of aid to the defenders to be stepped up. The 25th Infantry Division in Hawaii was alerted for a move to Guadalcanal, and the rest of the 2nd Marine Division and the Americal Division were also ordered forward.

Heartened by the promise of reinforcements, Vandegrift continued to keep the Japanese off balance with the troops he had. On November 3, six battalions under Colonel Edson probed forward and trapped a Japanese force near Point Cruz and eliminated another 300 men of Hyakutake's army. At the same time, on the eastern side of the perimeter, a reconnaissance in force by the 7th Marines, backed up by two battalions of the 164th Infantry, punished a 1,500-man Japanese reinforcement group from the 38th Division which landed near Koli Point, driving the enemy soldiers into the jungle. Partly as a result of this action, Hyakutake decided to abandon the concept of the two-sided attack on the American position and ordered the 38th Division's troops to move overland to Kokumbona. Five hundred of the retreating Japanese failed to complete the trip. They were hunted down and killed by the Marines of the 2nd Raider Battalion who landed at Aola Bay 40 miles west of the Lunga on November 4. These men were part of a project dear to Admiral Turner's heart, an attempt to set up another airfield on Guadalcanal. Vandegrift wanted nothing to do with any scheme that dispersed American ground forces on

▽ *"One of ours"–an American plane swoops over a Marine post at "Hell's Corner" on the Matanikau river.*

Guadalcanal, but lost the argument to his naval superior. He did, however, get permission for the raiders to patrol overland to the Henderson Field perimeter and they accounted for the Japanese straggling through the jungle.

Reinforcements pour in

The further landing of 38th Division troops on Guadalcanal was part of a massive reinforcement effort which included the daylight landing of Japanese forces on November 14. While shore-based aircraft and planes from the carrier *Enterprise* sank seven of 11 transports carrying the Japanese soldiers, Tanaka's destroyers were able to rescue many of the men and Hyakutake had 10,000 fresh troops. But Vandegrift had two new reinforced regiments too, the 8th Marines from Samoa and the 182nd Infantry from New Caledonia, and he retained his numerical advantage. He continued to pressure the Japanese, repeatedly probing and jabbing toward Kokumbona in November, using many of his newly arrived Army and Marine battalions.

The Marine general needed the fresh men. His own division, after four months of fighting in the jungle heat and humidity, was worn out; over half the men had contracted malaria or other tropical diseases. His original Marine units had suffered nearly 2,000 casualties, 681 of them killed in action or dead of wounds. The decision was made to withdraw the 1st Marine Division to Australia for rest and rehabilitation. On December 9, 1942, General Vandegrift turned over command of the troops on Guadalcanal to Major-General Alexander M. Patch of the American Division, and the 5th Marines boarded ship to leave the island, leading the exodus of the 1st Division.

Patch's mission was to drive the Japanese off Guadalcanal, and his forces were increased substantially to give him

▽ *Mute witness to the start of the campaign: the smashed Japanese base on Tanambogo Island.*

the means to carry out this task. Major-General J. Lawton Collins' 25th Infantry Division began landing on Guadalcanal on December 17 and the last elements of the 2nd Marine Division came in on January 4 under command of Brigadier-General Alphonse de Carre. New Army and Marine squadrons swelled the ranks of the Cactus Air Force and the situation was grim indeed for the Japanese.

By the beginning of January, General Patch had 50,000 men of all services under his command. Hyakutake's 17th Army troops amounted to about 25,000 men, but they were now cut off from effective reinforcement or resupply by Allied air power and a resurgent naval effort. His men were on short rations and low on ammunition; many were sick with the same tropical diseases that had ravaged the

▽ *Marines advance over a pontoon bridge across the Matanikau.*

Marines of Vandegrift's division, but there were not enough medical supplies to aid them back to health. While the Japanese were still capable of hard fighting, they could not sustain a serious offensive effort. The decision was made in Rabaul about mid-December to abandon the ill-fated attempt to recapture Guadalcanal and to rescue as many of Hyakutake's men as possible.

General Patch unwittingly reinforced the Japanese decision to get out. Commander since January 2 of a newly organised XIV Corps run by a skeletal staff from the Americal Division, he used his three divisions to drive unrelentingly west from the Lunga perimeter. Using Collins' 25th Division inland and de Carre's 2nd Division along the coast, he hammered steadily at the Japanese. The defenders fell back slowly, fighting hard but unable to hold any position long before the American troops, who used massive

artillery, air, and naval gunfire support, drove them out. Kokumbona, so long the objective of Vandegrift's attacks, was occupied by the 25th Division on January 23. Here Patch held up the attack, anxious because reports of a Japanese shipping build-up at Rabaul and in the Shortland Islands presaged another attempt to take Guadalcanal. Actually, this was the Japanese destroyer force that was intended to evacuate Hyakutake's men.

Patch cautiously resumed his advance on January 30. He had a small blocking force in the mountain passes inland to prevent the Japanese crossing to the other side of the island, and he sent an Army battalion around Cape Esperance to the western coast to block that route of escape also. By February 5, when the advance was held up again by reports of a large Japanese flotilla lurking in the northern Solomons, the lead Army regiment, the 161st Infantry, had reached positions 3,500 yards west of Tassafaronga and only about 12 miles from Cape Esperance.

On the night of February 7-8, Japanese destroyers under the command of Rear-Admiral Koniji Koyonagi executed a masterly evacuation of 13,000 Japanese troops from Guadalcanal. Many of these men would fight the Americans again on other battlefields in the Solomons and on New Britain. But there were many others who would fight no more. Almost 15,000 Japanese troops had been killed in action on Guadalcanal, 9,000 others had died of wounds and disease, and 1,000 had been taken prisoner. Against this toll, the American ground and air forces could balance 6,300 casualties, including almost 1,600 dead.

On January 8, 1943, the official ending of the Guadalcanal land campaign, General Patch could report "the complete and total defeat of Japanese forces on Guadalcanal." After the struggle for control of the island was decided, the Japanese never again advanced in the Pacific. The staggering Japanese losses of ships, planes, and pilots that were equally a feature of the Guadalcanal campaign with the bitter ground fighting were not replaceable in kind. Admiral Tanaka, whose Tokyo Express had done so much to sustain the Japanese on the island, considered that "Japan's doom was sealed with the closing of the struggle for Guadalcanal".

The scene was now set for the American offensives of 1943.

CHAPTER 96
Struggle for the Solomons
by Stanley L. Falk

By February 9, 1943 the battle for Guadalcanal was over. The campaign had cost the Japanese some 24,000 lives, including more than 2,000 skilled pilots and aircrew, who could probably never be replaced. American losses were about 1,600 men killed and over 4,000 wounded. Japanese aircraft losses, still difficult to assess precisely, were probably well over 800, far outnumbering American planes destroyed. Both sides suffered heavily in numbers of ships sunk, but the Americans could build new ones more readily.

The final action in the Guadalcanal campaign was the seizure of the Russell Islands, just north-west of Guadalcanal. The U.S. 43rd Infantry Division landed unopposed in the Russells at the end of February. As on Guadalcanal, the invaders quickly began the construction of air and naval bases to support the

projected advance up the Solomons.

The American victory at Guadalcanal was matched by similar gains in eastern New Guinea by General MacArthur's forces. By early 1943, then, the situation in the South Pacific had changed sufficiently for both sides to reassess their strategy. The Japanese, determined to hold the area at all costs, strengthened their defences and rushed in fresh troops, planes, and ships. Hoping to blunt the force of the Allied offensive, in April they launched a major air effort to destroy American bases, aircraft, and shipping in both the lower Solomons and New Guinea. Results were poor, however, and although Japanese pilots returned with great tales of success, the attackers actually sustained far greater losses than they inflicted – losses, again, that they could ill afford.

Perhaps the most damaging blow to the Japanese cause fell in mid-April. Gratified by the exaggerated reports of Japanese success, the commander of the Combined Fleet, Admiral Isoroku Yamamoto, planned to visit the island of Bougainville, in the northern Solomons, on a combination inspection-morale building tour. As Japan's foremost sailor, architect of the Pearl Harbor attack, and a source of inspiration for all, his arrival would be a major event. So, while security required the utmost secrecy, it was still necessary to inform local commanders. The appropriate messages accordingly went out. Unfortunately for Yamamoto, these messages were intercepted by American listeners, promptly decoded, and passed on to Admiral Halsey. The South Pacific commander now knew exactly when Yamamoto would arrive, his route of approach, and the number and types of planes in the flight. He immediately prepared an aerial ambush with Guadalcanal-based fighters.

Bougainville was at extreme range from Henderson Field, but Yamamoto had a reputation for punctuality, so the American pilots planned to waste no time at the fatal rendezvous. At 0930 on the morning of April 18, just as Yamamoto's plane began to land, and his own fighter escort turned to leave, the attackers struck. Eighteen Lockheed P-38 Lightnings swooped down on the two bombers carrying the admiral and his staff. Brushing aside the remaining Japanese fighters, they quickly struck down their targets. Yamamoto died in the wreckage of his bomber, a victim of able Intelligence

◁ ◁ *Marines struggle with the mud on Bougainville.*
△ *A brisk fire fight between Marine Raiders and Japanese snipers concealed in trees.*
◁ *New punch for the American infantry: a U.S. Marine rocket platoon moves up with its rockets and launchers during the battle for Bougainville.*

work and skilful timing.

The admiral's death was a great shock to Japanese morale, and an even greater loss to Japan's naval leadership. "There was only one Yamamoto," commented a saddened colleague, "and no one is able to replace him." His talents would be sorely missed in the coming months when the Americans resumed their offensive.

The details of this offensive had already been worked out. Despite the requirements of other areas, the two-pronged offensive against Rabaul would continue, with MacArthur advancing in New Guinea, and Halsey, still under Nimitz but subject to MacArthur's strategic direction, climbing the ladder of the Solomons. Halsey's objective was Bougainville, but to reach it he would first have to seize intermediate fighter bases from which to cover his final advance. So his initial target was New Georgia, in the central Solomons, with its vital airstrip at Munda.

Indirect attack

New Georgia posed a difficult problem. The centre of a small group of islands, shielded by coral reefs and accessible only through narrow channels, it was all but impossible to assault directly. Munda Point, moreover, site of the airstrip, could not be approached by large ships. It was clear to Halsey that he would first have to seize bases in the islands around New Georgia from which to mount and support his main attack. Making his task no easier were the Japanese defenders of the central Solomons, some 10,000 army and navy troops deployed in scattered detachments to deny airfields and harbours to any invader. Rabaul-based air and naval forces were also ready to assist these units.

The operation began late in June, with small unopposed American landings at the south end of New Georgia and on

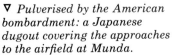

▽ *Pulverised by the American bombardment: a Japanese dugout covering the approaches to the airfield at Munda.*

adjacent Vangunu Island. Then, on the night of June 29-30, some 6,000 troops of Major-General John H. Hester's 43rd Infantry Division went ashore on Rendova Island, just across the channel from Munda Point and ideally located to support the final assault on the airstrip. The few defenders on Rendova were surprised, and offered little resistance, but Japanese airstrikes proved a nuisance and coastal defence guns on Munda Point dropped heavy shells on the American beach-head. Rendova, nevertheless, was securely in American hands.

The landings on New Georgia began on July 2, when the bulk of Hester's division splashed ashore without opposition at Zanana, on New Georgia's south shore, about five miles east of Munda. On the 5th, a small second force of soldiers and Marines landed at Rice Anchorage, on the island's north shore. While this group sought to cut off the approaches to Munda, the larger forces at Zanana struck out directly to capture the airstrip.

Almost immediately things went wrong. The fierce heat, jungle terrain, and stubborn Japanese resistance proved too much for the attackers. The 43rd Division's troops, in combat for the first time, suffered heavy casualties and morale dropped badly. Relieving one of the regimental commanders did little to help, nor did the arrival of reinforcing elements of the 37th Division. By July 7, the southern drive on Munda had halted, while the advance from Rice Anchorage, after some initial gains, was also stopped.

Major-General Noboru Sasaki, the Japanese commander on New Georgia, was so encouraged by his success that he began planning a counter-landing on Rendova. Higher headquarters overruled him, however, and instead decided to make a major effort to reinforce Sasaki's troops on New Georgia. As a result, for nearly two weeks the waters of the central and northern Solomons were violently disturbed by clashes between American warships and Japanese vessels engaged in a renewal of the "Tokyo Express". Two major battles, the Battles of Kula Gulf (July 5-6) and Kolombangara (July 12-13), were slight tactical victories for the Japanese. More important, they managed to land about 2,000 reinforcements, which made the American ground advance all the more difficult.

This advance continued to stumble against the fierce Japanese resistance.

△ Loading up Stuart light tanks to add more muscle to the offensive on New Georgia.
◁ Communications. This is a divisional message centre, charged with co-ordinating all reports on the progress of the troops for the commander.

▽ Stretcher cases from fighting in the central Solomons are unloaded on Guadalcanal.

BATTLE FOR THE SOLOMONS

Admiral Halsey, who bore the responsibility for the naval end of the long, painful advance along the Solomon archipelago. His South Pacific Force had been extended to the utmost during the struggle for Guadalcanal, but by January 1944 it had achieved naval and air superiority. His ships had to seal off the central Solomons while the land forces established themselves there, and had to fight several fierce engagements in the waters off New Georgia and Kolombangara. As during the Guadalcanal campaign, much of Halsey's intelligence about Japanese counter-moves came from the devoted coast-watchers, sending in reports from behind the Japanese lines. The Battle of Empress Augusta Bay, which sealed the fate of Bougainville, was the last major engagement between surface fleets in the South-West Pacific.

General MacArthur, overall commander in the South-West Pacific theatre. His basic task was to breach the Japanese perimeter at its south-eastern extremity in order to clear the way for his long-promised "return" to the Philippines. In this task the campaigns in New Guinea, Guadalcanal, and the rest of the Solomons merged together as the Allied pincers converged on the key base of Rabaul. MacArthur, however, was not given the bulk of the new naval and land forces which had been amassed since the late summer of 1942. These were earmarked for the forthcoming assault across the Central Pacific, which would take precedence over the South-West theatre.

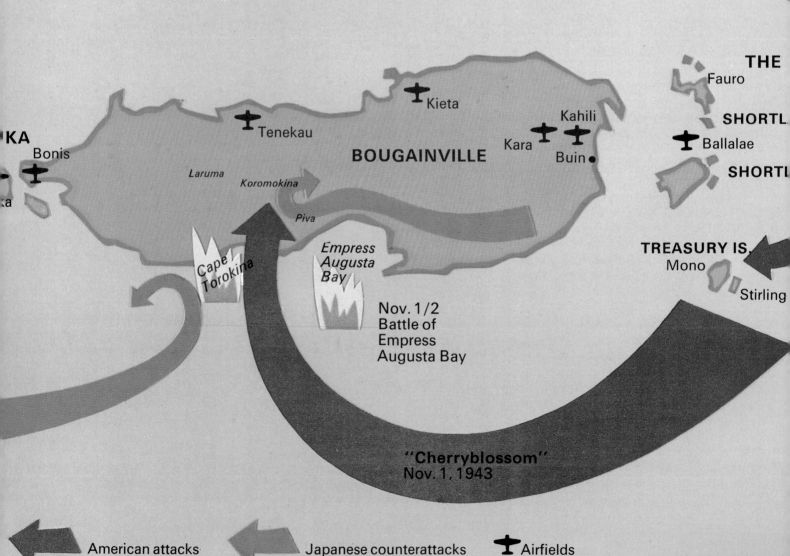

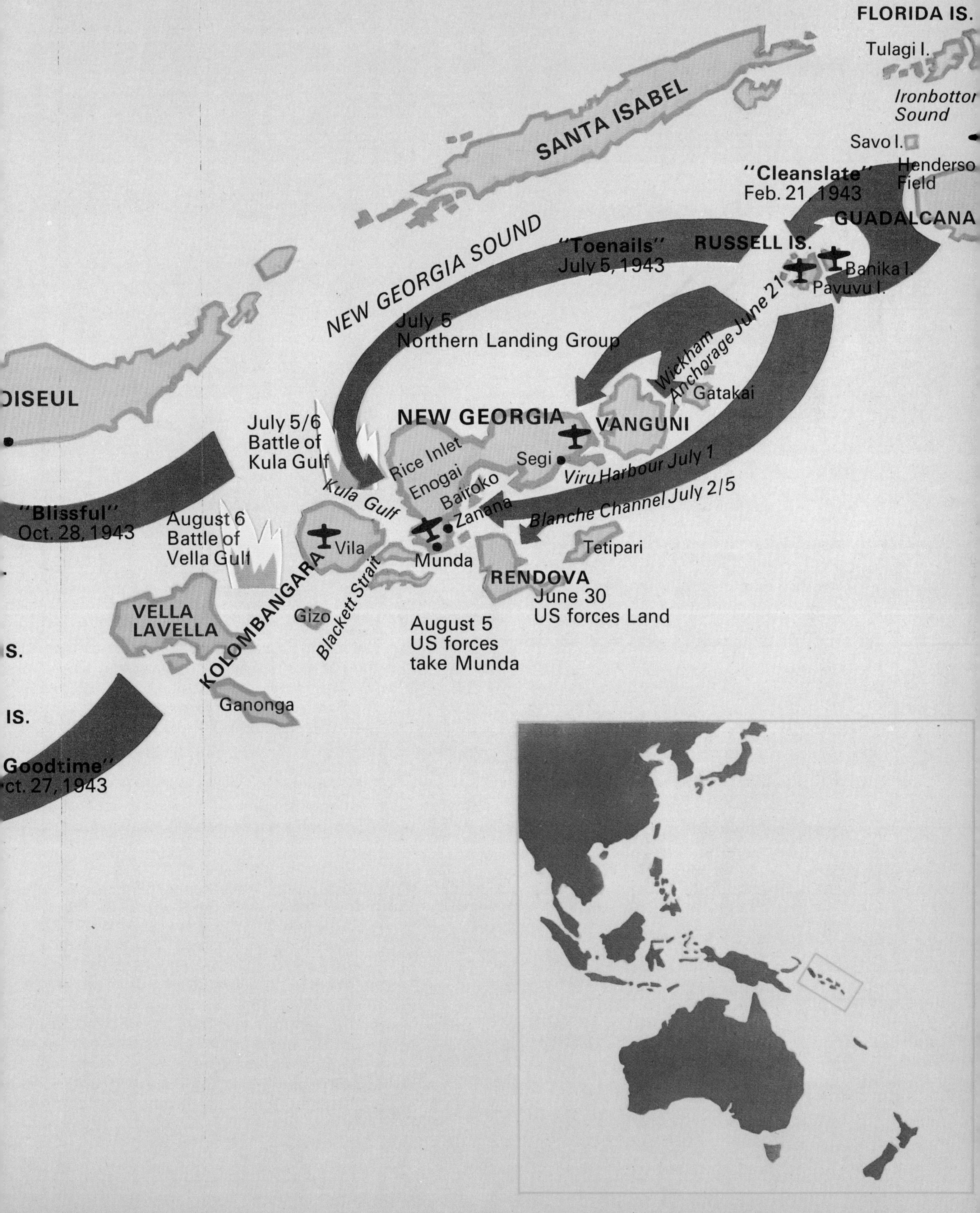

FLORIDA IS.

Tulagi I.

Ironbottor Sound

Savo I.

Henderso Field

"Cleanslate"
Feb. 21 1943

GUADALCANA

SANTA ISABEL

"Toenails"
July 5, 1943

RUSSELL IS.

Banika I.

Pavuvu I.

NEW GEORGIA SOUND

July 5
Northern Landing Group

Wickham
Anchorage June 21

Gatakai

July 5/6
Battle of
Kula Gulf

NEW GEORGIA

VANGUNI

Rice Inlet

Segi

Enogai

Viru Harbour July 1

OISEUL

Bairoko

Kula Gulf

Zanana

Blanche Channel July 2/5

"Blissful"
Oct. 28, 1943

August 6
Battle of
Vella Gulf

Vila

Munda

Tetipari

RENDOVA
June 30
US forces Land

KOLOMBANGARA

Gizo

Blackett Strait

August 5
US forces
take Munda

**VELLA
LAVELLA**

S.

IS.

Ganonga

"Goodtime"
ct. 27, 1943

The thick tropical vegetation and intense heat proved effective allies for Sasaki's men, who provided a bitter lesson in jungle warfare to the green American troops. If the Japanese were stubborn foes during the day, they were even more effective at night. Testing the American perimeters, throwing hand grenades, shouting, and dropping harassing fire on the exhausted men of the 43rd Division, they kept up a constant pressure. The inexperienced Americans, bewildered by the weird noises and intense darkness of the jungle night, were often terrified by their own imaginations. They mistook the slithering sound of land crabs for Japanese soldiers crawling to attack them, the phosphorescence of rotting logs for enemy signals, and the sick, dank smell of the jungle for poison gas. Fearing the nocturnal enemy who, it was said, would drag them from their foxholes with hooks and ropes, or at the least would knife or bayonet them while they slept, American troops fired wildly at the least sound, hurled grenades at each other, and suffered badly from combat neurosis.

Gradually they became accustomed to the worst aspects of fighting in the jungle, but they still made little progress in their efforts to reach Munda. By mid-July, despite another landing between Zanana and Munda, the main drive had advanced less than halfway to the airfield. To put new life into the offensive, therefore, Major-General Oscar W. Griswold, the new XIV Corps commander, took direct charge of the New Georgia operations. He immediately asked for reinforcements and set about reorganising for a major attack, in order, as he put it, "to crack [the] Munda nut".

It was ten days before he was ready. Then, on July 25, supported by artillery, airstrikes, and naval bombardment, the American infantry renewed its attack. Progress remained frustratingly slow, however, and on the 29th Griswold relieved General Hester and put Major-General John H. Hodge, a veteran of Guadalcanal, in command of the 43rd Division. Perhaps because of this change, or maybe because of a simultaneous Japanese decision – under the pressure of increasing casualties – to fall back toward Munda, the American drive gradually began to accelerate. By August 1, there was little doubt of the outcome. Three days later, the 43rd Division's

troops overran the airfield. The surviving Japanese made their way to other nearby islands or sought shelter elsewhere in the New Georgia jungles. Munda airstrip, after hasty reconstruction and widening, was in operation on August 14. By the end of the month, with the help of the newly arrived 25th Infantry Division, the entire island had been cleared of Japanese.

There remained one more island in the central Solomons with a strong Japanese garrison and a useful airstrip. This was Kolombangara, just north-west of New Georgia, where General Sasaki now had his headquarters and about 10,000 troops with which he hoped to counter-attack the Americans on New Georgia. To help in this projected operation, the Japanese had been trying to run troops in from Rabaul. On the night of August 1, they succeeded in landing a few bargeloads of reinforcements. When American motor torpedo boats from Rendova tried to stop them, a Japanese destroyer ran down the PT boat commanded by Lieutenant John F. Kennedy. Thrown into the water, the future president of the United States not only escaped with his life, but also succeeded in rescuing most of his crew

◁ ◁ △ *The way in: landing craft head in to the beaches of Vella Lavella.*
◁ ◁ ▽ *The way out: wounded are evacuated.*
△ *Major-General Oscar W. Griswold* (left), *commanding on Bougainville, confers with Lieutenant-General Millard F. Harmon, U.S. Army C.-in-C. in the South Pacific.*
▽ *An L.S.T. disgorges supplies on Bougainville, largest island of the Solomons chain.*

through a combination of bravery, determination, and several exhausting swims.

Five nights later, four fast Japanese troop-carrying destroyers again attempted to reinforce Kolombangara. Intercepted by American destroyers just as they were approaching their destination, three of the Japanese warships succumbed to a surprise torpedo attack before they knew what had hit them. The fourth made good its escape, but nearly two battalions of reinforcements drowned in the warm waters of Vella Gulf.

Sasaki's forces, nevertheless, still constituted a formidable challenge, for capture of the Kolombangara airstrip was the next scheduled operation. To Admiral Halsey, the prospect of another long and costly land battle against Sasaki seemed less and less palatable. After some consideration, and a daring advance reconnaissance, an alternative solution offered itself. This was to bypass Kolombangara in favour of seizing lightly-defended Vella Lavella, about 20 miles to the north-west, and building an airstrip there. From Vella Lavella and a few other small islands, Kolombangara could easily be cut off and neutralised. And since Vella Lavella was closer to Bougainville, its airstrip would be better located to support the subsequent invasion of the latter. Thus, a principle to be followed whenever possible for the rest of the Pacific war was established: it was easier to carve a new airstrip out of the jungle than to wrest one already built from the hands of its stubborn Japanese defenders.

More landings

Just after daylight on August 15, a reinforced regiment of the 25th Division landed on the beaches of southern Vella Lavella. Japanese dive-bombers and fighters constituted the only resistance, and these inflicted little damage on the invaders. Unloading proceeded rapidly. The troops

△ *Manhandling a 75-mm gun up "Snuffy's Nose" Hill on Bougainville.*
▷ *Into action.*

▽ *Manpower supply line on Bougainville: carrying rations and ammunition up "Hand Grenade Hill".*

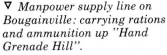

quickly established a defensive perimeter and then struck inland to secure the island. A few hundred Japanese survivors of the ill-fated August 6 destroyer run, and some other escapees from New Georgia, were the only enemy troops on the island. The Americans had more trouble finding them than defeating them. There was some Japanese discussion of making a counter-landing, but wiser heads at Rabaul suggested that this would simply be like "pouring water on a hot stone", and the idea died quickly.

The Japanese thus limited themselves to hit-and-run air raids on the beachhead and on American ships bringing supplies to Vella Lavella. These were a constant danger, inflicting some casualties on troops unloading supplies and damaging a few ships. But despite such problems, the end of September saw the island all but secured, by which time the airstrip was in action and New Zealand units had replaced the American troops. An attempt by the Japanese to evacuate survivors on the night of October 6 led to another fierce destroyer engagement. This time the Japanese got the better of the fight, rescuing their compatriots and inflicting greater losses on the American warships.

The decision to bypass Kolombangara proved to be doubly sound. For even as the Americans were securing Vella Lavella, General Sasaki, under orders from Rabaul to save his troops for another day, was shifting the Kolombangara force to Bougainville. On three nights at the end of September and in early October, Japanese barges, landing craft, and torpedo boats, escorted by destroyers and aircraft, managed to evacuate more than 9,000 troops. Attempts by American destroyers to thwart the withdrawal were frustrated by the Japanese escorts.

The fight for the central Solomons thus ended with New Georgia and all of the islands around it in American hands. More than 1,000 Americans had died in the battle, and nearly four times as many had been wounded. Japanese casualties probably totalled around 10,000, of which at least a quarter had been killed. Furthermore, continuing Japanese air and naval losses emphasised the growing attrition of these valuable resources. Still, the four months' defence of the central Solomons meant that much more time to prepare Rabaul for its final defence. And on Bougainville the Japanese hoped to delay the Americans even further.

Neutralise, not destroy

The importance of this was greater than perhaps they realised. Halsey's victories in the Solomons had been matched by impressive advances by MacArthur in New Guinea. As a result, the Joint Chiefs-of-Staff had concluded that it would be more advantageous to bypass and neutralise Rabaul than to capture it, thus freeing large forces for a more rapid drive on targets closer to Japan itself. This decision, ratified by Allied military leaders in late August 1943, left Bougainville as the last obstacle for Halsey to overcome before he could push on beyond Rabaul.

While American heavy bombers struck fiercely at Japanese air bases in the Bougainville area in late September, Halsey was planning his assault. There were about 40,000 Japanese soldiers on Bougainville, commanded by General Hyakutake, of Guadalcanal fame, as well as an additional 20,000 navy troops. Allied Intelligence had a fairly good appreciation of this strength, and Halsey, after his successful bypassing of Kolombangara, decided to attempt a similar strategy on Bougainville. What he sought was an air base from which Rabaul could be neutralised and from which the Japanese supply line between Rabaul

△ *Marine commander on Bougainville, Major-General Allen H. Turnage, gives his men some well-earned praise after the battle of Cape Torokina.*

▽ *The Marine advance continues, with the strain of combat beginning to show.*

and the Solomons could be severed. It was not necessary to crush all of Hyakutake's forces: only to bypass and isolate them. And this is exactly what Halsey proposed to do.

With most of the Japanese concentrated in southern Bougainville and at the island's northern tip, the practically undefended Empress Augusta Bay area, midway up the west coast, seemed an attractive target. The landing date was set for November 1, with the I Marine Amphibious Corps under General Vandegrift, who had also cut his combat teeth at Guadalcanal, given the assignment.

During October, American bombers continued to punish Japanese airfields on Bougainville, knocking out the last of them by the end of the month. To confuse the Japanese further, in the pre-dawn hours of October 27, a small force of New Zealand troops occupied the Treasury Islands, south of Bougainville. Then, later in the day, a battalion of U.S. Marines landed on the large island of Choiseul, to the east. This was merely a raid, to mislead the Japanese about American intentions, but in the week before they were evacuated the Marines stirred up enough trouble to make the defenders believe they had come to stay.

Whatever the effect of the Treasury and Choiseul landings, when the 3rd Marine Division landed on the north shore of Empress Augusta Bay early on November 1, there was very little opposition. Since the terrain around the bay was low and wet, the Japanese thought it unsuitable for offensive operations by an invader and thus ruled out the chances of an American landing there. General Hyakutake had stationed less than 300 men in the area, and these outnumbered troops were quickly overwhelmed by the attacking Marines. Within a few hours, Vandegrift's men had secured the area.

The Japanese counter-attack came by air and sea. Almost immediately, Rabaul-based bombers and fighters struck at the landing force, only to be driven off with heavy losses by defending American aircraft. At the same time, a strong cruiser-destroyer force sped down from Rabaul, hoping to smash American warships in a repeat of the Savo Island victory of the Guadalcanal campaign. The naval attack was also intended to cover the landing of Japanese ground troops at Empress Augusta Bay. But this time the Americans were ready. In the Battle of Empress Augusta Bay on the night of

August 1-2, the Japanese were driven off, with slightly heavier losses than those sustained by the American vessels. Repeated Japanese air attacks the next day were also defeated.

Crushing blows

Then it was the Americans' turn. Learning of a heavy Japanese naval build-up at Rabaul, Halsey despatched his fast carrier units against the enemy base. In two daring airstrikes, on November 5 and 11, the American carrier planes smashed Japanese naval and air targets at Rabaul. So effective were these blows, that they forced the surviving Japanese warships to retreat north to other bases, thus ending the chances of further attacks on the Marine beach-head from the sea.

Japanese air strength also suffered badly. A sustained air attack on Empress Augusta Bay, lasting for ten days after the Marine invasion, was a dismal failure. The Japanese sustained heavy losses, with little to show for them. By November 12, with the Japanese fleet withdrawn from Rabaul and little or no air strength left there, the great Japanese base was no longer an offensive threat.

The Americans were thus free to enlarge their beach-head. Army troops – the 37th Infantry Division – had begun landing on November 8, and within a few days there were more than 34,000 Americans at Empress Augusta Bay. By the beginning of 1944, the Army's Americal Division had replaced the

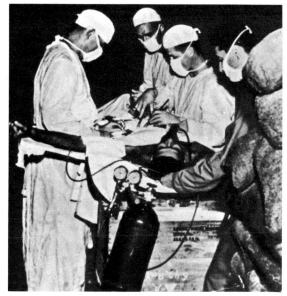

◁ ◁ △ *Countering a Japanese ambush which has knocked out the tank in the background.*
◁ ◁ ▽ *American tank men take a break for running repairs and taking on ammunition.*
△ *Rough, ready, and virtually out in the open, a field hospital.*
◁ *Sheltered in a dugout, surgeons carry out an emergency operation.*

▽ *Fire-fighting detail in a blazing fuel dump set ablaze by a surprise Japanese air raid.*

With the battle for Bougainville won, Marines march down to the water's edge to re-embark.

Commonwealth forces take a hand. These New Zealanders are landing on Green Island, February 16, 1944.

Marines, and the two army divisions, with strong artillery support, were defending a large beach-head that included a naval base, three airfields, and extensive supply installations.

Attempts by General Hyakutake to crush the American perimeter were to no avail. Japanese forces, pushing overland through the heavy Bougainville jungle and cut off from outside assistance, were unable to mount a co-ordinated and sustained offensive. There was considerable fighting during November and

December, but Hyakutake's efforts were futile, and the American beach-head gradually expanded. Content to hold this beach-head, the Americans made no further effort to enlarge it after the end of the year.

On March 9, 1944, Hyakutake launched his last attack. This was an all-out assault, with at least 15,000 troops, and what the Japanese lacked in air and naval support, they made up in ferocity. In a bitter struggle that lasted until the end of the month, the Japanese threatened but never succeeded in breaking the American lines. When the fight ended, Hyakutake had lost some 6,000 troops. He continued to peck away at the American perimeter, but the threat had ended. The Japanese on Bougainville were no longer a force to be reckoned with. Defeated and isolated from support or resupply, weakened by hunger and disease, they were doomed to sit out the rest of the war. The Americans, meanwhile, soon to be replaced in their perimeter by Australian units, were free once again to push on to other conquests.

The fight on Bougainville brought to a close the long struggle up the Solomons ladder from Guadalcanal. In conjunction with MacArthur's efforts in the New Guinea area, the successful campaign had isolated and neutralised Rabaul. That once great Japanese bastion no longer posed any danger to the great Allied Pacific offensive, and could be left to wither and rot away. No less important was the damaging attrition the Japanese had suffered in men and *matériel*. Thousands of soldiers had been killed or left to die in the Solomons. Even more crushing were the losses in warships and transport, which, at this stage of the war, could never be replaced. And finally, perhaps most significant of all, the tremendous Japanese losses in aircraft and trained pilots were decisive.

Japanese naval air power, which had once made the Combined Fleet one of the most effective fighting forces in the history of modern seapower, had now been all but wiped out. Without it, the Japanese would be unable to oppose the great central Pacific offensive that the Americans were now about to launch. Nor, for that matter, could they mount an effective air defence against MacArthur's projected drive to retake the Philippines. In this sense, the American victory in the Solomons was decisive, hastening and ensuring Japan's ultimate defeat.

CHAPTER 97

Allied problems, 1944

The Anglo-American summit conference at Quebec in August 1943 ("Quadrant") was born out of a need to take fresh grand-strategic decisions in view of the fast-changing situation in the Mediterranean after the fall of Mussolini – and also out of underlying mistrust between the Western Allies. Churchill had proposed the summit to Roosevelt, partly because he had been informed by Averell Harriman that Roosevelt was thinking of convening a purely Soviet-American meeting. As the Prime Minister telegraphed to the President: "I do not underrate the use that enemy propaganda would make of a meeting between the heads of Soviet Russia and the United States at this juncture with the British Commonwealth and Empire excluded. It would be serious and vexatious and many would be bewildered and alarmed thereby." (Michael Howard, *Grand Strategy* Vol IV, 559). Roosevelt replied that he had only intended to explore informally with Stalin the question of postwar Russian policy, and suggested that in the meantime he and the Prime Minister should confer in Quebec. Nonetheless here was the shadow of the future–Roosevelt's burgeoning belief that he could settle the postwar world with "Uncle Joe" on the basis of personal deals in mutual trust; the emergence of two super-powers, the U.S.A. and Soviet Russia, and the relegation of Britain to the second division, against which Churchill was to struggle with all the force of his personal prestige in a frantic but hopeless fight.

American suspicions

Yet while this political mistrust before the Quebec Conference was no more than a whisper, military mistrust between Britain and the United States had now reached crisis point. It turned on the perennial issue of the correct relationship between a Mediterranean strategy and a cross-Channel invasion (Operation "Overlord", as "Round-up" had been renamed). The American Joint Chiefs-of-Staff, and especially General Marshall and his own staff, were convinced that the

British were seeking to overturn the decisions first reached at Casablanca and confirmed at Washington in May whereby the Mediterranean was unequivocally subordinated to "Overlord". They feared that the British would drag them into an ever-deeper morass of involvement in the Mediterranean, so weakening and perhaps even ruling out "Overlord". They did not believe in fact that the British meant to attack across the Channel at all. The United States Secretary of War, Henry Stimson, reported to Roosevelt after a visit to London:

"We cannot now rationally hope to be able to cross the Channel and come to

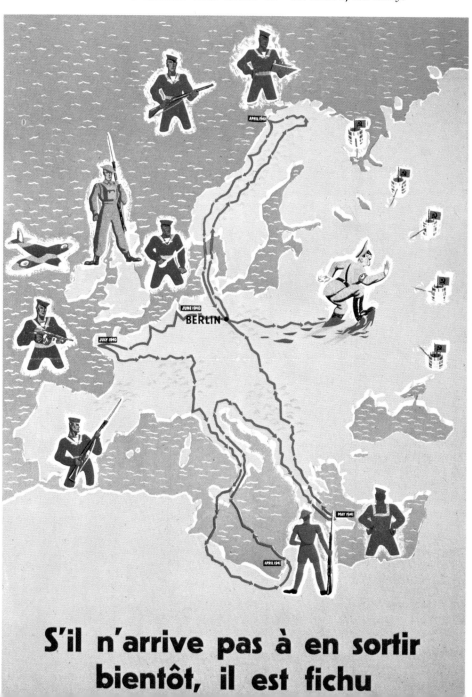

▽ *Caged in Europe, Hitler tries to break out of a cordon of Allied forces in this Free French poster. The Allies had halted all German offensives by August 1943; now they had to decide how best to strike back to the heart of Germany.*

S'il n'arrive pas à en sortir bientôt, il est fichu

Some of the men who were helping to shape future events now that the Allies were no longer losing the war, and had to decide how best to co-operate to win it.
▷ *General Jan Smuts, C.-in-C. and Prime Minister of South Africa. During the war he became the valued friend and adviser of Churchill.*
▷▷ *Generalissimo Chiang Kai-shek. He was a symbol of resistance for the Allies in the Far East, having been at war with the Japanese since 1937.*

grips with our German enemy under a British commander. His Prime Minister and his Chief-of-Staff are frankly at variance with such a proposal. The shadows of Passchendaele and Dunkerque still hang too heavily over the imagination of these leaders of his government. Though they have rendered lip-service to the Operation, their heart is not in it. . . ." (Henry L. Stimson and McGeorge Bundy *On Active Service in Peace and War*).

In particular Marshall's staff, educated in the American military tradition to think only in narrow military terms and to regard political considerations as irrelevant, believed that the British *penchant* for the Mediterranean was inspired more by postwar British political interests than by wartime strategy. The American Chiefs-of-Staff therefore went to Quebec in militant mood. That this would be the case was well known to the British delegation, for they had been forwarned by their Joint Staff Mission in Washington that they would encounter "some serious difficulties".

The four-day voyage amid the pre-war luxuries of the Cunarder *Queen Mary* gave Churchill and the British Chiefs-of-Staff an opportunity to clear their own minds.

For there appears to have been a divergence between the Prime Minister and his military advisers. Sir Alan Brooke apparently remained completely committed to "Overlord" as the primary war-winning strike against Germany, while still believing that German resistance must first be weakened by further operations in the Mediterranean which would exploit the opportunity now presented by Mussolini's fall and the impending collapse of Italy. But Churchill's imagination now encompassed the possibility of actually deciding the whole war by offensives in the Mediterranean and the Balkans. The Balkans had fascinated him as a potential theatre of war ever since 1915. If there was to be an invasion of Europe launched from Britain, Churchill favoured Norway as the objective (Operation "Jupiter") rather than France. As it happened, Hitler too was preoccupied by Norway and the Balkans. However, Churchill, in the chapters on the Quebec Conference in his war memoirs, makes no mention of Norway or of his far-reaching Balkan ideas, but gives the impression that his mind was wholly upon how to ensure the ultimate success of "Overlord", to which an advance up Italy at least to the line Leghorn-Ancona would be an essential

▷ *Sir Samuel Hoare, British Ambassador to Spain. Madrid, Stockholm and Berne were the main places in Europe where there could be any contact between Axis and Allied diplomats.*
▷▷ *General Sir Frederick Morgan. He was responsible for the preliminary planning for "Overlord". With the limited resources available in 1943, his plans were hedged with "ifs" and "buts", and only became viable with massive American support.*

ancillary. But in fact he had written to the Chiefs-of-Staff in July 1943:

"I have no doubt myself that the right strategy for 1944 is:

(a) Maximum post-'Husky'; certainly to the Po, with option to attack westwards in the South of France or north-eastward towards Vienna, and meanwhile to procure the expulsion of the enemy from the Balkans and Greece.

(b) 'Jupiter' prepared under the cover of 'Overlord'."

British plans to invade Italy

The Chiefs-of-Staff, and in particular Brooke, spent the voyage to Canada arguing the Prime Minister out of these propositions, but, as it proved, with only partial success since he was to insist on putting forward "Jupiter" late in the Conference. With regard to the Mediterranean, the agreed British case to be put at Quebec was that a campaign in Italy constituted an essential preliminary to "Overlord", both by dispersing and consuming German land forces and by providing bases from which Allied bombers could destroy fighter factories in south Germany.

On August 11 Churchill and his party, which included Brigadier Orde Wingate the Chindit leader (who, being a romantic and eccentric figure offering an unorthodox, offensive nostrum, much impressed Churchill), arrived in the Citadel at Quebec. The role of the Canadian Government was limited to that of host, for Roosevelt had feared that if Canada took part, other American allied states such as Brazil would expect to be present too. On August 14 the British and American Chiefs-of-Staff met in battle, Churchill himself having gone off to visit Roosevelt at his home, Hyde Park, while the military men hammered out an agreed paper for the political leaders to consider.

American demands

The Americans laid down their own views in a forthright memorandum submitted to their British colleagues the day before. They insisted that there must be no renunciation of the decisions reached in Washington, but on the contrary an end to

△ *Orde Wingate, whose ideas fascinated Churchill but found little favour in most of the British army.*
Previous page: *Mackenzie King, host to three illustrious guests. With Churchill and Roosevelt is Field-Marshal Sir John Dill, British military representative in the U.S.A. The Quebec conference laid down the principle of an invasion of Europe in summer 1944, provided that the Germans would be unable to oppose the landing with more than 12 mobile divisions and that their air fighter strength in the West should have been considerably diminished.*

what they called "opportunist strategy". "We must not jeopardise," they wrote, "our second overall strategy simply to exploit local successes in a generally-accepted secondary theatre, the Mediterranean . . ." They demanded that "Overlord" be given "whole-hearted and immediate support". Nevertheless they had no objection to further operations in Italy aimed at weakening German strength, bringing about an Italian collapse and at establishing airfields at least as far north as Rome. But they were careful to emphasise that, as between Operation "Overlord" and operations in the Mediterranean, "when there is a shortage of resources 'Overlord' will have an overriding priority". With regard to more distant objectives, any surplus Allied forces in Italy should, they stated, be allotted to the invasion of southern France rather than to the Balkans or a march on Vienna.

When in the meetings on August 14 and 15 Brooke and Air Chief Marshal Portal argued that the American proposals failed to acknowledge adequately the importance of an advance in Italy as an essential preliminary to "Overlord", especially in making it possible to bomb German fighter production, they merely exacerbated the profound American mistrust of British intentions. A key issue lay in the seven Allied divisions which it had been agreed at Washington should be transferred from the Mediterranean to the U.K. by November 1943 as part of the "Overlord" build-up. The American paper wanted this decision re-affirmed, while the British argued that these divisions should be retained in the Mediterranean where they would be more useful.

The Americans make plain their suspicions

On August 16 the American Joint Chiefs-of-Staff sent the British a formal memorandum couched in plain language:

"The discussion in the Combined Chiefs-of-Staff Meeting yesterday made more apparent than ever the necessity for decision now as to whether our main effort in the European Theater is to be in the Mediterranean or from the United Kingdom. The United States Chiefs-of-Staff believe that this is the critical question before the Conference . . ."

They proposed that the Conference formally reaffirm the decision to launch "Overlord" and "assign it an overriding priority over all other operations in the European Theater". They added that they believed that "the acceptance of this decision must be without conditions and without mental reservations".

Candid talk and a compromise solution

Thus came to a head the underlying differences of approach and military tradition that had divided the two allies ever since Marshall reluctantly accepted "Torch" as the operation for 1942 instead of "Roundup"; a matter now not so much for strategic argument as for candid talk about American suspicion of British good faith. The candid talk took place unrecorded in a closed session. According to Brooke's account, he went over "our whole Mediterranean strategy to prove its objects which they had never fully realised and finally I had to produce countless arguments to prove the close relations that exist between the cross-Channel and Italian operations. In the end I think our arguments did have some effect on Marshall." (Arthur Bryant *The Turn of the Tide*).

Next day, August 17, after more talk, a compromise strategic statement was agreed, but based largely on the American paper submitted at the start of the Conference. Instead of the original American phrase "'Overlord' will have an overriding priority" [over the Mediterranean in allotting limited resources], a British alternative was substituted, to the effect that "Available resources will be distributed and employed with the main object of ensuring the success of 'Overlord'. Operations in the Mediterranean theatre will be carried out with the forces allotted at 'Trident' [the Washington Conference in May 1943], except insofar as these may be varied by the decisions of the Combined Chiefs-of-Staff." Nevertheless, as Michael Howard points out, while the British had succeeded in getting written in a greater measure of flexibility as between "Overlord" and the Mediterranean, they gave up their own proposal that the seven battle-hardened divisions due for return to the U.K. should instead stay in the Mediterranean.

Brooke's opinions

The Quebec conference saw the rumbles of Anglo-American discord break forth again. Was the American suspicion about the sincerity of British intentions in regard to "Overlord" due to a misunderstanding, or was it in fact justified? Churchill certainly hoped that opportunities would now open up in the Mediterranean and the Balkans which would render unnecessary what he saw as a highly risky cross-Channel invasion. What of Brooke himself? At the time of the Quebec Conference his arguments in the meetings and the entries in his diary alike express a belief in "Overlord" as the paramount Allied stroke. Yet, as Michael Howard notes in *The Mediterranean Strategy in the Second World War*, Brooke wrote in his diary only a few months later, on October 25:

"Our build-up in Italy is much slower than that of the Germans and far slower than I expected. We shall have to have an almighty row with the Americans who have put us in this position with their insistence to abandon the Mediterranean operations for the very problematical cross-Channel operations. We are beginning to see the full beauty of the Marshall strategy! It is quite heartbreaking when we see what we might have done this year if our strategy had not been distorted by the Americans . . ."

"Overlord's" commander

And his diary entry for November 1 is even more revealing:

"When I look at the Mediterranean I realise only too well how far I have failed. If only I had had sufficient force of character to swing those American Chiefs-of-Staff and make them see daylight, how different the war might be. We should have had the whole Balkans ablaze by now, and the war might have finished by 1943." (Arthur Bryant *Triumph in the West*)

Light is cast on this whole question by the matter of the appointment of an Allied supreme commander for "Overlord". It had long been understood between Brooke and Churchill that Brooke should be that commander. At Quebec, however, Churchill told Brooke that because of the

△ *One for the camera: the Royal Canadian Mounted Police detachment at Quebec is inspected as a press photographer gets his picture.*

preponderance of American over British land forces in "Overlord" after the first few weeks, the appointee must be American. In his war memoirs Churchill states that "I myself took the initiative of proposing to the President that an American commander should be appointed for the expedition to France. He was gratified at this suggestion, *and I dare say his mind had been moving that way.*" [author's italics]. When Stimson's warning to the President about the prospects for the invasion under a British general is taken into account, it seems possible that it was not only the ultimate preponderance of American strength that dictated an American commander, but also the deep, ineradicable and perhaps justified American mistrust of Brooke's personal commitment to "Overlord".

European operations

The plenary sessions with Churchill and Roosevelt duly ratified the agreement on strategy in the European theatre reached by their military advisers. The intention was confirmed to advance as far north in

Italy as possible in order to weaken the Germany army before "Overlord", and with a view to invading southern France. Meanwhile the bomber offensive against the German economy (Operation "Pointblank") was to be stepped up. In regard to the Far East and Pacific, however, it was not mistrust between allies but the variety of strategic options that caused the problems.

The Far East

This was especially true of Burma. Sir Claude Auchinleck, the Commander-in-Chief in India and at present responsible for Burma operations, found himself – as in the Middle East in 1941 – acting as the unwelcome voice of realism. He had told London that poor rail and road communications, now severely interrupted by floods, necessarily laid tight logistic restrictions on stragety. He recommended a complete cessation of offensive operations until 1944, concentrating in the meantime on improving communications and building up supplies. Churchill re-

acted to this as he had to Auchinleck's similar advice in the Middle East – by writing Auchinleck down as a low-spirited obstructionist. Instead he lent a willing ear to the splendid scenario outlined by Orde Wingate for air-supplied long-range penetration offensives behind the Japanese front in northern Burma; a scenario which would have drawn in much of Allied resources in troops and aircraft and virtually handed over operations in Burma to Wingate himself. The

Prime Minister also strongly favoured Operation "Culverin", a plan for seizing the northern tip of Sumatra in 1944, which he saw as "the 'Torch' of the Indian Ocean". The British Joint Planners favoured a seaborne attack against the Burmese port of Akyab. The Americans simply wanted to re-open a land route between Burma and China; they also saw the Akyab operations as the touchstone of whether the British really meant to lend a hand in 1943 in the war against Japan at all. The British Chiefs-of-Staff had no very clear ideas, except that seaborne operations against Burma would be impossible without draining landing craft and naval forces from the European theatre, which they were determined must not occur. It was finally agreed by the Conference, though somewhat nebulously, that land operations should be pushed on in Upper Burma in order to press the Japanese and bring relief to China, Wingate playing a prominent part; but no conclusions were reached as to further operations.

South-East Asia and the Pacific

However, the Quebec Conference did come to the major decision, originating from a proposal by Churchill, to set up a South-East Asia Command under Vice-Admiral Lord Louis Mountbatten to run the Burma campaign and any other operations in the region. The Commander-in-Chief in India became responsible only for providing the new command's main base and training facilities. The directives of the Allied governments were to reach Mountbatten via the British Chiefs-of-Staff, so that the new organisation became the British equivalent of the American-controlled Pacific and South-West Pacific areas. "Vinegar Joe" Stilwell became Mountbatten's deputy as well as continuing as Chief-of-Staff to Chiang Kai-shek.

With regard to the Pacific, the Conference merely blessed the now agreed American strategy of two separate but converging axes of advance, one under MacArthur via the northern coast of New Guinea and the other under Nimitz via the Gilberts, Marshalls and Carolines, aimed at establishing a base on the Chinese mainland from which an invasion of Japan could be launched. Likewise the British acquiesced without much argument in the American proposal to set the target date for the final defeat of Japan at twelve months after the defeat of Germany.

So once again the two Allies had composed their differences and emerged with agreed formulas of strategy. In particular, if "Overlord" had indeed been in doubt, the British had now committed themselves to it morally and verbally more firmly than before, whatever reservations individuals might still hold.

Nuclear research

However, one of the most portentous decisions reached at Quebec, certainly in the long term, was not even recorded in the Conference proceedings, so secret was it. This was the so-called "Quebec Agreement" between Roosevelt and Churchill over the future of nuclear research and the development of the atom bomb. Up to early 1942 the British had been ahead in terms of original research, thanks to brilliant work done in British universities under the auspices of the Maude Committee in following up a paper drafted in spring 1940 by two German-born physicists at Birmingham University, Professor Rudolf Peierls and Dr Otto Frisch, which had first laid down how an atom bomb might be made. But by 1942 the sheer size of American research resources, especially in terms of experimental equipment, meant that the British lead was being fast overtaken. In July 1942 the British "Tube Alloys" (the codename for nuclear development) Council reported to the Prime Minister that if there were to be a merger between the two countries' efforts, it had better be effected quickly while the British side still had something to offer as part of a bargain. In the ensuing months the British found themselves more and more excluded from American information. In 1943 the Americans reached agreement with the Canadian Government for the entire Canadian output of uranium and the Canadian heavy-water plant, upon which the British themselves had been counting. Moreover, the British themselves, upon investigations, had come to realise that they could not spare the industrial resources in wartime to continue with their own nuclear development. It was therefore inevitable that Britain would have to accept that future research and development must be con-

centrated in the United States, albeit making use of British scientists and the fruits of British work.

Nevertheless the "Quebec Agreement" was reached on terms which really meant that Britain abdicated the hope and intention of becoming a leading independent postwar nuclear power, not only militarily but also industrially:

". . . in view of the heavy burden of production falling upon the United States as a result of a wise division of war effort the British Government recognise that any post-war advantages of an industrial or commercial character shall be dealt with as between the United States and Great Britain on terms to be specified by the President of the United States to the Prime Minister of Great Britain. The Prime Minister expressly disclaims any interest in these industrial and commercial aspects beyond what may be considered by the President of the United States to be fair and just and in harmony with the economic welfare of the world."
(Michael Howard *Grand Strategy* Vol IV)

So even in this uncharted field of the future Britain dwindled to the second rank of power, dependent on American resources and American good will.

△ *Indispensable companions to any great man, the wives of the three political leaders at Quebec. Their presence prompted a social round, which Brooke, for one, did not approve. "These continual lunches, dinners and cocktail parties were a serious interruption to our work. When occupied with continuous conferences, time is required to collect one's thoughts, read papers and write notes."*

CHAPTER 98

KATYN: the burden of guilt

As previously explained, the military situation, as it appeared at the time of the "Quadrant" Conference, was sufficiently hopeful to make the British and the Americans begin to think of the future of the European continent and its balance of power after German military might, which had changed the entire pre-war picture, had been reduced to dust and ashes.

There are two documents to be taken into account in this question. One comes from the pen of a senior American officer whom Robert E. Sherwood, editing the Harry Hopkins papers, could not identify. The other comes from a letter that Churchill sent to Field-Marshal Smuts personally on September 5, 1943.

When Harry Hopkins went to Quebec, he carried with him a note entitled "The Russian position", in which the anonymous American officer gave his views concerning post-war prospects in Europe and the chances of obtaining the help of Russia in the struggle against Japan:

"Russia's post-war position in Europe will be a dominant one. With Germany crushed, there is no power in Europe to oppose her tremendous military forces. It is true that Great Britain is building up a position in the Mediterranean *vis-à-vis* Russia that she may find useful in balancing power in Europe. However, even here she may not be able to oppose Russia unless she is otherwise supported.

"The conclusions from the foregoing are obvious. Since Russia is the decisive factor in the war, she must be given every assistance and every effort must be made to obtain her friendship. Likewise, since without question she will dominate Europe on the defeat of the Axis, it is even more essential to develop and maintain the most friendly relations with Russia.

"*Finally, the most important factor the United States has to consider in relation to Russia is the prosecution of the war in Pacific.* With Russia as an ally in the war against Japan, the war can be terminated in less time and at less expense in life and resources than if the reverse were the case. Should the war in the Pacific have to be carried on with an unfriendly or negative attitude on the part of Russia, the difficulties will be immeasurably increased and the operations might become abortive."

Churchill saw things in much the same light. His old South African friend, disappointed by the results of the Quebec Conference, which slowed down the war in the Mediterranean, cabled him on September 3:

"To the ordinary man it must appear that it is Russia who is winning the war. If this impression continues what will be our post-war world position compared with that of Russia? A tremendous shift in our world status may follow, and will leave Russia the diplomatic master of the world. This is both unnecessary and undesirable, and would have especially bad reactions for the British Commonwealth. Unless we emerge from the war on terms of equality our position will be both uncomfortable and dangerous."

Two days later, Churchill replied "after profound reflection", in a cable outlining eight points. Only the sixth is quoted here because it deals in particular with the question under discussion:

"I think it inevitable that Russia will be the greatest land Power in the world after this war, which will have rid her of two military Powers, Japan and Germany, who in our lifetime have inflicted upon her such heavy defeats. I hope however that the 'fraternal association' of the British Commonwealth and the United States, together with sea- and air-power, may put us on good terms and in a friendly balance with Russia at least for the period of rebuilding. Farther than that I cannot see with mortal eye, and I am not as yet fully informed about the celestial telescopes."

Anti-Russian consensus

So, it is evident that neither the anonymous American officer's memorandum nor the man responsible for British policy were fundamentally opposed to the opinions expressed on February 21, 1943 by General Franco in his letter to Sir Samuel Hoare, at the time British Ambassador in Madrid, on the consequence of the military collapse of the Third Reich. But, in contrast to the report entitled *The*

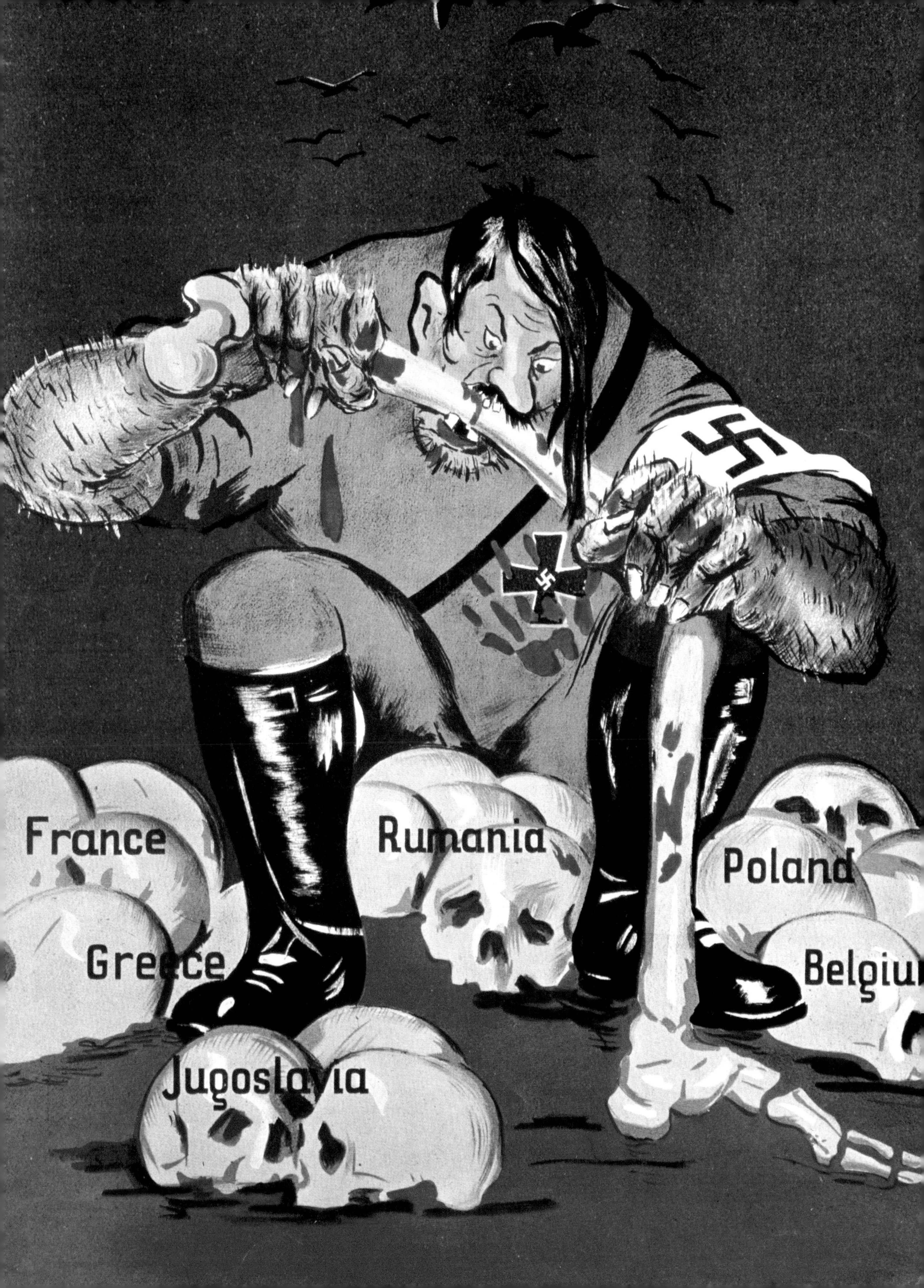
France
Rumania
Poland
Greece
Belgiu
Jugoslavia

position of Russia, Churchill could not so easily accept the upsetting of the balance of power, and took some care to think about easing its most unpleasant consequences. So, in his opinion, after the war it would not be a good policy to loosen the Anglo-American ties which would have helped to win it. On September 6, with this in mind, he spoke to the staff and students of Harvard University, which had just conferred on him an honorary doctorate. He recalled the linguistic, literary, and legal heritage common to the two English-speaking democracies and, speaking beyond his immediate audience, exhorted Great Britain and the United States to strengthen their common purpose even more. In particular, he expressed the wish that the "marvellous" system of the Combined Chiefs-of-Staff Committee would not wind up, once the last shot had been fired.

"Now in my opinion it would be a most foolish and improvident act on the part of our two Governments, or either of them, to break up this smooth-running and immensely powerful machinery the moment the war is over. For our own safety, as well as for the security of the rest of the world, we are bound to keep it working and in running order after the war–probably for a good many years, not only until we have set up some world arrangement to keep the peace, but until we know that it is an arrangement which will really give us that protection we must have from danger and aggression, a protection we have already to seek across two vast world wars."

But President Roosevelt acted on the advice of Harry Hopkins and had no intention of following Churchill's plans. This would mean engaging the United States in a "special relationship" with Great Britain after the war. And so, in his memoirs, Churchill concludes, speaking of the rejection of his suggestion: "Alas, folly has already prevailed!"

Stalin's ill-will

The word "folly" was perhaps an over-exaggeration because Roosevelt and Hopkins did not possess, any more than did Churchill, a crystal ball which would give them some insight into the murky future of the world.

All the same, just like Churchill, Roosevelt had on file a large bundle of letters sent to him by Stalin, beginning on the date when Hitler's attack had destroyed the German-Soviet Non-Aggression Pact. The least that can be said is that neither in the style nor the content of these letters was there any sign which might allow any optimism for the future, even though when he wrote to the White House, Stalin took care to express himself more tactfully than when he wrote to Churchill.

Reading this correspondence Stalin's tone is seen to be distinctly arrogant and sarcastic, with hostile accusation against his allies, statements which are extreme to say the least, an obstinate refusal to take any account of the opinions of others, a completely unconcealed expression of the most unpleasant suspicions, and an insatiable desire for revenge, sharpened by each concession or gift made by his Western partners.

From this time on, it was becoming abundantly clear that post-war relations between the Allies and peaceful collaboration between Moscow, London, and Washington would tend to be difficult, even supposing that the two English-

▽ *The horrifying extent of the Katyn massacre: an aerial view of the bodies, packed in rows like dried fish.*
▷ *The investigation begins. One of the bodies is uncovered under the supervision of Professor Orsōs from the University of Budapest, the Hungarian delegate on the European commission invited by the Germans to visit the Katyn site.*

continued on page 1293

"HONOUR TO THE RED ARMY!"

1. *An 82-mm mortar in action; used against troops in wooded areas, mortar bombs would burst amongst the branches giving an air burst effect.*
2. *Soviet infantry advance into the misty shadows of a Russian wood.*
3. *A Cossack patrol crosses the Don. Cavalry was used until the end of the war for reconnaissance and as mounted infantry.*
4. *A Russian assault group moves into position in a workers' settlement in the northern Caucasus.*

Between the German invasion of Russia in June 1941 and the Allied invasion of Italy in September 1943, the burden of the Allied war effort on the continent of Europe fell squarely on the shoulders of the Russian soldier. Rising above the murderous defeats of the first phase of "Barbarossa" in June–December 1941, the Red Army not only survived as a fighting entity but immediately proved itself to be the foremost instrument of armed resistance to Germany.

One of the greatest mistakes Hitler ever made was to underestimate the grass-root patriotism of the Russian soldier. Even in the weeks of apparent national collapse in 1941, the steadfastness of the Russian troops appalled the men of the Wehrmacht. Abominably led, thrown into the battle in driblets, the Red Army's infantry charged the German machine guns head-on with linked arms, cheering *"Za rodinu, za Stalina"* ("For the

motherland, for Stalin") until the sickened German gunners could hardly bring themselves to fire another shot.

If it was magnificent it was certainly not war, and yet within months the Red Army had gone over to the offensive and was threatening to annihilate the German Army Group "Centre". Only the self-destructive, wide-front strategy insisted on by Stalin, and the slap-dash tactics used during the offensive, robbed the Red Army of victory.

When the Germans attacked again in the summer of 1942 they soon found how much the Red Army had learned since its mauling in 1941. As Army Group "South" drove east to the Volga and south to the Caucasus, the Russians pulled back, refusing to get trapped in vast pockets and conserving their superiority in manpower. And at Stalingrad the incredible endurance and fighting spirit of the Russian soldier were

4

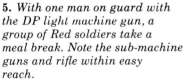

5. *With one man on guard with the DP light machine gun, a group of Red soldiers take a meal break. Note the sub-machine guns and rifle within easy reach.*
6. *The Morozov Cossack cavalry division attacks on the Voronezh front.*
7. *Russian soldiers bringing a mortar into action under fire.*
8. *A Soviet 76-mm gun in position to cover a bridge.*
9. *Czech troops fighting on the Eastern front with an ambulance presented by the Czech community of Canada.*

proved for all time in the vicious hand-to-hand fighting in the shattered ruins of the city.

The Red Army's successes at winter fighting were not caused by the immunity of the Russian soldier to cold, but were the result of sensible equipment. Nothing, however, can detract from the fact that right from the beginning of the war in Russia the men of the Red Army earned themselves a reputation for unbelievable toughness, which impressed even the veteran soldiers of the Wehrmacht.

Even when the Red Army went over to the offensive its losses remained high, owing to the sledgehammer tactics of the front commanders. Yet the Russian soldier was willing to endure this as well. All in all he certainly deserved the propaganda salute of "Honour to the Red Army!"

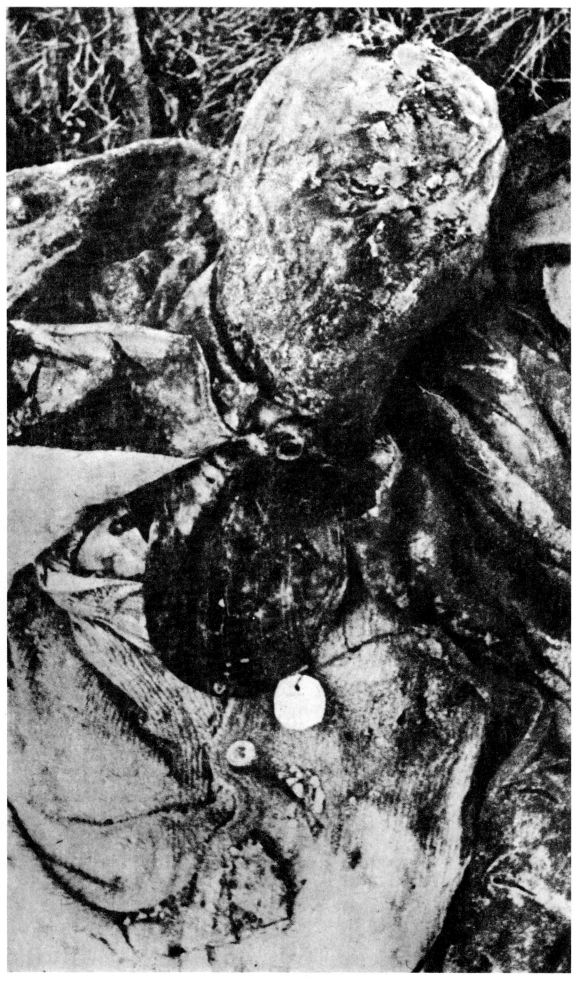

◁ *The body of a chaplain, identified as Jan Leon Zielkowski, still wearing his clerical bands.*
△ *The excavations revealed how the bodies were packed in parallel, stacked rows.*

continued from page 1286

speaking democracies surreptitiously abandoned the great humanitarian principles proclaimed to the world in August 1941 in the Atlantic Charter.

Massacre at Katyn

At this point, should the ghastly charnelhouse of Katyn be recalled? Here, six miles west of Smolensk, on April 13, 1943 the Germans found piled up 12 deep, the mummified bodies of 4,143 Polish officers, all felled by pistol shots in the back of the neck. It has been maintained that when the British and Americans learned of this example of Stalinist ferocity, they should have taken clear warning and had their eyes fully opened to the real nature of Soviet domination. Examination of the facts and the evidence require some modification of this opinion, however.

In fact, at the time neither Churchill nor Roosevelt had a complete dossier on the massacre which would clarify where the responsibility for Katyn lay. This

would come out in 1946 at the international trial in Nuremberg and would be completed in 1952, when a House of Representatives' Committee would carry out an investigation.

Certainly neither one nor the other believed the emphatic statements of Stalin in the least. He told them on April 21, 1943, that Moscow was breaking off relations with the Polish Government-in-Exile. The terms used merit quotation:

"The fact that the anti-Soviet campaign has been started simultaneously in the German and Polish press and follows identical lines is indubitable evidence of contact and collusion between Hitler – the Allies' enemy – and the Sikorski Government in this hostile campaign.

"At a time when the peoples of the Soviet Union are shedding their blood in a grim struggle against Hitler's Germany and bending their energies to defeat the common foe of freedom-loving democratic countries, the Sikorski Government is striking a treacherous blow at the Soviet Union to help Hitler's tyranny."

It seems likely that Churchill never

△ *Found in the winter clothing of Chaplain Zielkowski: a breviary and a miniature altar and rosary, made in the camp at Kozielsk in 1940.*
Overleaf: *The biggest of the seven mass graves at Katyn was found to contain 2,500 bodies in a row, stacked in five layers.*

▷ *The international committee at work, examining the personal effects found on the bodies.*

▽ *Professor Palmieri of Naples dissects a skull. He found that three bullets had been fired into the nape of the neck.*

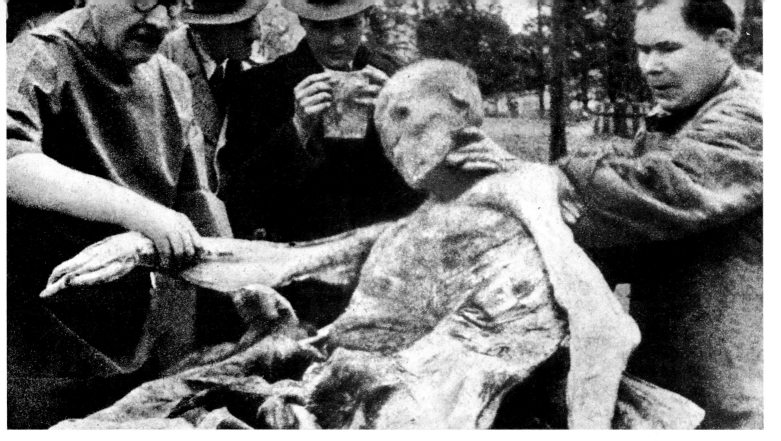

believed the Moscow version of the facts, which blamed the mass murder on the Germans. Perhaps it was the indignation caused by his conclusions on the massacre that was one of the motives which caused him to change his mind on the chances of co-operation between the Stalinist East and the Democratic West. But in the final analysis it had no influence on Anglo-American discussions.

President Roosevelt was the arbiter of the situation, and the many reports which arrived on his desk from the most reliable sources concerning the crimes perpetrated by the Nazis in most of the occupied countries led him to lay the massacre of the Polish officers at their door. Furthermore, perhaps his opinions were confirmed by a report on the massacre sent to him by Averell Harriman, his Ambassador in Moscow, on January 25, 1944, after the Red Army had retaken Smolensk.

On January 15, British and American press correspondents stationed in Moscow had travelled to Katyn to find out for themselves the conclusions reached by the committee appointed by the Soviet Government to clarify this frightful mystery and to hear some witnesses. The American Ambassador was permitted to send his daughter as one of his aides and, on the basis of her information, he formed his opinion. The prudence and intentional vagueness with which he expressed himself is noteworthy:

"None of the members of the group", he

wrote to the State Department, "was qualified to judge the scientific evidence deduced by the autopsies carried out in their presence. They were not allowed to make personal enquiries but they could address definite questions to certain witnesses with whom they were confronted.

"The correspondents made reports on what they had seen without expressing any personal opinion but for some reason the censor withheld their report. The proofs and evidence are not very conclusive but Kathleen [his daughter] and the representative of the Embassy believe that the massacre was probably committed by the Germans."

△ △ *A body is carefully stripped of its clothing. Professor Hajek of Prague examines documents found in the pockets.*
△ *Professor Milosavić of Zagreb tells Professor Buhtz, superintendent of the excavations, of his findings: death by shooting in the neck. Overleaf: One of the mass graves on the site is exposed.*

Le document de Katyn

This was followed by factual appendices supporting this opinion, assembled by Miss Harriman. She, however, recognised frankly and without restraint that they were not very consistent when, as Mrs. Mortimer, she gave evidence on November 12, 1952 before the Investigating Committee of the House of Representatives.

It has also been said that, towards the end of his life, Roosevelt no longer believed that the Katyn massacre had been perpetrated by the Germans. Nevertheless, for evident reasons, he was no more able than Churchill to make a public declaration on the matter.

Soviet responsibilities

However, the historian of today must note that Katyn was introduced, during the summer of 1945, into the charges preferred against the German leaders accused of war crimes before the Nuremberg International Military Tribunal, and that this was done at the request of the Soviet prosecutor. Furthermore, after long discussions, all the zeal of Colonels Pokrovsky and Smirnov could not establish conclusive proof, and the charge of the murder of 11,000 Polish officers was not even mentioned in the Tribunal's verdict on the condemned men.

And so it is valid to conclude that the Soviet accusation did not risk trying to contradict the report which had been signed by 12 forensic experts on April 30, 1943. These latter had been invited to Berlin to visit the charnel-house at Katyn and had been authorised to conduct post-mortems freely on whichever bodies they chose. With the exception of Professor Naville of the University of Geneva, they all belonged to occupied or German satellite countries. Yet, with the exception of a Bulgarian, later acquitted after a pitiful self-accusation before a Sofia court, and a Czech, none of the 12 signatories agreed to go back on the declaration he had made in 1943.

In spite of the accusations made against him by a Communist deputy from Geneva, Professor Naville confirmed his evidence in September 1946, and was completely exonerated by the cantonal authorities of the suspicions that Moscow had tried to throw on his scientific reputation and professional probity. In 1952, Dr. Milosavić, once Director of the Institute of

Criminology and Forensic Medicine of Zagreb, Professor Palmieri of the University of Naples, and Dr. Tramsen, Head of Medical Services of the Royal Danish Navy, deported for acts of resistance by the Gestapo in 1944, maintained their statements before the American Committee of Enquiry, as did Professor Orsōs, of the University of Budapest.

After having examined the bodies, their clothing and the documents found on them, they came to the unanimous conclusion that the crime of Katyn could not be dated later than the beginning of spring 1940. The Russians, on the other hand, claim that the massacre had been perpetrated during August 1941, that is just after the battle in which the Germans overran the entire Smolensk region.

The controversy stifled

These separate opinions, from Europe and from America, are confirmed absolutely independently by the evidence of Colonel van Vliet of the United States Army, in a report dated May 22, 1945. As a prisoner of the Germans he had been taken to the mass graves at Katyn, together with some other prisoners-of-war. He made the following observations which he revealed to nobody before his release:

1. The bodies wore winter uniforms.
2. The victims' boots and clothing were of excellent quality and showed no signs of wear.
3. "This was the way I saw it," continued van Vliet in his own words. "If the Germans had been responsible for the murders, they would have taken place at the time when the Germans invaded the Smolensk area, in other words in July and August 1941, and then the clothes and shoes would have looked much more used because they would have been worn for two years more. I had had personal experience in that connection. I wore out two pairs of shoes in two years while I was a prisoner (and they were army issue!), and those two years represent more or less the difference in time between the German and the Russian claims for the date of the massacre. So I was convinced without any doubt of Soviet guilt."

General Bissel, head of the United States Information Services, stifled the

△ The final page of the report of the European committee, bearing the signatures of its 12 delegates.
◁ ◁ △ Careful scrutiny of documents and personal effects found on the bodies.
◁ ◁ ▽ The bodies of Generals Smorawinski and Bochaterewicz are prepared for proper burial with the honours due to their rank.

▽ Checking the nationality. All were found to be Poles.

Les mŕtvych v Katyne

△ and ▷ *Posters distributed in occupied Europe capitalising on the Katyn atrocity. The grim facts lent themselves readily to anti-Soviet propaganda.*

SI LES SOVIETS GAGNAIENT LA GUERRE !

KATYN PARTOUT

report by Colonel van Vliet and went as far as ordering him to make absolutely no mention to anybody of his observations on the slaughter-house of Katyn. But did the former act on his own initiative, basing his decisions on reasons of major state interest about which he was not competent to judge? It seems reasonable to doubt this and to doubt it very strongly, because such a procedure is at variance with the normal practice of secret services.

Russia avoids the issue

Furthermore, and to bring this macabre question to a close, the extreme wariness shown by Soviet historical writing recently is noteworthy. When dealing with the breaking-off of diplomatic relations between Moscow and the Polish Government-in-Exile, the *Great Patriotic War* tells us simply that the U.S.S.R. could no longer tolerate the campaign of calumny indulged in at her expense by General Sikorski and his colleagues. But the history is very careful not to inform its readers of what these calumnies consisted and the name of Katyn is not even mentioned.

Not only was the question of the massacre removed from the attention of the Nuremberg court, but in Moscow, historians still attempt to remove it from the judgement of history!

CHAPTER 99
Cairo prelude

In the last two weeks of November and the first week of December 1943 took place two linked summit conferences in Cairo and Teheran which, taken together, decided the strategic shape of the remaining stages of the Second World War and traced the first vague outlines of the postwar world. For the first time too the Soviet and Chinese-Nationalist leaders were drawn into joint discussions with both the United States President and the British Prime Minister.

Like earlier purely Anglo-American summits, Cairo and Teheran witnessed the paradox of cordial personal relations between heads of state and between military staffs coupled with mistrust and manoeuvring behind the smiles because of differing national attitudes and interests. The British, as before Casablanca, had wanted there to be a preliminary exclusively Anglo-American summit in order to agree a basic grand-strategic package to put to Stalin. But Roosevelt, again as before Casablanca, wished to avoid giving any impression of an Anglo-American line-up that left the Russians on one side, for his ideas had further burgeoned with regard to a global postwar settlement, and he wanted to win Stalin's support for them. After some highly complicated correspondence between all the parties in order to find a *locale* and evolve arrangements agreeable to everyone, it was decided after all to hold an Anglo-American summit in Cairo, into the middle of which would be sandwiched a tripartite conference with Stalin in the Iranian capital Teheran; Stalin being unable to travel further because he was conducting major offensives against the German army in the East. Yet disagreements rumbled on between Churchill and Roosevelt. The President wanted to invite a Russian military observer to Cairo, but this was successfully resisted by the Prime Minister; the President also wanted Chiang Kai-shek, the Chinese leader, to take part in the conference, this being unwillingly accepted by the Prime Minister. But Churchill still desired that at least he and Roosevelt might meet privately in Malta before the main conference opened with Chiang among those present. This the President refused.

On November 12 Churchill set sail from Plymouth in the battlecruiser *Renown*, taking with him the American ambassador John Winant, as well as the Chiefs-of-Staff and Joint Planners. His daughter Sarah served as his ADC. As he wrote in his war memoirs: "I was feeling far from well, as a heavy cold and sore throat were reinforced by the consequences of inoculations against typhoid and cholera. I stayed in bed for several

▽ *Cheers for Churchill on his arrival at Alexandria on the* Renown. *On the journey he had called at Algiers where he invested Generals Eisenhower and Alexander with a special version of the North Africa ribbon bearing the numbers 1 and 8, signifying the two British armies in the campaign.*

△ △ *Generalissimo Chiang Kai-shek with Sir George Cunningham, the Governor of the North Western Frontier Province, visiting Jamrud Fort in the Khyber Pass.*

△ *Lord Louis Mountbatten joined Chiang Kai-shek and his wife when they visited a training centre in eastern India.*

▷ *With their son Major Chiang Wei-Kuo, the Generalissimo and Mme. Chiang watch an artillery demonstration given by American-trained and equipped Chinese troops.*

days." The new battleship *Iowa* raised anchor in Hampton Roads at 0001 hours next morning with Roosevelt, Admiral Leahy, Harry Hopkins and the Joint Chiefs-of-Staff aboard. Leahy records:

"President Roosevelt had no superstitions about the figure '13', which many people regard as an ill omen, but he did share the sailors' superstition that Friday is an unlucky day on which to start a long voyage. So the huge USS *Iowa* remained at her berth Friday night, November 12, 1943, and did not get under way for Oran, first leg of the trip to Cairo and Teheran, until 1201 am Saturday, November 13."

In Oran Roosevelt was able to confer with Eisenhower about operations in Italy before flying on to Cairo; Churchill had already paused in Malta likewise to confer with Eisenhower and Alexander.

The leaders assemble

The Cairo Conference ("Sextant") took place at Giza, where the Sphinx provided an object lesson to the participants on how to smile and yet remain inscrutable. As at Casablanca the VIPs were housed in luxurious villas amid palm-shaded gardens; the staffs were hardly less comfortable in the Mena House Hotel. Admiral Mountbatten, the Allied Supreme Commander South-East Asia, had flown in, as had his deputy "Vinegar Joe" Stilwell, also Chief-of-Staff to Chiang Kai-shek, whom Stilwell customarily referred to as "the Peanut". In the British delegation opinions on Chiang varied. The Prime Minister was impressed by his calm, reserved, and efficient personality. Sir Alan Brooke, however, was less impressed. "The Generalissimo", he wrote with the background knowledge of a keen naturalist, "reminded me of a cross between a pine-marten and a ferret. A shrewd, foxy sort of face. Evidently with no grasp of war in its larger aspects, but determined to get the best of all bargains."

British irritation at the Chinese presence

More important from the British point of view, Chiang's presence upset the order of priority of subjects to be discussed. The British were concerned above all with the question of the Mediterranean and its relationship with "Overlord". They had in mind further operations in Italy and in the Aegean: action to induce Turkey to enter the war. But instead, after item one on the agenda–"Reaffirm Overall objective, Overall Strategic Concept and Basic undertakings . . ."–it was South-East Asia that came next, with "Overlord" and the Mediterranean third. South-East Asia also took up a great deal of conference time. As Churchill testily wrote in his memoirs:

"All hope of persuading Chiang and his wife to go and see the Pyramids and enjoy themselves until we returned from Teheran fell to the ground, with the result that Chinese business occupied first instead of last place at Cairo."

Operation "Buccaneer"

When the first plenary session of the Cairo Conference opened in the President's villa on Tuesday, November 23, 1943, the topic for discussion was therefore South-East Asia in regard to China. Chiang Kai-shek did not stint himself with demands. He wanted an airlift of 10,000 tons over "the Hump" into China from India every month, an allied land offensive in 1944 aimed as far as Mandalay, and a naval operation to coincide with ground operations. In Chiang's words, "the success of

the operation in Burma depended, in his opinion, not only on the strength of the naval forces established in the Indian Ocean, but also on the simultaneous co-ordination of naval action with the land operations." The "naval action" being considered by the British and American Chiefs-of-Staff was Operation "Buccaneer", an amphibious attack on the Andaman Islands, which had replaced the now abandoned "Culverin" (an attack on northern Sumatra). The United States President, determined to bring aid to Chiang, was strongly in favour of "Buccaneer"; the American Chiefs-of-Staff, falling in with their President's view, had submitted a paper before the Conference which urged that "Buccaneer" be mounted as soon as possible and that the Combined Chiefs-of-Staff direct Mountbatten to submit plans for approval. But the British were by no means so keen. They considered that the final strategy for defeating Japan should be drawn up before deciding on an incidental operation like "Buccaneer", which might or might not fit in with that strategy. They also feared that "Buccaneer's" need for landing craft would have adverse repercussions on the Mediterranean and "Overlord". This question proved in fact to be the crux of the whole "Sextant" conference.

Agreement with Chiang

British and Americans alike swiftly rejected Chiang's demand for a monthly airlift of 10,000 tons, pointing out that there were insufficient aircraft both for that purpose and for sustaining land operations in Burma. Mountbatten made it clear to the Chinese also that an advance to Mandalay would be beyond his strength, especially in aircraft. Chiang settled for a lift over "the Hump" of 8,900 tons a month for the next six months, and for the already agreed offensive in northern Burma with the limited objective of gaining a line Indaw–Katha. But "Buccaneer" remained a controversial issue. The British succeeded in persuading the Conference to delay a final decision on it until it could be placed in the world picture of amphibious operations. However, as John Ehrman points out, suspending a decision did not mean that it was not still discussed. Throughout the Conference, therefore, discussion of the far

▽ "Madame was a study in herself; a queer character in which sex and politics seemed to predominate, both being used to achieve her ends." So Brooke described Mme. Chiang when he met her at Cairo. She acted as her husband's interpreter, and Brooke added after the war: "She was the only woman amongst a very large gathering of men and was determined to bring into action all the charms nature had blessed her with." Here she is seen apparently achieving her ends with Churchill.

Training the Chinese army

△ Weapon training under the eyes of an American instructor. Chinese troops practise the variations of bayonet drill.
◁ A U.S. Colonel explains artillery tactics to a group of Chinese officers.
▷ △ The mechanics of a medium machine gun are demonstrated by a U.S. captain.
▷ ▷ △ △ The officers and N.C.O.s of a training establishment in Kwangsi are addressed by Chiang Kai-shek in his capacity as head of state and C.-in-C. of China and her forces.

▷ ▷ △ Assisted by an interpreter, a captain briefs a Chinese officer on range practice. Note the China-Burma-India badge on the American's shirt.
▷ Curtiss P-40 Warhawks, sporting their Flying Tiger insignia under guard on their Chinese airstrip.

East and of the Mediterranean and "Overlord" proceeded day by day in parallel sessions with much overlap.

The British, mindful of current setbacks in the Aegean and, as they saw it, of missed opportunities in the Balkans during 1943, proposed further Mediterranean operations even at the expense of delaying "Overlord" from May to July 1944. Their strategy was well summarised by the Prime Minister: ". . . Rome in January, Rhodes in February, supplies to the Yugoslavs, a settlement of the Command arrangements and the opening of the Aegean, subject to the outcome of an approach to Turkey; all preparations for 'Overlord' to go ahead full steam within the framework of the foregoing policy for the Mediterranean." The American Chiefs-of-Staff did not, as might have been expected, pounce on this fresh British plea in favour of the Mediterranean, but accepted their ally's proposals as a basis for discussion with the Russians, subject to one proviso: that the Rhodes and Aegean operations "would in no way interfere with the carrying-out of 'Buccaneer'." General Marshall even expressed willingness to see "Overlord" postponed if that were necessary in order to make "Buccaneer" possible, and he revealed that President Roosevelt took a personal interest in the operation. In fact, during the conference Roosevelt went behind his British ally's back to promise Chiang that "Buccaneer" would take place. As John Ehrman writes: "On the eve of the Teheran Conference, the position seemed to be that the Americans (given the appropriate Russian pressure) might accept the British strategy for Europe, if the British would accept the Americans' strategy for south-east Asia."

A supreme commander?

The old question of the right relationship between "Overlord" and the Mediterranean came up at Cairo in a novel form. The United States Joint Chiefs-of-Staff submitted a long and elaborate paper arguing that a single Allied supreme commander "be designated at once to command all United Nations operations against Germany from the Mediterranean and the Atlantic under direction from the Combined Chiefs-of-Staff", in other words, much as in Nato today. They also wanted a single "strategic air force commander" to direct both Bomber Command and the U.S. 8th Air Force. The remainder of their proposals sketched a tidy organisational pyramid of the kind also now familiar in Nato. However, the British Prime Minister and Chiefs-of-Staff reacted vigorously against the American proposals, which they believed were clumsy and would produce confusion. Even Marshal Foch in the Great War had only been in command of the Western and Italian fronts, not the Aegean and Balkan, they pointed out. In a cogently argued memorandum the British Chiefs-of-Staff said that because total war was a matter of politics and economics as much as of purely military decisions, "it seems clear that the Supreme Commander . . . will have to consult both the United States and the British Governments on almost every important question. In fact, it boils down to this, that he will only be able to make a decision without reference to high authority on comparatively minor and strictly military questions, such as the transfer of one or two divisions, or a few squadrons of aircraft, or a few scores of landing-craft, from one of his many fronts to another. He will thus be an extra and unnecessary link in the chain of command." They could see no reasons for making a "revolutionary change" in the existing and well-tried machinery of Allied command, let alone by such cumbrous means as inserting a whole new command layer.

Churchill, in a paper of his own, deftly tackled the political aspects of the American scheme. Since in May 1944 Britain would be fielding larger forces than the U.S.A. on all fronts against Germany, it "would therefore appear that the Supreme Command should go to a British officer. I should be very reluctant, as head of His Majesty's Government, to place such an invidious responsibility upon a British officer." Moreover, he went on, a Supreme Commander, be he British or American, who took a major decision which one or other Allied government believed seriously damaged its interests, "would therefore be placed in an impossible position. Having assumed before the whole world the responsibility of pronouncing and being overruled by one Government or the other, he would have little choice but to resign. This might bring about a most serious crisis in the harmonious and happy relations hitherto maintained between our two Governments."

◁ *A fund-raising poster for China. She had suffered longer than any other ally in her war with Japan, and in 1942 she seemed to be the only one to have scored any successes.*
▽ *Admiral of the Fleet Sir Andrew Cunningham. On the death of Admiral Pound in late 1943, Cunningham became First Sea Lord.*
▽▽ *Mountbatten with General Joseph W. Stilwell. Stilwell had been in charge of the training of Chinese units and their operations in northern Burma, but Mountbatten was made Supreme Allied Commander, South-East Asia.*

CHAPTER 100
The Teheran conference

In Teheran, Stalin and Churchill took up residence in the adjacent Russian and British embassies, which were protected by a single perimeter under British and Russian guard. But Roosevelt, in the American embassy, lay a mile or so distant, entailing the inconvenience, if not the danger, of mutual journeyings to meet in session. Molotov, the Russian foreign minister, suggested that Roosevelt come to live in an annexe to the Russian embassy; Churchill backed the idea; and the President and his staff duly moved in. With hindsight and knowledge of Russian skills in "bugging", it may be surmised that Molotov was not only prompted by emotions of hospitality and concern for the President's safety; certainly the Russian delegation was to show itself acutely aware of the differences over strategy and policy between the British and Americans. Harry Hopkins wrote:

"The servants who made their beds and cleaned their rooms were all members of the highly efficient NKVD, the secret police, and expressive bulges were plainly discernible in the hip pockets under their white coats. It was a nervous time for Michael F. Reilly and his own White House secret service men, who were trained to suspect *everybody* and who did not like to admit into the President's presence anyone who was armed with as much as a gold toothpick."

On the afternoon of November 28 the first plenary session of the Teheran Conference ("Eureka") opened in the Russian embassy under, as with all the sessions, President Roosevelt's chairmanship. Flanked by Molotov and Marshal Voroshilov, Stalin was resplendent in a uniform, according to Lord Moran, "that looks as if it has not been worn before, and gives the impression that it has been specially designed for the occasion. It looks, too, as if the tailor has put on it a shelf on each shoulder, and on it dumped a lot of gold lace with white stars. And there is a broad red stripe down the trousers, which are immaculately creased. All this is crowned with a dreadful hat, smothered with gold braid." Gaudily uniformed or not, Stalin dominated the conference from the start. In his very opening statement he announced that after Germany's defeat Russia would join in the war against Japan, a development that at once threw Anglo-American grand strategy in the Pacific and Far East into the melting-pot.

Churchill's ideas

Churchill followed by putting forward the British concept for the war against Germany: "Overlord" in the late spring or the summer of 1944, to be undertaken by 35 strong divisions, of which 16 would be British; the capture of Rome and an advance to the Pisa–Rimini line, with the option of advancing later either into southern France or north-eastward towards the Danube; an attempt to bring Turkey into the war, followed by the capture of the Dodecanese. Hereupon Stalin moved in masterfully by cross-examining Churchill not only about the details of these operations, but also about the depth of the British commitment to launch "Overlord". In the first place he wanted to know the proportion of Allied land forces to be allotted to "Overlord" and the Mediterranean. Churchill confirmed that "Overlord" would have 35 "very strong" divisions, leaving 22 in the Mediterranean region. After questioning the Prime Minister further about the present state of plans for invading southern France and the number of divisions thought necessary for the support of Turkey and the capture of the Dodecanese (should Turkey enter the war), Stalin proceeded to lay down unequivocally his own conception of the right strategy for the Western Allies. According to the conference record:

"Marshal Stalin thought it would be a mistake to disperse forces by sending part to Turkey and elsewhere, and part to southern France. The best course would be to make 'Overlord' the basic operation for 1944 and, once Rome had been captured, to send all available forces in Italy to southern France. These forces could then join hands with the 'Overlord' forces when the invasion was launched. France was the weakest spot on the German front. He himself did not expect Turkey to enter the war."

◁ A new angle on the Teheran story. Cameramen cluster to get their pictures at a press reception. Churchill complained afterwards that the arrangements for his arrival provided "no kind of defence against two or three determined men with pistols or a bomb."

"The Big Three" as the world saw them. With Molotov and Eden in the background they were directing the war, and seeking the peace. But according to Brooke it was a case of "the more politicians you put together to settle the prosecution of the war, the longer you postpone its conclusion."

In a further exchange with Churchill, Stalin agreed that it was worthwhile taking the Dodecanese if this involved only three or four divisions, but "repeated that 'Overlord' was a very serious operation and that it was better to help it by invading the South of France . . ."

Stalin's influence

All this was congenial enough to Roosevelt, who now suggested that Stalin's suggestion of invading southern France two months before D-day should be examined by the military experts. Stalin added:

". . . the experience gained by the Soviets during the last two years of campaigning was that a big offensive, if undertaken from only one direction, rarely yielded results. The better course was to launch offensives from two or more directions simultaneously . . . He suggested that this principle might well be applied to the problem under discussion."

Thus, to the surprise of both Americans and British, Stalin had placed all the weight of the Soviet Union and his own formidable personality behind the American strategy of concentrating on "Overlord" and abjuring wider commitments in the Mediterranean and Aegean. Churchill, however, did not agree with them and he resorted to bluster about the size of British-Empire forces in the Mediterranean area:

". . . he did not disagree in principle with Marshal Stalin. The suggestions he [Churchill] had made for action in Yugoslavia and in respect of Turkey did not, in his view, conflict in any way with that general conception. At the same time, he wished it to be placed on record that he could not in any circumstances agree to sacrifice the activities of the armies in the Mediterranean, which included 20 British and British-controlled divisions, merely in order to keep the exact date of the 1st May for 'Overlord' . . ."

Brooke cross-examined

President Roosevelt now suggested that the question should be referred to the staffs for study and report. This vital session took place next day, when Marshal Voroshilov, following Stalin's line,

unmistakably sided with the Americans against the British. Sir Alan Brooke found himself the victim at Voroshilov's hands of the kind of suspicious cross-examination about the sincerity of the British commitment to "Overlord" that he had been forced to endure from his American colleagues at earlier summit conferences.

"Marshal Voroshilov said he understood from General Marshall that the United States High Command and United States Government considered 'Overlord' to be an operation of the first importance. He said he would like to know whether Sir Alan Brooke considered this to be an operation of the first importance; whether he both thought the operation was necessary and that it must be carried out, or whether, alternatively, it might be replaced by another operation if Turkey came into the war."

Voroshilov's arguments

When Brooke answered that Mediterranean operations were designed to ensure "Overlord's" success, Voroshilov did not disagree, but insisted that any such operations must be secondary to "Overlord" and not compete with it. He went on:

". . . the suggestion made yesterday by Marshal Stalin was that, at the same time as the operation in Northern France, operations should be undertaken in South-ern France. Operations in Italy and elsewhere in the Mediterranean must be considered of secondary importance, because, from those areas, Germany could not be attacked directly with the Alps in the way. Italy . . . offered great possibilities for defence. Defences should be organised there with the minimum of troops. The remaining troops would be used for the South of France in order to attack the enemy from two sides."

Voroshilov added that "Marshal Stalin did not insist on an operation against the South of France, but that he did insist that the operation against the North of France should take place in the manner and on the date already agreed upon".

Stalin and Churchill

That afternoon the second plenary session of the conference saw Stalin press even more strongly the Russian case for total concentration on "Overlord". Firstly, he wanted to know the name of the Allied supreme commander for the operation; an embarrassing question since the American proposal at Cairo for a super supremo had put the former appointment in the melting-pot. Roosevelt answered that a staff officer with an Anglo-American staff had already brought plans and preparations for "Overlord" to an advanced stage. But Stalin, justifiably enough, observed that the commander might want to alter

such plans, and should therefore be appointed at once so he could become responsible for the planning and execution of the operation. It was agreed that this appointment should be made within two weeks and the Russians informed of the name of the new supreme commander. In this case too, therefore, Stalin's intervention proved decisive.

When in the same plenary session Churchill tried yet again to make a case for the British Mediterranean strategy, Stalin simply ploughed on remorselessly:

"In his view there were three main matters to be decided. First, the date of the operation ['Overlord'] should be determined. This should be some time in May and no later. Secondly, Operation 'Overlord' should be supported by a landing in the South of France . . . He regarded the assault on the South of France as a supporting operation which would be definitely helpful to 'Overlord'. The capture of Rome and other operations in the Mediterranean could only be regarded as diversions.

"The third matter to be decided was the appointment of a Commander-in-Chief for the 'Overlord' operation. He would like to see this appointment made before the conclusion of the present conference. If this was not possible, at least within a week."

Churchill, still game, brought up the question of available landing-craft in relation to the timings of "Overlord", the invasion of southern France and "Buc-

caneer", and put in a last plea for his favourite Aegean and Turkish strategy. On his suggestion, amended by Roosevelt, it was agreed to refer the subsidiary operations to an *ad hoc* military committee (in fact the Combined Chiefs-of-Staff) which was to submit detailed recommendations for approval. But Stalin, like the Americans before him, was now deeply suspicious of the sincerity of the British belief in "Overlord". At the close of the session, according to the British official record:

"Marshal Stalin said . . . he wished to pose a very direct question to the Prime Minister about 'Overlord'. Did the Prime Minister and the British Staffs really believe in 'Overlord'?

"The Prime Minister replied that, provided the conditions previously stated for 'Overlord' were to obtain when the time came, he firmly believed it would be our stern duty to hurl across the Channel against the Germans every sinew of our strength."

British isolation

The British sense of isolation was enhanced by President Roosevelt's own conduct since arriving in Teheran. Churchill relates in his memoirs how he, Churchill, was led at this juncture to seek a personal interview with Stalin on account of the fact that "the President

was in private contact with Marshal Stalin and dwelling at the Soviet Embassy, and he had avoided ever seeing me alone since we left Cairo, in spite of our hitherto intimate relations and the way our vital affairs were interwoven." In this interview, which took place on Churchill's 69th birthday, the Prime Minister sought to destroy "the false idea" forming in Stalin's mind "that", to put it shortly, "Churchill and the British Staff mean to stop 'Overlord' if they can, because they want to invade the Balkans instead". Churchill argued that if Roosevelt could be persuaded to call off Operation "Buccaneer" in the Indian Ocean, there would be enough landing-craft both for the Mediterranean and a "punctual" (*sic*) "Overlord". And yet, given Churchill's predilections earlier in 1943 for a major Anglo-American effort to bring about a collapse of the German position in the Balkans, and given also the bitter regrets Sir Alan Brooke was confiding to his diary only a month before the Teheran Conference about the chances missed for achieving this, was Stalin's mistrust unjustified?

Agreement is reached on future strategy

At four o'clock that afternoon the final plenary session ratified the recommendations agreed after exhaustive argument by the military committee in the morning:

"(a) That we should continue to advance in Italy to the Pisa–Rimini line. (This means that the 68 LST's which are due to be sent from the Mediterranean to the United Kingdom for 'Overlord' must be kept in the Mediterranean until 15th January.)

"(b) That an operation shall be mounted against the South of France on as big a scale as landing-craft will permit. For planning purposes D-day to be the same as 'Overlord' D-day.

"(c)... that we will launch 'Overlord' in May, in conjunction with a supporting operation against the South of France..."

The military committee reported, however, that they were unable to reach agreement about operations in the Aegean until they received fresh instructions from the President and Prime Minister.

Thus, thanks to Stalin, the Western

Allies had finally agreed on their strategy against Germany in 1944. In military terms Teheran had been Stalin's conference all the way. Sir Alan Brooke, by now a connoisseur of politicians at war, later recorded his appreciation of Stalin's qualities:

"During this meeting and the subsequent ones we had with Stalin, I rapidly grew to appreciate the fact that he had a military brain of the highest calibre. Never once in any of his statements did he make any strategic error, nor did he ever fail to appreciate all the implications of a situation with a quick and unerring eye. In this respect he stood out compared with his two colleagues. Roosevelt never made any great pretence of being a strategist

Two views of the Allies.
◁ *A Soviet poster illustrating a quote by Stalin: "The Red Army with the armies of our Allies will break the back of the Fascist beast."*
△ *A German poster displayed in Poland: "The German soldier is the guarantor of victories." Here Russia becomes a ravening wolf, the American eagle a balding vulture, and Britain (perfidious Albion) a snake.*

and left either Marshall or Leahy to talk for him. Winston, on the other hand, was more erratic, brilliant at times, but too impulsive and inclined to favour unsuitable plans without giving them the preliminary deep thought they required."

It may be that Stalin so strongly urged concentration on "Overlord" at the expense of Italy and the eastern Mediterranean because Russia as a great land power had a natural affinity with America in preferring a massive offensive proceeding along one major axis, in contrast to the British preference for opportunistic, peripheral and relatively small-scale operations. Nevertheless, the decisions taken at Teheran at Stalin's instigation, by shepherding the Western Allies away from the Balkans and making it less likely than ever that the Anglo-American army in Italy would eventually advance northeastward towards the Danube, also paved the way for the unhindered extension of Russian dominion over Rumania, Hungary, Bulgaria and Yugoslavia.

Political considerations

Although no far-reaching political decisions were reached at Teheran, Stalin proved hardly less the master in this sphere than in the purely military. In particular, his ruthless and farsighted sense of Russia's postwar interests contrasted with Roosevelt's naïve idealism and goodwill. Much of the political talk took place informally at mealtimes, or in private à deux–Roosevelt courted Stalin behind Churchill's back, Churchill courted Stalin behind Roosevelt's back. After dinner on the opening night of the conference, Churchill led Stalin to a sofa and suggested that they should talk about the postwar world. Stalin agreed, and proceeded to outline a profound fear of Germany's capacity for recovery, citing her prewar resurgence despite the Versailles Treaty. When Churchill asked him how soon he expected such a recovery, Stalin answered: "Within fifteen to twenty years." The Prime Minister remarked:

". . . Our duty is to make the world safe for at least fifty years by German disarmament, by preventing rearmament, by supervision of German factories, by forbidding all aviation, and by territorial changes of a far-reaching character. It all comes back to the question whether Great Britain, the United States, and the USSR can keep a close friendship and supervise Germany in their mutual interest."

Postwar problems: the fate of Germany

When Stalin noted that control of this kind had failed after the last war, Churchill suggested that Prussia should be dealt with more harshly than the rest of Germany, and be isolated and reduced, while Bavaria might join Austria and Hungary in a broad, harmless Danubian confederation. But Stalin commented, "All very good, but insufficient."

The topic of postwar Germany came up for formal discussion at the very last plenary session of the Conference on December 1. Roosevelt put forward a plan to divide her into five self-governing parts, plus two areas–Kiel–Hamburg and the Ruhr/Saar industrial regions–under direct United Nations control. Churchill said again that the most important thing was to isolate and weaken Prussia; he believed Roosevelt's five independent German states would be too small to be viable, and that they should be attached to larger non-German groupings. In particular he put forward his idea of a Danubian confederation including southern Germany, whose population he reckoned to be less ferocious than the Prussians. However, in Stalin's estimation, north and south Germans, and Austrians, were equally ferocious. He expressed the fear that Germans would come to dominate Churchill's proposed Danubian confederation, and therefore he wanted there to be no more large combinations in Europe once Germany was broken up. The Germans themselves, even if split up, would always seek to re-unite themselves, a process Stalin thought must be neutralised by economic measures and if necessary by force. Churchill then asked Stalin if he contemplated a Europe of disjointed little states with no large units; a good question. According to Churchill's memoirs, Stalin replied that "he was speaking of Germany not Europe. Poland and France were large States, Rumania and Bulgaria were small States. But Germany should at all costs be broken up so that she could not reunite." Finally it was agreed to set up a special three-power committee under the European Advisory Commission to study the matter.

Déclaration

Nous, LE PRESIDENT DES ETATS-UNIS D'AMERIQUE, LE PREMIER MINISTRE BRITANNI-QUE, ET LE CHEF DU GOUVERNEMENT DE L'UNION SOVIETIQUE, VENONS DE CONFERER PENDANT QUATRE JOURS EN CETTE CAPITALE DE NOTRE ALLIÉ L'IRAN, ET AVONS DEFINI ET CONFIRME NOTRE POLITIQUE COMMUNE.

Nous affirmons notre résolution d'assurer la colla-boration de nos peuples dans la guerre comme dans la paix qui suivra.

EN CE QUI CONCERNE LA GUERRE: les Etats-Majors de nos trois pays ont participé à nos débats communs et nous avons tracé de concert nos plans destinés à assurer la destruction des forces armées allemandes. Nous avons abouti à un complet accord en ce qui con-cerne l'envergure et la synchronisation des opérations qui seront déclenchées de l'est, de l'ouest et du sud.

L'accord auquel nous avons abouti ici garantit notre victoire.

EN CE QUI CONCERNE LA PAIX: nous sommes certains que la concorde qui règne entre nous conduira à une paix durable. Nous sommes entièrement conscients de la responsabilité suprême qui nous incombe, de même qu'à toutes les Nations Unies: celle de bâtir une paix qui sera appuyée de plein gré par la majorité écrasante des peuples de la terre, une paix qui bannira le fléau et l'horreur de la guerre pour de nombreuses géné-rations.

Nous avons examiné avec nos conseillers diploma-tiques les problèmes de l'avenir. Nous ferons appel à la coopération et la participation active de tous les pays, grands et petits, dont les peuples comme nos propres peuples se consacrent de tout leur coeur et de toute leur volonté à la suppression de la tyrannie et de l'esclavage, de l'oppression et de l'intolérance. Nous les accueillerons, à mesure qu'ils choisiront de nous rejoindre, au sein de la famille mondiale des nations démocratiques.

Nulle puissance au monde ne saurait nous empêcher de détruire les armées allemandes sur terre, les sous-marins allemands en mer, les usines de guerre alle-mandes par la voie des airs.

Notre attaque sera implacable et d'une vigueur sans cesse accrue.

A L'ISSUE DE NOS CORDIAUX ENTRETIENS, NOUS ATTENDONS AVEC CONFIANCE LE JOUR OU TOUS LES PEUPLES DE LA TERRE POURRONT VIVRE LIBRE-MENT, A L'ABRI DE LA TYRANNIE, SELON LEURS DESIRS RESPECTIFS ET SELON LEUR CONSCIENCE.

Nous sommes venus ici pleins d'espoir et de résolu-tion. Nous repartons unis par l'amitié, la volonté et la communauté de nos buts.

Franklin D. Roosevelt
J. Staline
Winston S. Churchill

SIGNE A TEHERAN LE IER DECEMBRE 1943

PUBLIÉ PAR L'OFFICE D'INFORMATION DE GUERRE DES ETATS-UNIS

Poland

Tightly linked to these questions of the postwar anatomy of Germany and Stalin's anxiety over a revived German threat to Russia's western frontier was the question of Poland. Churchill brought the topic up unofficially during his conversation with the Soviet leader after dinner on the first night of the conference, proposing that the three powers should agree future Polish frontiers between themselves and put the result to the Poles. He suggested that Poland might sidestep westwards, giving up territory in the east to Russia in exchange for German territory; an idea which, in Churchill's words, "pleased Stalin". But postwar Poland, like postwar Germany, did not figure in official discussions until the final plenary session on December 1. Roosevelt opened the topic by expressing the hope that the Soviet and Polish governments would resume diplomatic relations (broken off by the Soviet Union because the Polish Government-in-exile in London had associated itself with the German claim that the Polish officers whose corpses had been found at Katyn had been murdered by the Russians). Churchill reminded his hearers of the importance to Britain of Poland's future, since Britain had originally gone to war on her behalf. He repeated his suggestion that Poland should be sidestepped westwards and reminded Stalin of his own remark earlier that he would not object if Poland reached the Oder. Stalin, however, now shrewdly drew a distinction between discussing the frontiers of a future Poland and discussing a future Polish government. According to Churchill's account, Stalin went on:

"Russia, even more than other States, was interested in good relations with Poland, because for her it was a question of the security of her frontiers. Russia was in favour of the reconstruction, development, and expansion of Poland mainly at the expense of Germany. But he separated Poland from the Polish Government-in-exile. He had broken off relations with the Polish Government-in-exile, not on account of caprice, but because it had joined with Hitler in slanderous propaganda against Russia. He would like to have a guarantee that the Polish Government in exile would not kill Partisans, but, on the contrary, would urge the Poles to fight the Germans ... He would welcome any Polish Government which would take such active measures, and he would be glad to renew relations with them. But he was by no means sure that the Polish Government-in-exile was ever likely to become the sort of Government it ought to be."

New frontiers

In this statement were all the essential clues to the policy Stalin was to pursue towards Poland in the coming years, and which would reduce her to a Russian satellite. At Teheran, however, neither western leader challenged Stalin's comments about the Polish Government-in-exile or seemed to perceive their significance. Instead the discussion turned to Poland's future frontiers. After much consultation of maps and dispute as to the exact course of the Curzon Line of 1920, fixing the Russo-Polish frontier, the three leaders and their advisers agreed to a formula devised by Churchill that "it was thought in principle that the home of the Polish State and nation should be in between the so-called Curzon Line and the line of the Oder, including, for Poland, East Prussia and Oppeln, but the actual line required careful study . . ." Stalin's only caveat was to state that Russia also wanted Königsberg. All this was duly to come to pass.

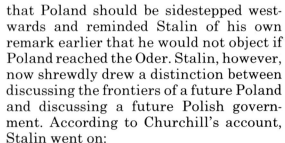

▽ Churchill's 69th birthday, which on November 30 came as finale to the Teheran conference. For Churchill it was "a memorable occasion in my life. On my right sat the President of the United States on my left the master of Russia. Together we controlled a large preponderance of the naval and three-quarters of all the air forces in the world, and could direct armies of nearly twenty millions of men."

Roosevelt's suggestions for world peace

At a private meeting on November 29 with Stalin and Molotov, Roosevelt had unveiled his ideas for a world peace-keeping organisation after the war which would avoid the built-in weaknesses of the League of Nations created by his predecessor President Woodrow Wilson. The preservation of peace would be entrusted to the "Four Policemen": the Soviet Union, the United States, Great Britain and China. But Stalin, more realistic than Roosevelt about the status of Chiang Kai-shek's China as a great power, did not respond to the President's visionary scheme. He doubted whether China would be very powerful after the war; he thought that European states would in any case resent being policed by China. Instead he suggested regional committees for Europe and the Far East, the Soviet Union, the United States and Britain being members of both. This, as Roosevelt acknowledged, tied in with a similar idea of Churchill's, although the Prime Minister wanted a supreme United Nations Council as well (an item which Roosevelt omitted to pass on to Stalin). But Roosevelt went on to tell the Soviet leader that the American Congress would be unwilling to sanction American participation in an exclusively European committee, which might demand the despatch of American troops to Europe. When Stalin pointed out that the same objection applied to the President's own concept of the "Four Policemen", Roosevelt, in an unguarded admission potentially dangerous for the future, answered that he had only considered committing American air and sea power; it would be up to Britain and the Soviet Union to find the land forces to deal with a future threat to peace in Europe. No doubt all this was carefully stored away in Stalin's memory and helped formulate his postwar policy.

The Teheran Conference concluded with a dinner at which friendly and flattering mutual toasts were exchanged by the three leaders, expressing the satisfaction felt by all of them at the results of their meetings; indeed expressing at that moment a true comradeship in the face of the enemy. But beyond the joint strategy and operations now agreed for the defeat of Germany and Japan lay the

undecided questions of postwar Europe and the postwar world. Churchill wrote later in his memoirs: "It would not have been right at Teheran for the Western democracies to found their plans upon suspicions of the Russian attitude in the hour of triumph and when all her dangers were removed." But with hindsight it might be argued that it would have been just as "right" for the Western democracies to look shrewdly to their own long-term interests as it was for Stalin to look to those of Soviet Russia.

Back to Cairo

On December 2, 1943, Roosevelt and Churchill arrived back in Cairo to thrash out with the Combined Chiefs-of-Staff the details of the operations agreed on at Teheran and to settle the question of the supreme command. Once again the military staffs and the plenary sessions

△ △ *General Wladyslaw Sikorski, Premier of the Polish Government-in-exile. He was killed in an air crash on July 4 1943.*
△ *His successor Stanislas Mikolajczyk. Relations between the Poles and the Russians broke down after the Katyn disclosures.*

According to Robert Sherwood, this was the only time during the war that Roosevelt overruled his chiefs-of-staff.

Eisenhower or Marshall?

There remained the question of a supreme commander for "Overlord". In the face of the strong British objections, the Americans had quietly given up their idea of a super supremo responsible for all operations everywhere against Germany. Yet only such a post would have been important enough to warrant moving General Marshall from Washington, where he was a key figure, and without giving the impression of a demotion. Roosevelt therefore came to another hard decision, this time one taken against the advice of Hopkins and Stimson as well as the known preference of Churchill and Stalin. He told Marshall, "I feel I could not sleep at night with you out of the country." Next day Roosevelt informed Churchill that Eisenhower would command "Overlord". It had already been agreed to create a single Mediterranean theatre command under a British supreme commander, who was named on December 18 as General Sir Maitland Wilson.

Final agreement

Thus the "Sextant" and "Eureka" conferences, when taken together the longest, toughest inter-Allied meeting ever held, came to an end with all the great strategic issues at last resolved. For all the arguing and bargaining, the British and Americans parted in amity, as the concluding remarks of the final session record:

"Sir Alan Brooke said he would like to express on behalf of the British Chiefs of Staff their deep gratitude for the way in which the United States Chiefs had met their views...

"General Marshall said that he very much appreciated Sir Alan Brooke's gracious tributes..."

On his way home Roosevelt summoned Eisenhower to Tunis, and as soon as Eisenhower had joined him in his car, he said: "Well, Ike, you are going to command 'Overlord'!" Eisenhower replied:

"Mr. President, I realise that such an appointment involved difficult decisions. I hope you will not be disappointed."

△ *General Dwight D. Eisenhower. He was promoted to command the Allied invasion force for operation "Overlord", a move which was politically expedient, but which disappointed Brooke, who had been promised the command by Churchill.*
▽ *General Sir Henry Maitland Wilson, who succeeded Eisenhower as Supreme Allied Commander in the Mediterranean theatre of operations.*

grappled with the old question of available landing-craft in relation to "Buccaneer", "Overlord", the invasion of southern France and the residual operations in the eastern Mediterranean. Fresh examination of the "Overlord" plan in the light of the experience of the invasion of Sicily and Italy suggested that a larger initial assault force was desirable, and that meant yet more landing-craft. The British Chiefs-of-Staff therefore once more sought to get "Buccaneer" abandoned, and with it the planned concurrent land offensive in northern Burma; their American opposite numbers nevertheless still argued that these operations were politically and militarily essential. Three days of discussion led only to deadlock. But on the evening of December 5, after hard thinking in private, Roosevelt came to a difficult decision. He sent Churchill the terse message "Buccaneer is off" Next day he signalled Chiang that European commitments left no margin for the operation.

CHAPTER 101
Smashing the Dniepr front

The first five months of 1944 were marked by new Red Army offensives to the south of the Pripet Marshes. The offensives led to the liberation of the Ukraine and Crimea as well as to the conquest of the northern part of Rumanian Moldavia, while in the Leningrad region they succeeded in throwing the Germans back from a line linking Oranienbaum–Volkhov–Novgorod–Lake Ilmen onto one linking Narva–Lake Peipus and Pskov. At the same time, the Western Allies were also putting the pressure on Germany.

Further south, General Sir Henry Maitland Wilson, new Allied Commander-in-Chief in the Mediterranean, endeavoured to carry out the limited mission which had been entrusted to him in implementation of decisions recently taken at the Teheran Conference. Two days before the Normandy landings, the advance guard of his 15th Army Group under General Sir Harold Alexander had entered Rome hard on the enemy's heels. Thereby the allies had achieved their strictly geographical objective, but arguably at the price of sacrificing their strategic objective in Italy, namely the destruction of the enemy forces.

Parallel to this, in Great Britain the preparations for Operation "Overlord", with all their attendant difficulties, were rapidly approaching their climax. While the divisions taking part in the landings by sea and by air were undergoing intensive training, in London Generals Eisenhower and Montgomery were putting the final touches to the invasion plans drawn up by the American and British Combined Chiefs-of-Staff, C.O.S.S.A.C., and submitted for their approval by General Morgan.

Bombing stepped up

Anglo-American bomber formations intensified their missions by day and by night over the Third Reich as well as over occupied Europe. Most probably the results obtained over the first six months were no more significant in their impact on German war production than during the previous year. However, systematic pinpointing of synthetic oil plants from spring onwards, as well as of the Ploiești oil-wells, enabled the Allied air forces for the first time to influence events on land directly by precipitating an extremely serious fuel crisis in the Wehrmacht. Furthermore, in the western and southern theatres British and American fighter-bombers and medium bombers constantly pounded the enemy's communications

▽ *"Crush the Fascist Reptile!" A typically virulent Russian poster. In the early days of the war, when they were exhibited near the front line, posters were used to demoralise the attacking Germans in addition to whipping the Russians into greater hatred of the invaders.*

БЕЙ ФАШИСТСКОГО ГАДА!

U-boats of the excellent XXI type under construction in a Bremen yard at the time of Germany's capitulation.

system. In France and Belgium their aim was to obstruct rapid reinforcement of the German 7th Army, which was in position on the coast between Cabourg and St. Nazaire; in Italy their main targets were the Po bridges and the course of the Adige, the route by which enemy supplies and reinforcements moved after crossing the Brenner Pass. Moreover, the Luftwaffe was being forced to sacrifice itself against the mass American daylight raids escorted by long-range fighters.

War in the Atlantic

On June 22, 1941, Hitler became involved unwisely in a "war on two fronts" such as had cost Wilhelm II his throne, in spite of the fact that the Emperor's ghost might have seemed to have been exorcised by the Soviet-German Pact of August 23, 1939. And now on January 1, 1944, the Third Reich and its Führer were in a position of having to conduct a "war on all fronts" (*Allfrontenkrieg*).

The only way in which Germany might have escaped the inevitable consequences of the powerful efforts of the Allies to surround and close in on her, would have been to resume the U-boat offensive in the Atlantic with the same success as in 1942. But for all his energy, intelligence, and experience, Grand-Admiral Dönitz was unable to stem the swelling tide of troops, war *matériel,* and supplies converging on Europe from America.

The facts are made clear in the following table, based on figures supplied by Captain Roskill, of Allied mercantile losses in 1942 and 1944 in the North Atlantic:

	1942		1944	
	tonnage	ships	tonnage	ships
January	276,795	48	36,065	5
February	429,891	73	12,577	2
March	534,064	95	36,867	7
April	391,044	66	34,224	5
May	576,350	120	0	0
Totals	2,208,144	402	119,733	19

The figures show the extent to which Britain and America recovered complete supremacy in the North Atlantic, with consequent complete freedom of manoeuvre and strategy. Although Grand-Admiral Dönitz was keeping new and unpleasant secret weapons up his sleeve, they were not as yet ready, and until they were there was a great deal that could happen.

Hitler's predictions

The immediate consequences of this complete reversal of the situation were perfectly clear to Hitler. One only need refer to the arguments propounded on November 3, 1943 in support of measures prescribed by his Directive No. 51, as regards the conduct of the war; in his own words:

"The hard and costly struggle against Bolshevism during the last two-and-a-half years, which has involved the bulk of our military strength in the East, has demanded extreme exertions. The greatness of the danger and the general situation demanded it. But the situation has since changed. The danger in the East still remains, but a greater danger now appears in the West: an Anglo-Saxon landing! In the East, the vast extent of the territory makes it possible for us to lose ground, even on a large scale, without a fatal blow being dealt to the nervous system of Germany.

"It is very different in the West! Should the enemy succeed in breaching our defences on a wide front here, the immediate consequences would be unpredictable. Everything indicates that the enemy will launch an offensive against the Western front of Europe, at the latest in the spring, perhaps even earlier.

"I can therefore no longer take responsibility for further weakening the West, in favour of other theatres of war. I have therefore decided to reinforce its defences, particularly those places from which the long-range bombardment of England will begin. For it is here that the enemy must and will attack, and it is here–unless all indications are misleading–that the decisive battle against the landing forces will be fought."

On December 20 following, Hitler returned to the question in the presence of his generals. It appears from the shorthand account of his statement that, while he was convinced that the invasion would take place, he was less than convinced that the British would have their hearts in it:

"It stands to reason that the English have less confidence in this enterprise than has Eisenhower. Eisenhower has effected one [sic] successful invasion, but this was solely due to the work of traitors. Here with our soldiers he will find none to help him. Here, we mean business, make no mistake! It is a totally different matter to invade North Africa and be greeted by Monsieur Giraud or be confronted by the Italians who for the most part stay in their holes without firing a single shot, and to set foot in the West in the face of unrelenting fire. And so long as a battery is capable of firing, it will continue firing. That is a certainty."

German misconceptions

The above extract from Directive No. 51 is interesting from more than one aspect. Its third paragraph adds a further reason to those normally advanced by way of explaining why O.K.W. situated the centre of gravity of its western defensive system between Le Havre and the Pas-de-Calais. The argument at Rastenburg ran as follows: the fact that the launching sites for the V-1 and V-2, whose effect was directed against Britain, were in this area would in all probability lead the British to urge their allies that this was the best place to make the landings. This argument was plausible enough, but its effectiveness required one condition,

▽ *Evidence of the Red Air Force's growing power – German transport destroyed during the retreat in the Ukraine. From now on the Luftwaffe could only very rarely assure the ground forces of any useful air cover.*

△ *German and satellite infantry wait to board a train leaving for the Russian front.*

namely that the Germans should be the first to open fire. Yet Hitler knew perfectly well that the V-1 missiles (let alone V-2) would not be operational before the date when he expected his enemies to attempt invasion across the Channel.

Furthermore, insisting as he did on the peril that was looming in the West to the extent of giving it priority in the short run over the Soviet threat, Hitler's judgement was correct. On the basis of this eminently reasonable view of the situation, seen from the perspective of O.K.W., Hitler went on to deduce that the Anglo-American attempt at invasion would fail so long as he did not, as he had done during the winters of 1941–2 and 1942–3, prop up the now tottering Eastern Front with troops from among those guarding the Atlantic battlements.

Thence it follows that he to whom the directive of November 3, 1943 was principally addressed, that is Hitler himself, this time in his capacity as Commander-in-Chief of German land forces, would draw the logical conclusions from the premises he had just himself stated in his office at Rastenburg.

At O.K.H., Colonel-General Zeitzler perhaps flattered himself for several weeks that he would be given more freedom of action than hitherto in the conduct of operations. Was it not there in writing, in Hitler's own hand, that if it were a case of absolute necessity on the Eastern Front, withdrawals on a fairly considerable scale could be countenanced without necessarily putting the "nervous system" of the Third Reich in mortal danger?

The Führer and Russia

But when it came down to it, the Russians' third winter offensive, the Führer showed the same persistent and mistaken obstinacy as he had done in the previous years, bringing his familiar arguments of high politics and the war economy to bear against his army group commanders every time one of them sought to advise him of a suitable chance to disengage in the face of the sheer weight, regardless of cost, of the Soviet onslaught.

And evidence of this came with the fresh disasters that occurred, principally to the south of the Pripet Marshes, when towards the end of January 1944 Kanev and Korsun' and, on the following May 13, Sevastopol' found their doleful place in the annals of German military history. So it was again a case of immediately arresting the possible consequences of these new defeats sustained by the Third Reich and, since the few reinforcements still available on the Eastern Front were quite inadequate, Hitler the head of O.K.H. sought help from Hitler the head of O.K.W. in order to avert imminent catastrophe. In these circumstances, born of his quite inexcusable obstinacy, Hitler the supreme commander had no alternative but to depart from the principle he had laid down in his Directive of November 3, 1943. At the end of the winter of 1943, the *Waffen*-S.S. II Panzer Corps had to be transferred from the Alençon sector, and hence missed the rendezvous of June 6, 1944 in Normandy.

Manstein's impossible task

The Soviet winter offensive began on December 24, 1943 on either side of the Kiev-Zhitomir road and within a few weeks involved the whole of Army Group "South" which, at that time, stretching as it did between the estuary of the Dniepr and the Mozyr' region, comprised the 6th Army (General Hollidt), the 1st *Panzerarmee* (General Hube), the 8th Army (General Wöhler), and the 4th *Panzerarmee* (General Raus). The entire group, commanded as before by Field-Marshal Erich von Manstein, was made up of 73 of the 180 understrength divisions that were then engaged on the front between Kerch' Strait and the Oranienbaum bridgehead on the Baltic.

In particular, 22 of the 32 Panzer and *Panzergrenadier* divisions on the Eastern Front were allocated to Army Group "South".

The 18th Artillery Division had also been assigned there, with its eight tracked or motorised battalions, comprising nine 21-cm howitzers, plus 30 15-cm, 48 10.5-cm, and 12 10-cm guns. This was a new formation, based on similar ones in the Red Army, and much was expected of it. But it proved disappointing and was disbanded after a few months. A total of 73 divisions seems impressive, but the figure is mis-

leading. Between July 31, 1943 and July 31, 1944, Manstein lost 405,409 killed, wounded, and missing, yet in the same period his reinforcements in officers, N.C.O.s, and other ranks amounted to only 221,893. His divisions, particularly the infantry ones, were thin on the ground. It was the same story with the Panzer divisions, which in spite of increased production of tanks, were 50 to 60 per cent below complement. And the front to be defended, in the Führer's words "with no thought of retreat", measured a good 650 miles.

4th *Panzerarmee* defeated

As has been noted, the 1st Ukrainian Front (General N. F. Vatutin) inaugurated the Soviet winter offensive on December 24. With fire support from four artillery divisions and ten artillery regiments (936 guns and howitzers) assigned from general reserve, Vatutin launched an attack on an 18-mile front in the direction of Zhitomir, with 18 divisions (38th Army and 1st Guards Army) backed by six armoured or mechanised corps. The XXIV Panzer Corps (General Nehring: 8th and 19th Panzer

△ Colonel-General P. S. Rybalko, twice a "Hero of the Soviet Union", was one of Stalin's most able and respected tank generals.

▽ A German 15-cm gun battery on the move on one of Russia's better roads. With the already efficient Russian artillery growing ever stronger, German artillery now found itself in very dire straits.
Overleaf: *Russian infantry move in to dislodge the Germans from a village they are holding.*

Divisions and *Waffen*-S.S. 2nd Panzer Division *"Das Reich"*) put up a stubborn resistance for 48 hours, then, in spite of being reinforced by XLVIII Panzer Corps (General Balck) broke under the impact. The 3rd Guards Tank Army (General Rybalko) stormed through the breach and on the last day of the year recaptured Zhitomir and by January 3 reached Novograd-Volinskiy, over 85 miles from its jumping-off point. Further to the right, the Soviet 60th and 13th Armies, comprising 14 infantry divisions, had retaken Korosten and were close to the Russo-Polish frontier of the pre-war period. On Rybalko's left, Vatutin's centre was overwhelming the defenders of Berdichev.

Hence the defeat of the 4th *Panzerarmee* took on a strategic dimension, and in the event of Vatutin exploiting his success to the south-west resolutely and with vigour, could have led to the total destruction of Army Groups "South" and "A". As early as December 25, Manstein had been aware of the possibility of such a danger and had alerted O.K.H. to this effect, confronting it with the following dilemma: "The 4th Army was no longer capable of defending the flank of Army Groups 'South' and 'A'; effective reinforcements were vital. If O.K.H. was unable to provide these, we would be obliged to take five or six divisions at least from our right wing, which clearly could not then maintain its positions inside the Dniepr loop. We sought our liberty of movement for that wing."

Hitler reminisces

During the period when he was writing his memoirs, Manstein had no knowledge of the disobliging, indeed absurd, comments that his report had drawn from the Führer: that Manstein had inflated the enemy numbers knowingly in the hope of imposing his personal decisions on O.K.H. Furthermore, the troops were bound to mirror their commander's attitude, and if some divisions failed to measure up to the standards needed, it was because Manstein, lacking in conviction, had failed to inspire his men.

Hitler went on, in the presence of Zeitzler, who must have been somewhat dumbfounded, about the heroic times when the party assumed power, capturing in turn Mecklenburg, East Prussia ("refractory and reactionary"), Cologne ("red

△ A small party of Germans pulls back past the wreckage of a shot-up motor convoy.
▷ "Dniepropetrovsk is ours!" thunders this Kukryniksy cartoon of the "Bandit of Melitopol" being driven back out of Russia.

and black"), and – according to the stenographic account of the meeting – "Thuringia was dyed a deep red, but then I had a Koch at the time I wanted him, at another time a Ley or a Sauckel. There were men for you. When, by some mischance, I didn't have the right men at hand, there was trouble. I took it as axiomatic that good *Gaus* made good *Gauleiters*. And it's not a jot different today."

Manstein pleads for reinforcements . . .

In any case, whatever the parallel between the situation of the Nazi Party in its electoral campaigns and the Russian campaign, Manstein, who had been offered two or three divisions by Hitler with which to plug the two breaches, each 45 to 50 miles in width, to right and left of the

4th *Panzerarmee,* proceeded on December 29 to carry out the manoeuvre he had proposed in his report of December 25. The 1st *Panzerarmee* command was switched from right to left of the 8th Army, transferring III Panzer Corps (General Breith) with its four divisions from the Dniepr loop and completing the movement by shifting VII Corps and XXIV Panzer Corps, which formed Raus's right flank, to the south-east of Berdichev. This manoeuvre, which was approved by O.K.H., provided some relief for Army Group "South", added to the fact that Vatutin failed to exploit his opportunity to drive to the Dniestr from Kamenets-Podolskiy. Hitler, however, had not let pass without response Manstein's proposal to evacuate the Dniepr loop and the Nikopol' bridgehead. It so happened that on January 3, General Konev himself launched an attack in the Kirovograd sector, where the German 6th Army had just relieved the completely exhausted 1st *Panzerarmee.*

... and tries to convince Hitler

A clear decision was called for and with the object of obtaining one, Manstein went to Rastenburg in person, hoping that he would carry more weight with the Führer than his teletype messages. He put his case as follows:

"If the high command could not bring up strong reinforcements immediately, our Southern wing would have to fall back, abandoning Nikopol', and hence the Crimea, simply in order to make good the deficiency; and this in our opinion was only a first step. We had reconnoitred positions in the rear and given orders for their preparation. These positions more or less followed the course of the Bug, making use of any high ground that seemed advantageous, up to a point south of the sector where our Northern wing

ДНЕПРОПЕТРОВСК НАШ!

ПРОКЛЯТЫЙ ФАКЕЛЬЩИК, БАНДИТ,
ИЗ МЕЛИТОПОЛЯ ДАВ ТЯГУ,
ПОПАЛ В ДРУГУЮ ПЕРЕДРЯГУ.
—ДНЕПРОПЕТРОВСК,—ПОДЛЕЦ ТВЕРДИТ,
Я ВВЕРИЛ АРМИИ НЕРОБКОЙ!—
И ВОТ, ТЕРЯЯ ВЕСЬ КРЕДИТ,
УЖ ОН ЛЕТИТ ОТТУДА ПРОБКОЙ!

△ *Maintenance work in progress on a Büssing-NAG SWS heavy gun tractor fitted with a ten-barrel 15-cm* Nebelwerfer *battery.*

was at the moment engaged in fighting. Occupation of these new positions would reduce the 600 mile front by almost half, held too thinly by the 6th and 8th Armies. Such a drastic reduction, and the availability of the 17th Army once it was withdrawn from Crimea, would enable us to achieve the degree of consolidation required in the Northern wing."

And anticipating the likely objection of the Führer, he added: "Naturally the Russians would also benefit by the operation, but since our front would thereby achieve greater solidity, its defensive capacity would be enhanced – and this is the greatest asset in war – so as to be able to resist even massive assault. Furthermore, the destruction of the railway system would prevent the enemy moving the forces now available to him with sufficient speed to allow him to maintain his superiority to west of Kiev."

Hitler stubbornly opposed the propositions made to him in these terms. The need for Nikopol' manganese, whose mining had been suspended for several weeks, prohibited him from abandoning the Dniepr loop. And as for evacuating the Crimea, the idea should be totally excluded; it could well bring about the defection of Bulgaria and a declaration of war on Germany by Turkey. Nor was

there any question of finding reinforcements from Army Group "North": if Field-Marshal von Küchler was forced to abandon his positions dominating the Gulf of Finland, Russian submarines would operate freely in the Baltic and cut the supply lines for Swedish iron-ore between Luleå and factories in Germany.

Manstein returned, disabused and empty-handed, to his H.Q. at Vinnitsa. From one of his several meetings with Hitler, the Field-Marshal took away the following impression of the dictator's face gripped, as was then the case, with inner fury:

"I saw Hitler's features harden. He threw me a glance which signified 'there is no further argument'. I cannot remember ever in my life having seen anyone portray such force of character. One of the foreign ambassadors accredited to Berlin speaks in his memoirs of the effect produced on him by Hitler's eyes. Alone in a coarse and undistinguished face they constituted the single striking feature, certainly the only expressive one. Those eyes fixed me as if they would annihilate me. The comparison with a Hindu snake-charmer suddenly struck me. For the space of a few seconds a kind of mute struggle took place between us. That gaze told me how he had contrived to dominate so many people."

The intervention of the 1st *Panzerarmee*, under the command of the gallant General Hube, may have allowed Manstein both to contain the centre of the 1st Ukrainian Front and even make it give ground a little after sustaining heavy casualties (during the second half of January on the furious Pogrebishche sector), but General Raus's northern wing, which presented a ragged line northwards to the Pripet Marshes, proved unable to resist the pressure applied on it by General Vatutin's right wing. On the previous January 4, in the course of his visit to O.K.H., Manstein had urged Hitler to build up a strong reserve in the Rovno region. His advice had not been followed, and this important fortress-town fell to the Russians on February 5, 1944. Since its breakthrough on December 24, the 1st Ukrainian Front had thus far advanced 170 miles westwards, with the result that the line Army Group "South" was required to hold was vastly lengthened from its furthest point at Nikopol', without receiving proportionate reinforcement. Also, lines of communication were increasingly under threat to the extent that the Russians exploited their gains in the direction of Tarnopol', only 90 miles to the south of Rovno.

Dangerous salient

In the immediate future, the situation was still more serious. On Hitler's express orders, the right of the 1st *Panzerarmee* and the left of the 8th Army were maintained on the banks of the Dniepr between Kanev and upstream of Cherkassy. With Vatutin's advance as far as Zhachkov and with Konev in possession of Kirovograd on January 10 a dangerous salient 100 miles wide and some 90 miles deep had formed in this sector, which gave the enemy the opportunity for a pincer movement. The reduction of the front (on the lines proposed to the Führer by Manstein at their meeting on January 4 at Rastenburg, a course which he continued to advocate in notes and personal letters) brooked no further argument; and subsequent events show that the whole manoeuvre, delicate though it was, might well have succeeded with the least cost; reckoning from January 4, there was an effective delay of three weeks, while the 1st and 2nd Ukrainian

Fronts together cut off the area between Kanev and Cherkassy; of almost four weeks before the 3rd Ukrainian Front (under General Malinovsky) attacked the Nikopol' bridgehead; and of nearly five weeks before General Vatutin's armoured and mechanised advanced units reached the Rovno–Shepetovka line.

The weather takes a hand

Soviet commentators attribute the relatively slow progress of the Russians to the constant changes in temperature and alternation of rain and snow recorded in the west of the Ukraine during the months of January and February 1944.

Writing in 1956, Colonel A. N. Grylev of the Soviet Army has this to say:

"Unfavourable weather conditions created more difficulties for our troops than did the crossing of rivers. An unusually early spring caused the snow to melt as early as the end of January. Rain and melting snow aggravated the difficulties. Rivers overflowed their banks.

▽ *Hungarian artillerymen move a somewhat antiquated piece of field artillery into position.*

Roads and tracks became as impracticable for vehicles as was the terrain for infantry. These various factors had a considerable effect on our military activities, limiting the possibility of manoeuvre and hampering supplies of food, fuel, and munitions."

Lest it should be felt that the writer is trying to excuse the purely relative failure of the Soviet armies to annihilate the German army groups facing the four Ukrainian Fronts, Colonel Grylev's testimony is borne out in detail by General

Воюют не числом, а умением!
(СУВОРОВ)

ТРОЕ ПРОТИВ ДВАДЦАТИ СЕМИ!

△ *A Russian poster extols the Red Air Force, now master of the skies over Russia.*

▽ *Soviet artillery batters away at the German positions near Leningrad.*

von Vormann, who was in the same area as commander of the hard-pressed XLVII Panzer Corps:

"The *rasputitsa* (thaw) had set in astonishingly early; everywhere it is spring mud . . . Worked on by the sun, the rain, and the warm winds, the heavy, black Ukraine earth turns into thick sticky mud during the day. There is not one metalled road in the country. On foot you sink down to your shins and after a few steps lose shoes and socks there. Wheeled vehicles stall and get stuck. Suction by the mud tore away the too-narrow tracks of our all-purpose transports. The only machines capable of making any headway were the tractors and the tanks, which rolled their way forwards at a maximum speed of 3 miles an hour but at the cost of tremendous strain on the engine and huge petrol consumption."

At all events, it is clear that the mud worked more to the disadvantage of the Russians than of the Germans, since in their task of attack and pursuit they also had to cope with the battlefield debris left by the retreating enemy, who destroyed everything of any value behind him.

Manstein a defeatist?

In Manstein's dispute with Hitler, are there grounds for accusing the former—as has been alleged from time to time—of having been obsessed with withdrawal in the face of any build-up in enemy strength or else of having been unjustifiably alarmed by the spectre of encirclement?

It is clear that at this juncture Manstein no longer displayed the genius for bold moves that had characterised his performance between 1941 and 1943; yet it is also abundantly clear that he was no longer in a position where he could act boldly. Apart from XLVI Panzer Corps, which had recently been assigned to him, he knew that he could expect no further reinforcements from the west and that on the Eastern Front it was a case of robbing Peter to pay Paul. The liquidation of a pocket containing half a dozen divisions would mean not only the loss of some 60,000 men and most of their *matériel,* but, further, a breach of 75 to 90 miles in his now dangerously reduced defensive system. The battle of Korsun'-Shevchen-

kovskiy would show that his appreciation of the situation – and he had vainly tried to prevail on Hitler to accept it – was the correct one.

On January 25, Marshal Zhukov, who had been delegated by *Stavka* to co-ordinate operations, threw the troops of the 1st and 2nd Ukrainian Fronts into an assault on the Kanev salient. General Vatutin brought his 40th Army (Lieutenant-General E. F. Zhmachenko) and 27th Army (Lieutenant-General S. G. Trofimenko) to bear on the western front of the salient. They had a considerable job in overcoming German resistance so as to open a breach for brigades of the 6th Tank Army (Lieutenant-General A. G. Kravchenko) to move south-eastwards. The 2nd Ukrainian Front, under General Konev, seems to have had an easier task; delivering its attack at the point of junction of XLVII Panzer Corps and XI Corps, the 4th Guards Army (Major-General A. I. Ryzhov) and 53rd Army (Major-General I. V. Galanin) swiftly broke through the lines held by the 389th Infantry Division, thus enabling the 5th Guards Tank Army, under the command of General P. A. Rotmistrov, to be unleashed without further ado.

"There could be no other adequate analogy. The sea-dikes had given and the tide, interminable and vast, spread across the plain, passing either side of our tanks which, with packets of infantry round them, had the appearance of reefs rising from the swell. Our amazement was at its peak when in the afternoon cavalry units, galloping westwards, broke through our screen of fire in close formation. It was a sight long-forgotten, almost a mirage – V Guards Cavalry Corps, with the 11th, 12th, and 63rd Cavalry Divisions under the command of Selimanov." Thus, in a monograph dealing with this episode, the former commander of XLVII Panzer Corps describes the breakthrough at Krasnosilka (30 miles north-west of Kirovograd). In these conditions, it is not surprising that Vatutin's and Konev's tanks effected a meeting on January 28 in the region of Zvenigorodka. XI Corps, which formed the left of the German 8th Army, and XLII Corps, on the right of the 1st *Panzerarmee,* were caught in the trap along with four infantry divisions (the 57th, 72nd, 88th, and 389th), the 5th S.S. *Panzergrenadier* Division "*Wiking*" and the S.S. *Freiwilligen Sturmbrigade "Wallonie",* which Himmler had recruited in the French-speaking provinces of Belgium.

By virtue of seniority over his comrade Lieutenant-General T. Lieb, General W. Stemmermann, commander of XI Corps, assumed command of those encircled.

Hitler hangs on to Kanev

Hitler was determined to defend the Kanev salient at all costs, as he considered it the base for launching an offensive which would force the Russians to cross back over the Dniepr in the region of Kiev. Hence orders were given to Stemmermann to hold his positions and to establish himself so as to be able to repulse any attacks from the south; to General O. Wöhler, commanding the 8th Army, to hurl his XLVII Panzer Corps, reinforced to a strength of five Panzer divisions, at the eastern face of the pocket; and to General H. V. Hube, to drive his III Panzer Corps, comprising four Panzer divisions (among them the 1st S.S. Panzer Division "*Leibstandarte Adolf Hitler*") at the western face of the pocket.

Such a plan, involving the concentration of nine Panzer divisions against

the Kanev pocket, was nevertheless doomed to failure within the time limit imposed by the defenders' capacity to hold out, though an airlift was being organised to keep them in supplies. Moreover, most of the Panzer divisions designated by Hitler were already engaged elsewhere, and hence it was a case of relieving them, pulling them out of line, and moving them to their jump-off

△ *Russian peasant women greet the arrival of liberating Soviet armour, complete with tank-riders.*

△ *Not all the Russians welcomed the Red Army as liberators, however, and many, particularly from the western regions, fell back with the retreating Germans.*

points. Furthermore, they were far short of complement; in particular their grenadier regiments were reduced to only several hundred rifles, and there were grounds for feeling some apprehension that they lacked the resilience necessary for a rapid thrust. Yet in counter-attacks speed is all.

Indeed, on February 2, XLVII and III Panzer Corps still had only four Panzer divisions and, what is more, one of them was immediately withdrawn from General N. von Vormann's XLVII Panzer Corps by special order of the Führer, on receipt of the news that units of the 3rd Ukrainian Front were advancing on Apostolovo, which lies half-way between Nikopol' and Krivoy-Rog. The following night, the *rasputitsa* arrived, covering the western Ukraine with the sea of mud described above. Now the unseasonable weather worked to the advantage of the Russians, delaying their enemy's movements still further. When the earth grew hard again, around February 10, the Soviet encirclement of the Korsun' pocket was con-

solidated to such an extent that III Panzer Corps only managed to reach the area of Lysyanka, eight miles from the lines held by the besieged forces.

Break-out attempt

General Stemmermann, as one might expect, had not succeeded in forming a front to the south as he had been enjoined to do in his orders from Rastenburg, without at the same time abandoning Kanev and the banks of the Dniepr, which would have been in defiance of these orders. On February 8 he gave no reply to a summons to capitulate transmitted to him from General Konev, under orders to reduce the pocket. Both Stemmermann and his subordinates turned a deaf ear to the exhortations made to them by representatives of the "Committee for a Free Germany" who had been conveyed to the battlefield on Moscow's orders and were led by General von

were called upon to give. The attempt took place in the night of February 16–17, but at first light Soviet artillery, tanks, and aircraft were able to react with vigour and immediate effect:

"Till now," writes General von Vormann, "our forces had dragged all their heavy equipment across gullies filled with thick, impacted snow. But then enemy shelling proved our undoing. Artillery and assault guns were abandoned after they had exhausted their ammunition. And then the wounded moving with the troops met their fate . . . Veritable hordes of hundreds of soldiers from every type of unit headed westwards under the nearest available officer. The enemy infantry were swept out of the way by our advancing bayonets; even the tanks turned in their tracks. But all the same Russian fire struck with impunity at the masses, moving forward with heads down, unevenly and unprotected. Our losses multiplied . . . "

This hopeless charge by 40,000 men foundered on the natural obstacle of the Gniloy-Tikich, a stream which had thawed only a few days previously, and was now 25 feet wide and just deep enough for a man to drown in. And it heralded a fresh disaster, which the Belgian Léon Degrelle, fighting in the ranks of the S.S. Sturmbrigade "Wallonie", describes in unforgettable terms:

"The artillery teams which had escaped destruction plunged first into the waves and ice floes. The banks of the river were steep, the horses turned back and were drowned. Men then threw themselves in to cross the river by swimming. But hardly had they got to the other side than they were transformed into blocks of ice, and their clothes frozen to their bodies. They tried to throw their equipment over the river. But often their uniforms fell into the current. Soon hundreds of soldiers, completely naked and red as lobsters, were thronging the other bank. Many soldiers did not know how to swim. Maddened by the approach of the Russian armour which was coming down the slope and firing at them, they threw themselves pell-mell into the icy water. Some escaped death by clinging to trees which had been hastily felled . . . but hundreds were drowned. Under the fire of tanks thousands upon thousands of soldiers, half clothed, streaming with icy water or naked as the day they were born, ran through the snow towards the distant cottages of Lysyanka."

Seydlitz-Kurzbach, former commander of LI Corps, who had been taken prisoner at Stalingrad. The tracts and individual free passes scattered among the soldiers with a view to encouraging surrender were equally ignored.

Notwithstanding, the airlift worked poorly in the face of an abundant and highly effective Soviet fighter force, and those encircled at Korsun' saw their strength diminish further each day. It was inevitable that the order should come to attempt to break out towards III Panzer Corps, which had been conclusively halted by the mud. It was the only chance left.

To this effect, General Stemmermann reassembled the remnants of his two corps round the village of Shanderovka and organised them in three echelons: at the head the grenadiers, bayonets fixed, next the heavy infantry units, and then finally the artillery and service troops. The 57th and 88th Infantry Divisions protected the rear and showed themselves equal to the sacrifice they

Part of the German bag taken in the Korsun'-Shevchenkovskiy pocket.

The hecatomb of Lysyanka

In short, between February 16 and 18, III Panzer Corps at Lysyanka retrieved only 30,000 survivors, unarmed for the most part; among them, General Lieb, commander of XLII Corps. The valiant Stemmermann had been killed by a piece of shrapnel. According to the Soviet historian B. S. Telpukhovsky, of the Moscow Academy of Sciences, on this one occasion the Russians accounted for more than 52,000 dead and 11,000 prisoners but his German colleagues Hillgruber and Jacobsen take issue with him: "Just before the investment occurred the two German corps numbered 54,000 all told, including rear area troops, some of whom escaped encirclement."

Allowing for the 30,000 or 32,000 survivors of this 21-day tragedy, German losses in the sector could barely have risen to more than one third of the total claimed by Moscow nearly 15 years after Germany's unconditional surrender. Hillgruber's and Jacobsen's figures are beyond question.

Alexander Werth quotes the account of a Soviet eye witness of these tragic events which confirms General von Vormann's account. On the day following, Major Kampov told Werth:

"I remember that last fateful night of the 17th of February. A terrible blizzard was blowing. Konev himself was travelling in a tank through the shell-shattered 'corridor'. I rode on horseback from one point in the corridor to another, with a dispatch from the General; it was so dark that I could not see the horse's ears. I mention this darkness and this blizzard because they are an important factor in what happened . . .

"It was during that night, or the evening before, that the encircled Germans, having abandoned all hope of ever being rescued by Hube, decided to make a last desperate effort to break out . . .

"Driven out of their warm huts they had to abandon Shanderovka. They flocked into the ravines near the village, and then took the desperate decision to break through early in the morning . . . So that morning they formed themselves into two marching columns of about 14,000 each . . .

"It was about six o'clock in the morning. Our tanks and our cavalry suddenly appeared and rushed straight into the thick of the two columns. What happened then is hard to describe. The Germans ran in all directions. And for the next four hours our tanks raced up and down the plain crushing them by the hundred. Our cavalry, competing with the tanks, chased them through the ravines where it was hard for the tanks to pursue them. Most of the time the tanks were not using their guns lest they hit their own cavalry. Hundreds and hundreds of cavalry were hacking at them with their sabres, and massacred the Fritzes as no one had ever been massacred by cavalry before. There was no time to take prisoners. It was the kind of carnage that nothing could stop till it was all over. In a small area over 20,000 Germans were killed."

In connection with this episode, General von Vormann, in the study mentioned above, raises an interesting question. Observing that the encirclement of XI and XLII Corps on January 28 had opened a 65-mile breach between the right of III Panzer Corps and the left of XLVII, he considers why the Soviet high command failed to exploit the opportunity of a breakthrough afforded. In his opinion, on that day there was nothing to prevent Stalin driving his armoured units towards Uman' and across the Bug, assigning to them distant objectives on the Dniestr, the Prut, and in the Rumanian Carpathians. This not impossible objective would have sealed the fate of Army Groups "A" and "South".

This question was raised in 1954, but it is still impossible to provide an answer which documents can verify. We must be content with the supposition that Stalin acted with extreme prudence, by annihilating the Korsun' pocket before embarking on more hazardous enterprises, and it should be noted that 12 months from then Chernyakhovsky, Rokossovsky, Zhukov, and Konev had far more freedom of action. But by then, from Tilsit to the Polish Carpathians, the German Army was little more than a ruin.

What is certain is that Stalin showed himself eminently satisfied by the way in which Zhukov and those under him had conducted the business; the proof of it being that on February 23, 1944 a decree of the Praesidium of the Supreme Council of the U.S.S.R. conferred upon General of the Army Konev the title of Marshal of the Soviet Union and upon General Rotmistrov that of Marshal of Tank Forces. Even if the generals had missed a golden opportunity, they had certainly won a great victory.

The German Panzerjäger 38(t) Marder III

Weight: 11.6 tons.
Crew: 4.
Armament: one 7.62-cm PaK 36(r) gun with 30 rounds and one 7.92-mm machine gun with 1,500 rounds. (The main armament was a rechambered Russian FK 296 or 297 anti-tank gun.)
Armour: hull front 52-mm, sides and rear 15-mm, decking 10-mm, and belly 8-mm; superstructure front and sides 16-mm; gun shield 11-mm.
Engine: one Praga EPA 6-cylinder inline, 125-hp.
Speed: 26 mph on roads, 9 mph cross-country.
Range: 115 miles on roads, 87 miles cross-country.
Length: 21 feet $1\frac{1}{4}$ inches.
Width: 7 feet 1 inch.
Height: 8 feet $2\frac{1}{2}$ inches.

CHAPTER 102
Exit Manstein

No sooner had the Russians closed the ring around XI and XLII Corps, than Field-Marshal von Manstein, just installed in the H.Q. which he had had transferred from Vinnitsa to Proskurov, learnt that the 3rd and 4th Ukrainian Fronts' forces had begun a combined attack on the Nikopol' bridgehead. But he was soon spared the anxiety of having to wage two defensive battles simultaneously, for on February 2, by order of O.K.H., the 6th Army, which was fighting in this sector, was transferred from Army Group "South" to Army Group "A".

Due to Hitler's obstinacy, Manstein left a rather poor legacy to Field-Marshal von Kleist, since the four corps comprising the 6th Army were completely worn out and, in addition, were firmly held in a pincer movement between the 3rd and 4th Ukrainian Fronts' forces; though the thick mud would soon thwart Generals Malinovsky and Tolbukhin in their attempt to benefit strategically from the

▽ and ▷ Once again the spring rasputitsa *engulfed the Eastern Front battlefields in mud and slush. In the spring of 1943 it had caused Manstein's great counter-offensive to peter out; now, in 1944, the slowing-down of the war of movement favoured the hard-pressed Wehrmacht.*
▷ ▽ Victims of the winter fighting are brought to light by the thaw.

tactical advantages which their superior resources had given them.

On February 3, General Malinovsky's 46th and 8th Armies reached Apostolovo, 30 miles from Nikopol', at the same time as the 4th Ukrainian Front's forces were going into storm this latter town's defences on the left bank of the Dniepr. Whereupon a command from the Führer ordered General von Vormann to send in his 24th Panzer Division; but this formation, though most ably commanded by Lieutenant-General M. von Edelsheim, arrived too late to plug the gap in the line at Apostolovo, as Wöhler and Manstein had tried to tell Hitler it would.

Against the Nikopol' bridgehead General Tolbukhin sent in no fewer than 12 infantry and two armoured divisions; General F. Schörner defended it with six infantry divisions and the two Panzer divisions of his XXX Corps. However, the strength of the former had been reduced to that of just one regiment, whilst on the day of the attack, the Panzer divisions had only five sound tanks. Despite the strong Nazi convictions which imbued Schörner and made him resist with great courage, he was pushed back from the right bank of the Dniepr, leaving behind him large quantities of *matériel;* on February 9, the 4th Ukrainian Front's forces liberated Nikopol', though the important engineering centre of Krivoy-Rog was not taken by the 3rd Ukrainian Front forces until February 22. By the end of the month the German 6th Army, in considerable disarray, had taken up positions behind the Ingulets, a tributary of the Dniepr, which flows into it just east of Kherson.

The Russians roll on

Whilst the 6th Army's retreat considerably shortened the line that Kleist now had to hold, Manstein's stretched between Vinnitsa and Rovno; furthermore, there had been heavy losses in the fighting at Korsun', Nikopol', and Krivoy-Rog, with the Panzer divisions in particular being reduced to an average of about 30 tanks, about 20 per cent of their normal strength

of 152 Pzkw IV and V tanks.

According to the calculations of Army Group "South", January and February had been expensive months for the enemy, who had lost 25,353 prisoners, 3,928 tanks, and 3,536 guns; but as Manstein rightly points out in his memoirs:

"These figures only served to show the enormous resources at the Red Army's command. The Russians were no longer merely hurling in infantrymen–the drop in the number of prisoners to the amount of arms captured or destroyed showed either that they had been able to save men by sacrificing arms and equipment, or that they had suffered enormous losses in manpower."

At Rastenburg, the Germans were counting upon the combined effects of these losses and of the thaw to slow down, then halt, the Russian advance. The staff sections of Army Group "South" were much less optimistic: the Russians still had 50 to 100 tanks per tank corps, making a total of 1,500 against less than 400 for the Germans. Secondly, radio Intelligence showed that between Rovno and Mozyr' another front, the 1st Belorussian Front (commanded by General Rokossovsky) was coming into being.

Faced with this information, Manstein reformed as best he could to reinforce his 4th *Panzerarmee,* which barred the enemy's advance towards Tarnopol' and Chernovtsy. Thus Generals Wöhler and Hube were forced to give up five Panzer divisions to Raus, who also received three infantry divisions from O.K.H.

Vatutin's death

Despite these reinforcements, the 4th Army was destroyed on the very first day – March 4 – of the new offensive launched by the 1st Belorussian Front's armies, now commanded by Marshal Zhukov. What, then, had happened to his predecessor, General Vatutin? The only thing one can state for sure is that he died at Kiev on April 14, 1944. But how? At the time of his death, a Moscow communiqué stated that it was from the after effects of a chill caught at the front. But the Soviet academician Telpukhovsky affirms "that this ardent defender of his socialist mother-country, this eminent general and Soviet army commander" – a judgement with which none will disagree – died as the result of bullet wounds inflicted by the enemy. In November 1961, however, during the twenty-second Congress of the Russian Communist Party, Nikita Khruschev, who had been Vatutin's political aide, revealed to an astonished audience that the liberator of Kiev had committed suicide whilst suffering from a fit of nervous depression. This is the version related by Michel Garder in his book *A War Unlike The Others,* published in 1962. It should be noted, however, that he does not accept this story himself, and in fact declares it to be highly unlikely. Finally, Alexander Werth, who during the war was the *Sunday Times'* Russian correspondent, brought out yet another explanation. According to him, Vatutin had been ambushed and killed by a band of Ukrainian nationalists: a version which has the advantage of explaining why Khruschev, himself a Ukrainian, might have distorted the facts.

The offensive restarts

At all events, Zhukov, on going into battle on March 4, 1944, had under him three tank and six rifle armies, i.e. about 60 divisions and at least 1,000 tanks. Attacking on both sides of Shepetovka on a front of about 120 miles, he gained between 15 and 30 miles in less than 48 hours, so that by March 6 his 3rd Guards Tank Army was approaching the L'vov – Odessa railway line at Volochisk, the last but one communication and supply link for Army Group "South" before the Carpathians.

By March 9, having covered some 80 miles in less than six days, General Rybalko's tanks came up against the hastily improvised Tarnopol' defences. At the same time, the 1st *Panzerarmee* and the German 8th Army were being severely mauled by the left wing of Zhukov's forces and the 2nd Ukrainian Front, numbering seven rifle and two tank armies. Immediately the forces of Generals Hube and Wöhler, which had not yet recovered from their losses at Korsun', and had had part of their Panzer units transferred to Raus, buckled under the

▽ *A knocked-out German Pzkw IV. Notice the curved "skirt armour" around the turret, intended to explode anti-tank shells before they reached the main armour.*
▽▽ *Czech troops, serving with the Red Army, break cover for the attack.*

shock. In particular, the 8th Army was forced to withdraw towards Uman'.

Manstein, however, was not surprised by this new Russian offensive, whose purpose he saw only too clearly. *Stavka's* aim was, in fact, nothing less than the cutting off of Army Groups "South" and "A" from the rest of the German troops fighting on the Eastern Front, pushing them south-west, as far as Odessa on the Black Sea, where they would stand no more chance of being evacuated than the defenders of the Crimea at Sevastopol'.

Manstein withdraws

The Soviet offensive of March 1944 put great pressure on the whole German line; and faced with such an overwhelming threat, Manstein did not hesitate. First, he ordered Generals Hube and Wöhler to withdraw immediately; then he decided to mass his troops around General Raus to stop Zhukov taking the most threatening route across the Dniestr to the Carpathians via Chernovtsy. With his XIII Corps covering L'vov in the Brody region, he ordered XLVIII Panzer Corps, then fighting 120 miles to the east, southwest of Berdichev, to go to the defence of Tarnopol'. To carry out such an order, it first had to slip through the columns of the northbound 1st Ukrainian Front armies and do so without being engaged by the enemy. That it succeeded was due to the coolness and skill of its commander, General Balck, and also to errors committed by the Russians. Mellenthin, chief-of-staff of XLVIII Panzer Corps makes the following remark in this connection: "Since Russian attacks were nearly always aimed at large centres – probably because the Soviet generals wanted to attract attention to themselves by having their names inserted in special communiqués – we avoided such centres like the plague." Their manoeuvre was successful, and Manstein was able to ward off the catastrophe that had seemed so near, making the Russians fight for more than a month before they could enter Tarnopol'. However, it was not his responsibility to impose his views on Kleist, and he was not going to abandon his fellow-officer, just when the latter's 6th Army was locked in battle with the 50 or 60 divisions of the 3rd and 4th Ukrainian Fronts' armies.

At O.K.H., where the actions of the two army groups ought to have been co-ordinated, Hitler obstinately refused to allow the 6th Army to abandon the Bug line and strengthen Manstein's right wing. The consequence was that on March 13 Marshal Konev had pierced the defences that the 8th Army had hastily improvised on the right bank of the Bug, and had crossed the river on a 100-mile wide front. This breakthrough cruelly exposed the right wing of the *1st Panzerarmee*, whilst its left wing was also under pressure.

Ordered to Obersalzberg on March 19 to take part in a ceremony during which Rundstedt, on behalf of his fellow officers, presented vows of loyalty to the Führer, Manstein took advantage of the occasion to put his point of view: in his opinion four decisions had to be made, and quickly: "1. Immediate withdrawal of the 6th Army behind the Dniestr. The salient it occupied on the Bug was still much too pronounced and demanded too many troops for its defence. It was Kleist himself, commanding Army Group 'A', who had proposed this;
2. The units thus freed would then be rapidly transferred to the area between the Dniestr and the Prut, preventing the 8th Army from being pushed back from the Dniestr towards the south-east;
3. Army Group 'A' to be given the clear responsibility, in liaison with Rumanian forces, for covering Rumania on the Dniestr or the Prut; and
4. A rapid strengthening of the northern wing of Army Group 'South', to prevent its being pushed back into the Carpathians, or to prevent a Russian advance on L'vov."

▽ *More mobile artillery for the Panzer arm. This is a* Hummel – *"bumble-bee" – which mounted a 15-cm gun on a Pzkw IV hull. This weapon was officially classified as* schwere Panzerhaubitze – *"heavy armoured howitzer". The 15-cm gun had been the mainstay of the German medium artillery for years.*

Jetsam of defeat: German prisoners savour Russian hospitality at ration time.

Keeping up the momentum: Russian infantry, backed by armour.

But Hitler remained intractable; there were to be neither substantial reinforcements, nor freedom of manoeuvre for his generals.

The Soviet Blitzkrieg

Meanwhile, in the 2nd Ukrainian Front's sector, operations were taking place at Blitzkrieg speed, and even so farseeing a commander as Manstein was being left behind by events. Almost at the same time as he was suggesting to Hitler that the 6th and 8th Armies be withdrawn behind the Dniestr, Marshal Rotmistrov's 5th Guards Tank Army and General Kravchenko's 6th Army reached and crossed the river on either side of the town of Soroki.

Worse still, on March 21, Marshal Zhukov, who had regrouped his forces after his moderate success at Tarnopol', attacked the point just where the commands of General Raus and Hube came together. Throwing three tank armies into the attack, he broke through and immediately advanced south; by the 23rd his forward troops had reached the Dniestr at Chernovtsy, with the resultant

danger that the 1st *Panzerarmee*, fighting near Proskurov on the Bug, would be cut off. It had to be ordered to move west and try to make contact with the 4th Army, for already the only means of supplying it was by airlift.

After a whole day spent in sending and receiving a series of curt telephone calls, Manstein was peremptorily summoned to the Berghof. Here he was received by Hitler at about noon on March 25, and it was only after hours of discussion, and Manstein's threat to resign his command, that Hitler gave in on the two points he was most insistent upon: firstly, he was authorised to tell Hube to fight his way through to the west, and secondly he was assured that he would very soon be reinforced by the *Waffen*-S.S. II Panzer Corps which, in case there was a cross-Channel landing, was stationed near Alençon.

But this meeting had lost the Germans 48 hours, of which the Russians took full advantage: on March 27, the Russian 1st and 4th Tank Armies, commanded respectively by Generals D. D. Lelyushenko and K. S. Moskalenko, joined up at Sekiryany, on the Dniestr's right bank, and behind the 1st *Panzerarmee*. Hube was thus caught in a trap near

The Russian T-34/85 medium tank

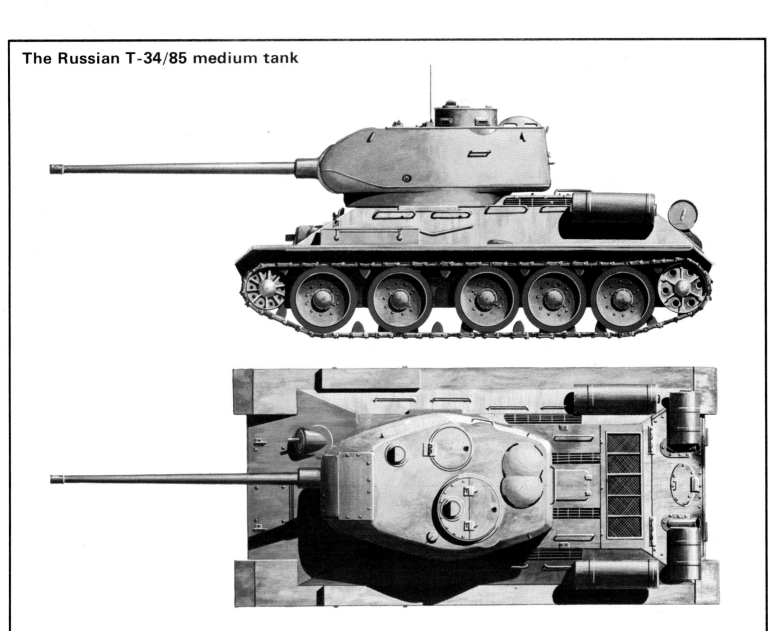

Weight: 32 tons.
Crew: 5.
Armament: one M1944 85-mm gun with 56 rounds and two 7.62-mm Degtyarev machine guns with 2,745 rounds.
Armour: hull glacis, nose, sides, and rear 47-mm, decking 30-mm, belly 20-mm; turret front 90-mm, sides 75-mm, rear 60-mm, and roof 20-mm.
Engine: one V-2-34 12-cylinder inline, 500-hp.
Speed: 32 mph on roads, 10 mph cross-country.
Range: 220 miles on roads, 125 miles cross-country.
Length: 24 feet 9 inches.
Width: 9 feet 10 inches.
Height: 7 feet 11 inches.

Skala-Podolskaya with about ten divisions, including three Panzer divisions, there is no doubt that everything south of the Pripet would have collapsed if this brave general, who had lost an arm in World War I, had not shown such optimism, resolution, and skill, and inspired such confidence in his troops, both officers and other ranks.

Manstein finally sacked by Hitler

Did Hitler regret having agreed to Manstein's suggestions, or did he think him less capable than General Model of lessening the damage that his own stubbornness had caused in the first place? Whatever the reason, on March 30, Manstein, the victor of Sevastopol' and Khar'kov, took the plane to Obersalzberg, where at one and the same time, he was awarded the Oak Leaves to the Knight's Cross of the Iron Cross and relieved of the command which he had assumed in such grim circumstances on November 24, 1942.

"For a long time Göring and Himmler had been conspiring towards my downfall," wrote Manstein. "I knew this. But the main reason was that on March 25 Hitler had been obliged to grant me what he had previously, and in public, refused me. On shaking hands to take leave of him, I said 'I hope your decision today will not turn out to be mistaken.'

"Kleist was received after me and

dismissed in like fashion. As we left the Berghof, we saw our successors, Colonel-General Model, who was going to take over my army group which would now be called Army Group 'North Ukraine' and General Schörner, Kleist's replacement, already waiting at the door!''

And so, on April 2, Colonel-General Walther Model, in whom Hitler recognised the best repairer of his own mistakes, took command of what a few days later was rather pompously re-christened Army Group "North Ukraine".

Major-General Mellenthin who, as chief-of-staff of XLVIII Panzer Corps, got to know Model well, describes him as a "small thin man, jovial and lively, whom one could never have imagined separated from his monocle. But, however great his single-mindedness, his energy or his courage, he was very different from Manstein. In particular, Model was only too prone to busy himself with every tiniest detail, and to tell his army commanders, and even his corps commanders, where and how they were to draw up their troops. General Balck, for example, the commander of XLVIII Panzer Corps, considered this tendency in his new chief to be most irritating."

Hube wins through

At the same time as Hube's "mobile pocket" was painfully fighting its way west, Zhukov had crossed the Dniestr and reached the foothills of the Carpathians, first having captured Chernovtsy, Kolomyya, and Nadvornaya. It was at this time that the II S.S. Panzer Corps, comprising the 9th and 10th *"Hohenstaufen"* and *"Frundsberg"* Panzer Divisions, arrived in the L'vov region, under the command of Colonel-General P. Hausser. In addition Hitler had made available to Army Group "South" the 367th Division and the 100th *Jäger* Division, which had taken part in the occupation of Hungary. Thanks to these reinforcements, Generals Model and Raus succeeded on April 9 in re-establishing contact at Buchach on the River Strypa (one of the Dniestr's left bank tributaries) with the 1st *Panzerarmee* which, despite a retreat of some 120 miles through enemy territory, and having to cross four rivers, had managed to save most of its equipment. A few days later Hube was killed in an air accident *en route* to receive promotion from Hitler.

▽ *Weary and dispirited German infantry reveal the strain of the fighting for the Dniepr bend. Only the man on the left has managed to crack a smile for the camera.*

STALIN
RUSSIA'S OVERLORD

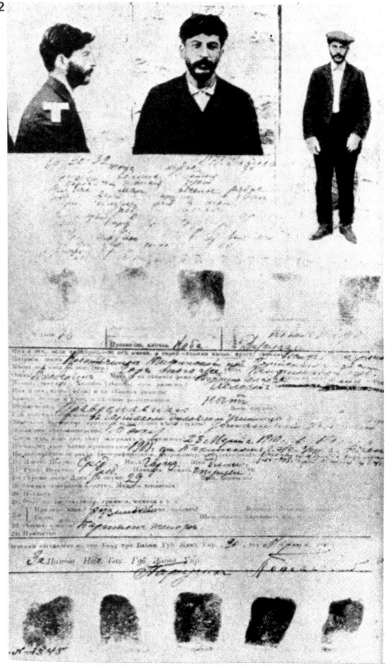

1

From Georgian political agitator to party boss.
1. *Joseph Vissarionovich Stalin, successor to Lenin and one of the eight men who spurred on the October Revolution.*
2. *From the Tsarist police files: Stalin's record as a subversive agitator, complete with finger-prints, photographs, and full details of past convictions. He was exiled to Siberia twice.*
3. *Stalin with Lenin and Kalinin. When Lenin fell ill in 1922, Stalin became one of the five committee members who assumed collective leadership in his stead.*

To Roosevelt he was "Joe", a man with whom one could "do business"; to Churchill he was first a much-needed ally, and then a long-term menace even greater than Hitler. And Joseph Stalin wasted no time in exploiting the differences between his allies to the full. This came naturally, after decades of consolidation and advancement which had made him Lenin's unchallenged successor and absolute master of the Soviet Union.

Stalin started life as Joseph Vissarionovich Dzhugashvili, the son of a Georgian shoemaker. Born at Gori on December 21, 1879, he was originally intended to study for the priesthood in the Georgian Orthodox Church. In 1894 he entered the theological seminary at Tiflis and soon made his mark as an industrious and keen-minded student. However, he soon began to dabble in socialist ideas and was expelled from the seminary for "disloyal" views, in 1899.

Dzhugashvili threw himself into the revolutionary movement and became an enthusiastic supporter of Lenin's journal *Iskra* ("The Spark"). Elected to the Social Democratic Party in 1901

3

4. *Biding his time. Stalin with Lenin in Gorky in 1922. With Zinoviev, Kamenev, Bukharin, and Rykov, Stalin embarked on a cautious policy in economics and foreign affairs. Lenin remained as an elder statesman until his death in January 1924.*

5. *Ten years after Lenin's death, and Stalin has moved into a position of prominence. In the front row Ordzhonikidze, Stalin, Molotov, and Kirov whose assassination was used as one of the justifications for the purges of 1934-1938. Back row: Yenukidze (later purged), Voroshilov, Kaganovich, and Kuibishev, who died in an alleged medical murder. His ruthlessness with his comrades was reflected in the rigorous way he enforced a policy of industrialisation and collectivisation which displaced about 25,000,000 peasants. He justified these moves by stating that Russia was 50 or 100 years behind other countries, and they undoubtedly gave the U.S.S.R. the industrial resources necessary to prosecute the war.*

he was soon arrested as a subversive and was deported to Siberia; but he escaped and returned to Tiflis shortly after the Social Democrats had split into the Bolshevik and Menshevik factions. Dzhugashvili supported the Bolsheviks and first met Lenin in 1905. Between then and 1914 he emerged as the Bolshevik leader of Baku and participated in party congresses held in Sweden and Britain.

In 1912 Lenin and the Bolsheviks finally broke with the Mensheviks and formed a central party, with Lenin making

6. "Uncle Joe" as seen in a contemporary propaganda poster.
7. Stalin with Maxim Gorky the writer. Stalin was active in the preparations for the October Revolution as the editor of the party paper Pravda.
8. Molotov and Stalin and other party leaders on Lenin's tomb. Stalin was less concerned with revolutionary ideals than with maintaining his own authority over the Communist world.
9. Dictator at work: Stalin signs a death warrant. Opposition was removed by trial or murder.

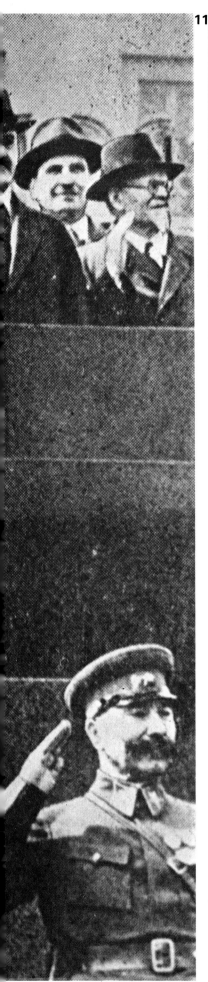

Dzhugashvili a member of the central committee. He was the first editor of the party newspaper *Pravda*, which appeared in 1912. In the following year he was arrested again and spent the next four years in Siberia, where he adopted the pseudonym "Stalin", the "man of steel".

Returning from Siberia in March 1917, Stalin resumed the editorship of *Pravda*. He played no direct part in the Bolshevik revolution of 1917, but Lenin appointed him Commissar of Nationalities after the Bolshevik seizure of power. Later he was appointed Commissar of the Workers' and Peasants' Inspectorate, with the power to supervise the other branches of the new administration. In the civil war (1918-1920) Stalin was a member of the Council of Defence, a political commissar, and inspector of fronts. He played a key rôle in the defence of the young Bolshevik state, organising the defence of Petrograd (later Leningrad), Tsaritsyn (later Stalingrad), and Orel. He also served during the war with Poland in 1920. It was during these years that his clash with Trotsky, the founder of the Red Army and Lenin's generally-accepted heir-apparent, began. In 1922 Stalin was appointed secretary-general of the party— an important stage in his advancement, for it gave him eventual control over both party and government.

After Lenin's death (January 1924) the power struggle began in earnest, with Stalin, Zinoviev, and Kamenev closing ranks against Trotsky. While extending his control over the party by abolishing its freedom of expression, Stalin managed to oust Trotsky. He then turned against Zinoviev and Kamenev by allying himself with the three key party "right-wingers", Bukharin, Rykov, and Tomsky. After expelling Trotsky, Zinoviev, and Kamenev from the party he turned against his former allies and meted out similar treatment to them. When he expelled Trotsky from Russia in 1929 Stalin remained as the undisputed overlord of the U.S.S.R.

In the next decade Stalin's energy and utter ruthlessness transformed Russia from its backward state into a modern industrial power. It was an agonising process, involving the forcible transfer of millions of peasants to industrial centres, but without it Russia would never have been able to survive the war. At the same time, however, the despotic nature of his rule revealed itself in the mass purges of 1936-38, which broke the last shards of possible opposition.

The crisis of 1941 brought out all Stalin's bedrock qualities: tenacity, iron nerves, and willpower. These qualities he never lost—and they paid dividends.

10. *The last parade. The generals at the foot of Lenin's tomb in this May Day Parade were nearly all to be executed as traitors. The only survivors, Budenny and Voroshilov, were unable to cope with the German advances of 1941, though Voroshilov later became a capable diplomat. The generals are, from left to right, Tukhachevsky, Byelov, Voroshilov, Yegorov, and Budenny. In his purges Stalin destroyed the "brains" of the Red Army of the 1930's.*
11. *Leaders and advisors. Stalin and Churchill with Hopkins and Eden at Teheran.*
12. *Stalin's son Vasily as a pilot during the war. He was to die in disgrace in a home for alcoholics.*

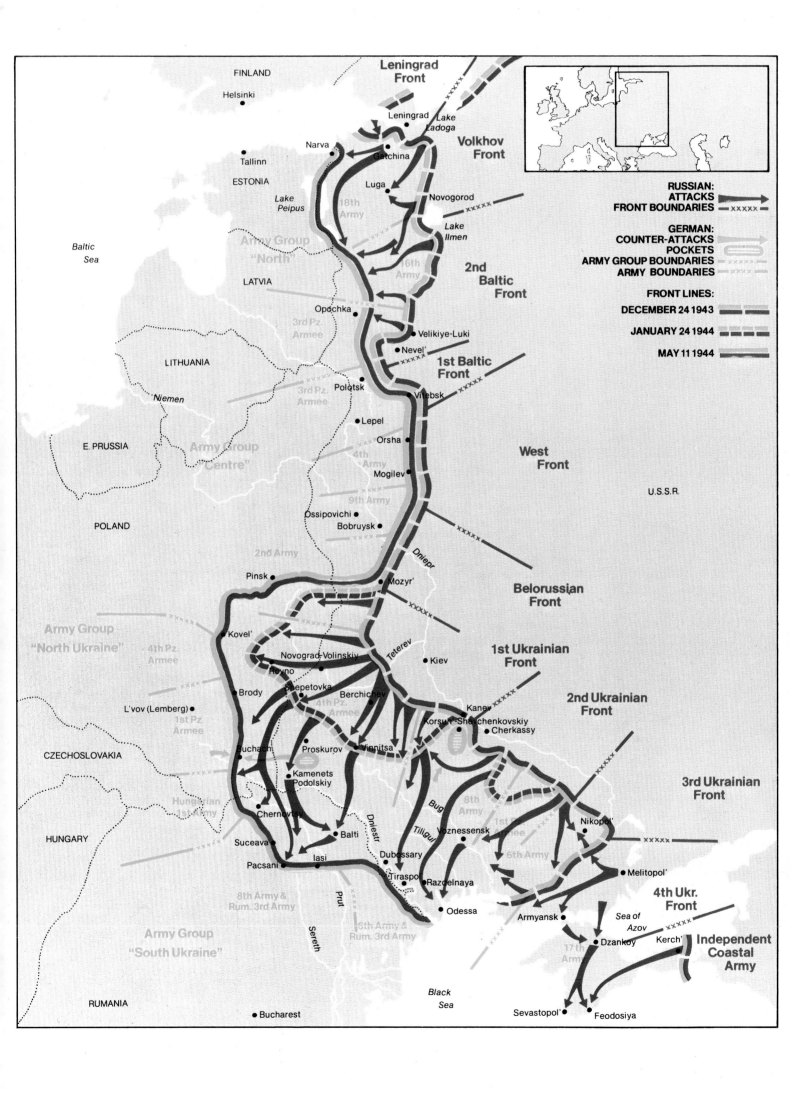

CHAPTER 103
Back to the Crimea

On March 30, like his colleague Manstein, Kleist had at the same time been decorated and dismissed; fortunately his successor, General Schörner, was a man after his own heart. A few days earlier, the 8th Army had been transferred to Army Group "A", which a week later was renamed Army Group "South Ukraine". But by the end of the month Schörner no longer held a square inch of Ukrainian territory–in fact, he considered he had done well to save the 6th and 8th Armies from complete disaster.

The Dniestr having been forced by Konev's armour, the 8th Army was soon face to face with the prospect of being cut off from all contact with Army Group "South", and of being pushed right back to the mouth of the Danube. Thanks, however, to the rapidity with which Marshal Antonescu moved his Rumanian 4th Army into the line, and to the splendid tactical sense of General Wöhler, not only was this disaster avoided, but also a break between Model and Schörner, who maintained contact at Kuty, 40 miles west of Chernovtsy.

This success, however, was obtained at the cost of northern Bessarabia and Moldavia, for the Prut was no more successful than the Dniestr in halting the Soviet tank advance. In fact, all that the stiffening of Germano–Rumanian resistance managed to accomplish, in mid-April, was to stop the Russians in front of Chişinau in Bessarabia and Iaşi in Moldavia, though the towns of Botoşani, Paşcani, and Suceava fell into their hands.

The German 6th Army, which by Hitler's express command had been kept on the lower Bug beyond all reasonable limits, almost suffered the same fate near Odessa as had its predecessor at Stalingrad. Malinovsky and the 3rd Ukrainian Front tried to turn a good situation to their advantage by pushing through the gap that had been made between the 6th Army's left flank and the right of the 8th Army as a result of the Uman' breakthrough, with the obvious aim of cutting it off from the Dniestr; and it has to be admitted that it had plenty of resources to accomplish this.

However, Hitler, judging by the direc-tive he issued on April 2 to the commanders of Army Groups "A", "South", and "Centre", did not seem to think the situation so dangerous, since he ordered Schörner to hold "for the time being, the line of the Tiligul estuary to Dubossary on the Dniestr until such time as it would be possible to supply the Crimea independently of Odessa. The retreat to the Dniestr ought, however, still to be prepared."

The position to be occupied by the 6th

▽ *Russian poster: the bayonet of the Red Army tears into the Nazi beast.*

Army between the estuary of the Tiligul and Dubossary on the Dniestr's left bank, level with the city of Chişinau, was about 120 miles long. With the completely worn-out troops that General Hollidt had, such a line could not be held indefinitely, even if he had been allowed sufficient time to dig himself in and organise himself.

The enterprising Malinovsky took good care, however, to allow him no time; on April 5, supported by the guns of a whole corps of artillery, he captured the Tiligul position, whilst the squadrons and tanks of the Kuban' Cavalry Corps, commanded by Lieutenant-General Pliev, took the railway junction of Razdelnaya by surprise, thus cutting off the enemy's access to the Dniestr crossings at Tiraspol. Faced with these reverses, which placed him in a catastrophic position, the 6th Army's commander took it upon himself, on April 9, to evacuate Odessa. Crossing the Dniestr, his troops, in collaboration with the Rumanian 3rd Army, organised the defence of the river's right bank, between the Black Sea and the Dubossary region. North of Chişinau, Hollidt's left flank once more made contact with General Wöhler's right. In Stalin's special com-muniqué, which described the liberation of Odessa in particularly glowing terms, the honour of this victory went to the gallant defenders of Stalingrad: Colonel-General Chuikov and his 62nd Army.

Crisis in the Crimea

The April 2 directive, from which we have just quoted, showed Hitler's resolution to defend the Crimea at all costs. Less than a week later, the storm clouds which Kleist and Manstein had seen gathering burst with irresistible force. Within Army Group "A", it was the German 17th Army, under the command of Colonel-General C. Jaenecke, and comprising V and IL Corps and the Rumanian I Mountain Corps, themselves made up of five German divisions and seven Rumanian divisions, which had the task of defending the peninsula. It must, however, be said that two of the Rumanian divisions were in action against the partisans who, since November 1943, had held the Krimskiye massif, whose peaks dominate the southern coast of the Crimea. The key to the Crimea,

▽ *The inevitable* rasputitsa *of spring. Here German troops are attempting to extricate a half-track stuck in the mud somewhere near Lake Ilmen.*

the Kamenskoye isthmus, was held by IL Corps (General R. Konrad), who had established his 50th, 111th, and 336th Divisions in soundly fortified positions defending this tongue of land, whilst the Rumanian 9th Cavalry Division kept watch on the Black Sea, and the Rumanian 10th and 19th Divisions performed the same task on the shore of the Sivash Lagoon. V Corps (General K. Allmendinger) kept an eye on the small bridgehead which the Russians had taken the previous autumn beyond the Kerch' Strait, a task in which it was helped by the 73rd and 98th Divisions, and the 6th Cavalry Division and 3rd Mountain Division of the Rumanian Army.

Stavka's plan

Stavka's plan to reconquer the peninsula meant the simultaneous action of the 4th Ukrainian Front and a separate army, known as the Independent Coastal Army. The first, with 18 infantry divisions and four armoured corps, would storm the Kamenskoye isthmus, whilst the second, 12 divisions strong, would break out of the Kerch' bridgehead, and they would then together converge upon Sevastopol'. As will be noted, the Russians had ensured a massive superiority in men and matériel.

On April 8, General Tolbukhin unleashed the offensive, the 4th Ukrainian Front attacking under an air umbrella as large as it was powerful.

On the right, the 2nd Guards Army, under Lieutenant-General G. F. Zakharov, was hard put to it to storm the Kamenskoye defences, and took 48 hours to reach the outskirts of Armyansk. On the left, breaking out of the small bridgehead on the Sivash Lagoon, which it had succeeded in linking to the mainland by means of a dike, the 51st Army, commanded by Lieutenant-General Ya. G. Kreizer, which had the main task, had in fact a much easier job, faced as it was by only the two Rumanian divisions. By midday on April 9, the 10th Division was submerged, and its collapse enabled the Soviet tanks to capture two days later the important junction of Dzhanskoy, where the railway leading to Sevastopol' divides from that leading to the town of Feodosiya and the port of Kerch'.

On April 11, in the Kerch' peninsula, the Independent Coastal Army, under General Eremenko, attacked in its turn; and

when one realises that Hitler, a prey to hesitation, thought he could conduct the Crimea campaign from Obersalzberg, it was little short of a miracle that General Jaenecke was able to withdraw his troops to their Sevastopol' positions without being intercepted by the combined forces of Tolbukhin and Eremenko, who had linked up on April 16 near Yalta. To defend its 25-mile long front before Sevastopol', the 17th Army could now count only upon the five German divisions already mentioned above. But they had been reduced, on average, to something like a third of their normal strength and were already tired. Therefore Schörner flew to see the Führer personally and put the case for the evacuation of his troops. In vain, however, and when Jaenecke, in his turn, went to Berchtesgaden to put the same arguments, he was even refused permission to return to Sevastopol', and was succeeded as head of the 17th Army, on April 27, by General Allmendinger.

On May 7, after artillery had softened up the positions for 48 hours, the 2nd Guards Army attacked the northern flank, as Manstein had done in 1942; but the Germans were too few to rival the

▽ German rolling stock destroyed by the Russians' tactical air forces. These, combined with the increasing success of partisans behind the German lines, made supply a constant problem for the army.

▷ *May 8, 1944: Soviet sailors enter Sevastopol'.*
▷ ▷ *An exhausted German soldier rests on the trail of a destroyed gun.*

heroic exploits of General Petrov's men. Thus, when General Allmendinger finally received a message on May 9 from the Führer authorising evacuation, it was already too late for it to be properly organised, especially since the Soviet Air Force, completely dominating the air, fired at anything that tried to take to the sea. On May 13, all resistance ceased in the region around the Khersonesskiy (Chersonese) peninsula, now (as in 1942) the last defence position.

The evacuation of the Crimea gave rise to dramatic scenes such as those described by Alexander Werth:

"For three days and nights, the Chersonese was that 'unspeakable inferno' to which German authors now refer. True, on the night of May 9–10 and on the following night, two small ships did come and perhaps 1,000 men were taken aboard. This greatly encouraged the remaining troops." But the Russians had no intention of letting the Germans get away by sea:

"And on the night of May 11–12 the *katyusha* mortars ('the Black Death' the Germans used to call them) came into action. What followed was a massacre. The Germans fled in panic beyond the second and then the third line of their defences, and when, in the early morning hours, Russian tanks drove in, they began to surrender in large numbers, among them their commander, General Böhme, and several other staff officers who had been sheltering in the cellar of the only farm building on the promontory.

"Thousands of wounded had been taken to the tip of the promontory, and here were also some 750 S.S.-men who refused to surrender, and went on firing. A few dozen survivors tried in the end to get away by sea in small boats or rafts. Some

of these got away, but often only to be machine-gunned by Russian aircraft. These desperate men were hoping to get to Rumania, Turkey, or maybe to be picked up by some German or Rumanian vessel."

The 17th Army's losses were very heavy. On April 8 it had comprised 128,500 German and 66,000 Rumanian troops; of these, 96,800 Germans and 40,200 Rumanians were evacuated, leaving behind 31,700 German and 25,800 Rumanian dead or missing. But it must be remembered that of the 137,000 evacuated, more than 39,000 were wounded and all their equipment lost. This was the terrible price of Hitler's intransigence.

The struggle in the north

Let us now turn from the Soviets' winter offensive south of the Pripet to the campaigns which, between January 15 and March 15, resulted in the complete relief of Leningrad through the rout of Army Group "North".

At the beginning of the year, Field-Marshal von Küchler, with his right flank at Polotsk and his left up by the Gulf of Finland, to the west of Oranienbaum, was holding a front of more than 500 miles with 40 divisions, all infantry. This line of defence was dangerously exposed, both at Oranienbaum and south of Leningrad, as well as on the left bank of the Volkhov. Which is why, on December 30, the commander of Army Group "North" suggested to Hitler that he withdraw his 16th and 18th Armies to the "Panther" position which was then being prepared; this would reduce the front by more than 60 miles; and of the remaining 440 miles,

△ A Panther tank meets its end.
△▷ A Russian anti-tank gun
and its crew lie in wait for prey.
▷▷ German Panzergrenadiers
aboard their battlefield transport.

more than 120 miles consisted of Lake Peipus and 50 of the expanse of water formed by the junction of the Gulf of Finland with the mouth of the Narva.

Although such a withdrawal would have saved eight divisions, Hitler rejected Küchler's suggestion, for he was fully aware that the Russian and Finnish Governments had resumed diplomatic contact at Stockholm; thus to abandon the positions held by Army Group "North" might encourage Finland to bow out of the war.

The 18th Army caught

In the meantime, on January 14 the Leningrad Front's armies, under General Govorov, attacked the left wing of the German 18th Army, commanded by Colonel-General von Lindemann. According to German authorities, Govorov commanded a force of 42 infantry divisions and nine tank corps, though these figures cannot be checked since Soviet historians such as Telpukhovsky give no information on the strength of the Red Army forces on this occasion. Simultaneously, General

Meretskov's Volkhov Front forces, with 18 infantry and 15 tank divisions, attacked the right wing of the 18th Army in the Novgorod sector.

Thus this offensive planned by *Stavka* took the form of a pincer movement, with Govorov and Meretskov trying to meet at Luga, so catching Lindemann's 18 divisions in the trap.

On the Leningrad Front, the Soviet aim was to reduce the Peterhof salient, and to this end, General Fedyuninsky's 2nd Shock Army, from the Oranienbaum bridgehead, and General Maslennikov's 42nd Army were to aim for the common objective of Gatchina. The Germans, behind well-established defensive positions, put up a very stubborn resistance, and held out for nearly a week. But once the 126th, 170th, and 215th Divisions collapsed, a large gap was opened up in the German positions. On January 26, Govorov reached Pushkin, formerly Tsarskoye-Selo, and extended his offensive right up to the Mga region, a victory which enabled the Russians to capture large quantities of arms, in particular 85 guns of greater than 10-inch calibre.

On the Volkhov front, General Meretskov's capture of Lyuban' enabled direct

railway communication between Moscow and Leningrad to be re-established; whilst north of Lake Ilmen, his left flank, comprising the 59th Army, commanded by General Korovnikov, punched a gaping hole in the German defences, recaptured Novgorod, and speeded up its advance towards the west. On January 21 the plan prepared by Marshal Zhukov entered the phase of exploitation.

Küchler sacked

With both wings of his army in disarray, and no reinforcements except the single 12th Panzer Division, Küchler realised the necessity of withdrawing the 18th Army to the Luga as a matter of urgency, only to see himself immediately relieved of his command in favour of Colonel-General Model. Monstrously unjust as this decision was, it nevertheless helped to save Army Group "North", since Hitler showed himself more ready to listen to a commander of working-class origin than to the aristocratic Küchler; and the day after his appointment, Model was given two more divisions.

△ *Field-Marshal Erich von Manstein. Sacked in April 1944, his dismissal was permanent, unlike that of several other senior commanders. Liddell Hart described him as "the Allies' most formidable military opponent—a man who combined modern ideas of manoeuvre, a mastery of technical detail and great driving power".*

Field-Marshal Walther Model was born in 1891. He was chief-of-staff of IV Corps in the Polish campaign and of 16th Army in the French. He commanded the 3rd Panzer Division in "Barbarossa" and 9th Army in 1942. Always in favour with Hitler, Model was instrumental in getting *"Zitadelle"* postponed until July 1943, when he failed to stem the Russian counter-offensive at Orel. In 1944 he was successively head of Army Groups "North", "South", and "Centre". Model was then transferred to the West as supreme commander and then head of Army Group "B".

On the whole, Model, a capable soldier, adopted the arrangements made by his predecessor, and moreover managed to get them approved by Hitler. However, hardly had he got his army from out of the clutches of Govorov, than the latter, enlarging the radius of his activities, crossed the River Luga to the left of the town of the same name; Pskov, the main supply base of Army Group "North" seemed to be the objective of this push, but at the same time it seriously exposed Colonel-General Lindemann's rear. Furthermore, the left wing of General Hansen's 16th Army was beginning to wilt under the attacks of General Popov and his Baltic Front, and to make matters worse, was in great danger of being flooded by the waters of Lake Ilmen.

This last extension of the Soviet offensive forced Model to abandon his intention of placing his 18th Army as a defensive barrier between Lake Ilmen and Lake Peipus. He asked for, and obtained, permission from O.K.H. to withdraw all his forces back to the "Panther" line, which, stretching from a point west of Nevel', passed through Opochka and Pskov, then followed the western bank of Lake Peipus, finally reaching the Gulf of Finland at Narva. Begun on February 17, this withdrawal was concluded by mid-March without any untoward incident. When Model was called upon to replace Manstein a fortnight later, Lindemann succeeded him at the head of Army Group "North", being in turn succeeded at the head of the 18th Army by General Loch.

For the German Army, therefore, the first quarter of 1944 was marked by a long series of reverses, which, although their worst effects had been avoided, had nevertheless been very costly in terms of men and materials. And many reports originating at the front showed that reinforcements were arriving without the necessary training.

The threat to Rumania

Furthermore, the protective glacis of *"Festung Europa"* was being seriously encroached upon. Bucharest and the vital oil wells of Ploieşti, Budapest and the Danube basin, Galicia with its no less vital wells at Borislaw, Riga and the central Baltic, were all coming within the compass of Soviet strategy. So that these further defeats of the Third Reich had far more than merely military significance, and encroached upon the diplomatic and political plane.

As we have seen, Hitler was afraid that the withdrawal of Army Group "North" to its "Panther" defensive position might tempt Finland, which he knew to be engaged in discussions with Russia, to get out of the war and conclude a separate peace. Küchler's defeat and the battered state in which the 16th and 18th Armies reached the "Panther" line encouraged the Finns to continue their negotiations. These were broken off, however, on April 1, when the Russians insisted that all German troops should be evacuated or interned within 30 days, and that the Finns should pay them 600 million dollars in reparations, to be paid in five annual instalments.

Hungary occupied

On March 27, 11 German divisions began Operation *"Margarethe"*, the occupation of another satellite, Hungary.

"What was I to do?" asks the former Regent in his memoirs. "It was quite clear that my abdication would not prevent the occupation of Hungary, and would allow Hitler to install a government entirely composed of Nazis, as the example of Italy clearly showed. 'Whilst I am still Regent,' I told myself, 'the Germans will at least have to show some consideration. They will be forced to keep me at the head of the army, which they will not be able to absorb into the German Army. Nor will they be able to place at the head of the government Hungarian Nazi puppets, who would hunt down, not only many Hungarian patriots, but also 800,000 Jews, and tens of thousands of refugees who had found shelter in our country. I could very conveniently have abdicated at that time and saved myself many criticisms. But I could not leave a sinking ship which at that moment had the greatest possible need of its captain.'"

In line with this reasoning, Horthy accepted the *fait accompli,* and on March 23 swore in a new cabinet, whose prime minister was General Döme-Sztojay, his ambassador in Berlin. But Hitler's Klessheim trap freed him from any obligation *vis-à-vis* the Third Reich, and henceforth the old Admiral was to embark upon a policy of resistance.

CHAPTER 104
ANZIO: failure or foundation?

A map on the scale of 1:1,000,000 is sufficient to give us an immediate picture of the results of the Soviet winter offensive in the first quarter of 1944, but to follow the Allies' progress in Italy the scale would have to be at least 1:100,000. Even on this scale we would not find all the heights and place names we shall be mentioning in our narrative.

A cartoonist in the Third Reich showed a map of Italy at this time as a boot, up which a snail, wearing the Allied flags, is slowly climbing. At about Easter, Allied public opinion did not attempt to conceal its disappointment, not to say impatience, at the results of Anglo-American strategy in the Mediterranean. As can well be imagined, political and military leaders in London and Washington were hardly able to pacify these frustrations by making public the vast organisation, training, and preparation then going on towards an operation which was to bear its first fruits at dawn on June 6. Certainly after five months of marking time the Allies scored a decisive victory over their enemy in Italy, but only less than 30 days before the Normandy landings and thus a little late in the day. The normal course of development of Allied strategy was hindered by a chain of unfortunate circumstances which, it must be said, had nothing to do with politics.

On January 16, 1944 the American 5th Army, still under the command of Lieutenant-General Mark Clark, renewed its attack on the Cassino redoubt, which was defended by XIV Panzer Corps from the 10th Army (General von Vietinghoff-Scheel). The main objective of this under-

▽ *American soldiers splash ashore at Anzio on January 22. The Allies gained complete strategic surprise by the landing, which went in against negligible opposition. It took the Germans some six hours to realise that an invasion was in progress behind the Cassino front.*

taking in such difficult terrain was to force Kesselring to move up the reinforcements at present around Rome to strengthen his front. When this had been achieved, the American VI Corps (Major-General John P. Lucas), which was to effect a surprise landing on the beaches at Anzio and Nettuno, would find the way open to drive inland and attack the enemy's communications. This was the fundamental idea of Operation "Shingle", a pet scheme of Churchill, who had succeeded in winning over both Roosevelt and Stalin. He had even agreed to sacrifice to it the amphibious forces collected together for a landing on Rhodes. Did Churchill see further than his Allies? It seems likely that had the German 10th Army been annihilated during the first two weeks of February, nothing would have prevented Churchill from renewing his demands on his Allies and perhaps demanding an exploitation of this victory in the direction of Ljubljana and the abandonment of a landing in Provence, as planned at Teheran.

But everything was to go against him. First of all, General Clark considerably toned down the instructions given to him on January 12 by Sir Harold Alexander, commanding the 15th Army Group. Alexander saw the mission of the American VI Corps as follows: "to cut the enemy's main communications in the Colli Laziali (Alban Hills) area southeast of Rome, and threaten the rear of the XIV German Corps". Clark's directive of the same date to General Lucas merely required him "to seize and secure a beachhead in the vicinity of Anzio" and thence "to advance on the Colli Laziali".

This threefold manoeuvre (seize, secure, and advance) clearly did not reflect Alexander's original intention, but Alexander did not order Clark to change his directive so as to bring it into line with his own. As we shall see him giving in to his subordinate again on the following May 26, we can take it that it was not merely an oversight. We must believe that in acting as he did, General Clark was still under the strain of the Salerno landings, though he says nothing of this in his memoirs. John Lucas, entrusted with carrying out Operation "Shingle", noted in his diary: "It will be worse than the Dardanelles". His friend George S. Patton, spitting fire and smelling a fight in the offing, had said to him:

"'John, there is no one in the Army I

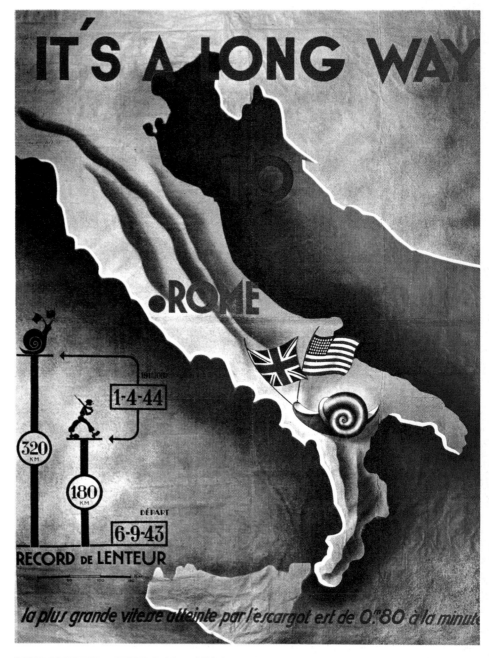

△ *For the benefit of the Allies in Italy: a cynical German comment on the slow pace of the march on Rome.*
◁ ◁ *G.I.s plod through the gaping jaws of a landing ship with their equipment.*
◁ *A landing ship heads inshore, packed with motor transport.*

would hate to see killed as much as you, but you can't get out of this alive. Of course, you might be badly wounded. No one ever blames a *wounded* general!' He advised Lucas to read the Bible when the going got tough, and then turned to one of the VI Corps commander's aides and said, 'Look here; if things get too bad, shoot the old man in the backside; but don't you dare kill the man!'"

About a week before D-day, an ill-fated landing exercise hastily carried out in the Gulf of Salerno only served to confirm Major-General Lucas's pessimistic forecast.

The wrong analysis

The 5th Army plan to take the Cassino defile placed the main burden on the American II Corps (Major-General Geoffrey Keyes). Forcing the Rapido at San Angelo, five miles south of Cassino, it would drive up the Liri valley and its tanks would exploit the success towards Frosinone then Anzio. This action was to be supported on the right by the French Expeditionary Corps (General Juin) and on the left by the British X Corps (Lieutenant-General Sir Richard McCreery).

"It was a somewhat simple concept," wrote Marshal Juin, "revealing a bold temperament which everyone recognised in the 5th Army commander, but at the same time it was at fault in that it ignored certain strategic principles and betrayed a false notion of distances and especially of the terrain in this peninsula of Italy where mountains—and what mountains! —dominate the landscape."

Sure enough the British X Corps, though it established a bridgehead on the right bank of the Garigliano (resulting from the confluence of the Liri and the Rapido), came to grief on the slopes of Monte Maio. The American 36th Division (Major-General F. L. Walker) of II Corps was even less fortunate, losing the strip of land it had won two days before on the right bank of the Rapido with casualties of 143 dead, 663 wounded, and 875 missing. On the right the 3rd Algerian Division (General de Monsabert) and the 2nd Moroccan Division (General Dody), attacking in line abreast, captured the heights of Monna Casale and Costa San Pietro (4,920 ft). But the French Expeditionary Corps did not have the reserves to exploit this success in the direction of

Atina, from where it might have been possible to get down into the Liri valley behind the defence line along the Rapido.

General Clark had six divisions (54 battalions) and his opponent, General von Senger und Etterlin (XIV Panzer Corps), had four with only six battalions apiece. This indicates how the terrain favoured the defenders, who were also valiant, well-trained, and better led. They were, however, stretched to the limit and Vietinghoff had to ask Kesselring for reinforcements. Kesselring took it upon himself to send him the 29th and the 90th *Panzergrenadier* Divisions from Rome, where they had been stationed in reserve.

"Considering what happened," General Westphal, at the time chief-of-staff of Army Group "C", wrote in 1953, "it was a mistake. The attack and the crossing at the mouth of the Garigliano were only a diversion intended to pin down our forces and to get us to drain our resources away from Rome as far as possible. The Allied commander's aim was fully achieved." Three years later Kesselring answered this charge, though without naming Westphal, to some point:

"I was well aware of the enemy's possible moves. One of these possibilities always stood out more clearly than the others. The attack by the American II Corps and the French Expeditionary Corps on positions north of Monte Cassino was clearly linked to the fighting on the Garigliano and increased its chances of success.

"Another possibility, that is the landing, was still only a faint one. We did not know yet when or where this would be. If I had refused the request of the 10th Army's commander, his right flank could have been dented and there seemed to be no way of knowing how it could have been restored." The German field-marshal seems to have been right in his judgement

△ ◁ *On the quayside.*
▽ ◁ *Down the ramp and into Anzio town.*
▽ *Kesselring's gunners wake up: a German shell scores a near hit on D.U.K.W.s heading in towards the beaches.*
Overleaf: *Extending the limited accommodation of Anzio harbour: a floating causeway from ship to shore.*

because on the eve of the event Admiral Canaris, head of the *Abwehr,* had told him that in his opinion no Allied landing was to be expected in Italy in the near future.

The Anzio landings

No other landing in Europe or the Pacific was initially as successful, and at such little cost, as that at Anzio-Nettuno in Operation "Shingle". By midnight on January 22, that is after 22 hours of operations, Rear-Admirals Frank J. Lowry of the U.S. Navy and Thomas H. Troubridge of the Royal Navy had landed 36,034 men, 3,069 vehicles, and 90 per cent of the assault equipment of the U.S. VI Corps. This comprised the British 1st Division (Major-General W. Penney), the American 3rd Division (Major-General L. K. Truscott), a regiment and a battalion of paratroops, three battalions of rangers, and a brigade of commandos. Losses amounted to 13 killed, 44 missing, and 97 wounded. The supporting naval forces, four light cruisers and 24 destroyers, had neutralised the fire of the shore batteries and two German battalions had been overrun on the beaches. "And that was all," wrote General Westphal as he reckoned up his weak forces. "There was nothing else in the area we could have thrown against the enemy on that same day. The road to Rome (37 miles) was now open. No-one could have prevented a force which drove on hard from entering the Eternal City. For two days after the landing we were in a breath-taking situation. Our counter-measures could only take effect after 48 hours."

Kesselring musters his strength

The General Staff of Army Group "C" had made several studies of a possible Allied landing of some strategic importance. For each hypothesis envisaged (Istria, Ravenna, Civitavecchia, Leghorn, Viareggio), the formations which would fight it had been detailed off, the routes they would have to take marked out, and their tasks laid down. Each hypothetical situation had been given a keyword. Kesselring only had to signal "*Fall*

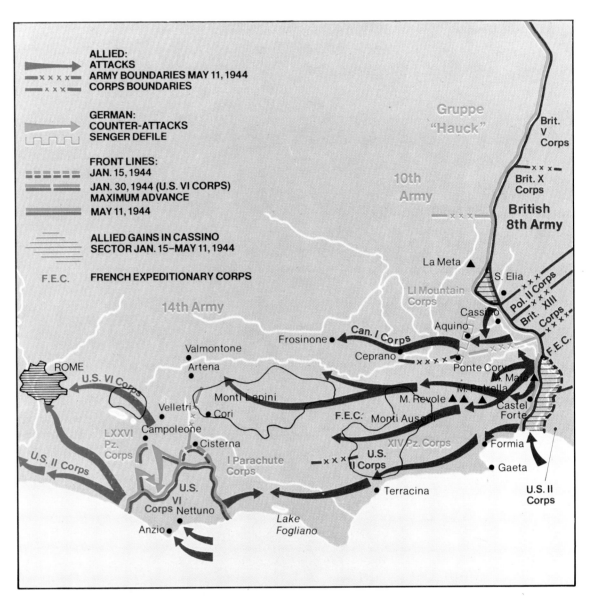

▷ *The Anzio landings and the break-through at Cassino.*

ALLIED:
ATTACKS
ARMY BOUNDARIES MAY 11, 1944
CORPS BOUNDARIES

GERMAN:
COUNTER-ATTACKS
SENGER DEFILE

FRONT LINES:
JAN. 15, 1944
JAN. 30, 1944 (U.S. VI CORPS)
MAXIMUM ADVANCE
MAY 11, 1944

ALLIED GAINS IN CASSINO
SECTOR JAN. 15–MAY 11, 1944

F.E.C.   FRENCH EXPEDITIONARY CORPS

Gruppe "Hauck"

Brit. V Corps

10th Army

Brit. X Corps

British 8th Army

La Meta ▲

S. Elia

LI Mountain Corps

Pol. II Corps

Brit. XIII Corps

Cassino

Aquino

F.E.C.

14th Army

Frosinone   Can. I Corps

Valmontone

Artena

Ceprano

Ponte Corvo

M. Maio ▲

M. Petrella

ROME

U.S. VI Corps

Monti Lepini

M. Revole ▲ ▲ ▲

Castel Forte

Velletri

Cori

F.E.C.

Monti Ausoni

LXXVI Pz. Corps

Campoleone

Cisterna

I Parachute Corps

XIV Pz. Corps

Formia

U.S. II Corps

U.S. II Corps

Gaeta

U.S. VI Corps

Nettuno

Terracina

U.S. II Corps

Anzio

Lake Fogliano

▽ *A Sherman tank heads inland from the beach-head. With the forces, both infantry and tank, available to him soon after the initial landings, could Lucas have pressed on inland and cut the Germans' communications between Rome and Cassino?*

Richard" for the following to converge on the Anzio bridgehead:

1. the "Hermann Göring" Panzer Division from the area of Frosinone and the 4th Parachute Division from Terni, both in I Parachute Corps (General Schlemm)
2. from the Sangro front LXXVI Panzer Corps (General Herr: 26th Panzer and 3rd *Panzergrenadier* Divisions); from the Garigliano front the 29th *Panzergrenadier* Division, newly arrived in the sector; and
3. from northern Italy the staff of the 14th Army and the 65th and 362nd Divisions which had crossed the Apennines as quickly as the frost and snow would allow them.

But O.K.W. intervened and ordered Field-Marshal von Rundstedt to hand over to Kesselring the 715th Division, then stationed in the Marseilles area, and Colonel-General Löhr, commanding in the Balkans, to send him his 114th *Jäger* Division.

On January 23, when Colonel-General von Mackensen arrived to take charge of operations against the Allied forces, all that lay between Anzio and Rome was a detachment of the "Hermann Göring" Panzer Division and a hotchpotch of artillery ranging from the odd 8.8-cm A.A. to Italian, French, and Yugoslav field guns. Despite the talents of Kesselring as an improviser and the capabilities of his general staff, a week was to pass before the German 14th Army could offer any consistent opposition to the Allied offensive.

On the Allied side, however, Major-General John P. Lucas thought only of consolidating his bridgehead and getting ashore the balance of his corps, the 45th Division (Major-General W. Eagles) and the 1st Armoured Division (Major-General E. N. Harmon). It will be recognised that in so doing he was only carrying out the task allotted to the 5th Army. On January 28 his 1st Armoured Division had indeed captured Aprilia, over ten miles north of Anzio, but on his right the American 3rd Division had been driven back opposite Cisterna. On the same day Mackensen had three divisions in the line and enough units to make up a fourth; by the last day of the month he was to have eight.

Was a great strategic opportunity lost between dawn on January 22 and twilight on the 28th? In London Churchill was champing with impatience and wrote to Sir Harold Alexander: "I expected to see a wild cat roaring into the mountains—

and what do I find? A whale wallowing on the beaches!"

Returning to the subject in his memoirs, Churchill wrote: "The spectacle of 18,000 vehicles accumulated ashore by the fourteenth day for only 70,000 men, or less than four men to a vehicle, including drivers and attendants . . . was astonishing."

Churchill might perhaps be accused of yielding too easily to the spite he felt at the setbacks of Operation "Shingle", for which he had pleaded so eagerly to Stalin and Roosevelt. These were, however, not the feelings of the official historian of the U.S. Navy who wrote ten years after the event:

"It was the only amphibious operation in that theater where the Army was unable promptly to exploit a successful landing, or where the enemy contained Allied forces on a beachhead for a prolonged period. Indeed, in the entire war there is none to compare with it; even the Okinawa campaign in the Pacific was shorter."

We would go along with this statement, implying as it does that the blame lay here, were it not for General Truscott's opinion, which is entirely opposed to Morison's quoted above. Truscott lived through every detail of the Anzio landings as commander of the 3rd Division, then as second-in-command to General Lucas, whom he eventually replaced. He was recognised by his fellow-officers as a first-class leader, resolute, aggressive,

△ *Part of 5th Army's complement (over-extravagant according to Churchill) of soft skinned and armoured vehicles.*

and very competent. His evidence is therefore to be reckoned with:

"I suppose that armchair strategists will always labour under the delusion that there was a 'fleeting opportunity' at Anzio during which some Napoleonic figure would have charged over the Colli Laziali (Alban Hills), played havoc with the German line of communications, and galloped on into Rome. Any such concept betrays lack of comprehension of the military problem involved. It was necessary to occupy the Corps Beachhead Line to prevent the enemy from interfering with the beaches, otherwise enemy artillery and armoured detachments operating against the flanks could have cut us off from the beach and prevented the unloading of troops, supplies, and equipment. As it was, the Corps Beachhead Line was barely distant enough to prevent direct artillery fire on the beaches.

"On January 24th (i.e. on D+2) my division, with three Ranger battalions and the 504th Parachute Regiment attached, was extended on the Corps Beachhead Line, over a front of twenty miles ... Two brigade groups of the British 1st Division held a front of more than seven miles."

In his opinion again the Allied high command overestimated the psychological effect on the enemy's morale of the simple news of an Anglo-American landing behind the 10th Army. This is shown by the text of a leaflet dropped to German troops, pointing out the apparently impossible strategic situation in which they were now caught, pinned down at Cassino and outflanked at Anzio, and urging them to surrender.

Kesselring beats Alexander to the punch

But far from allowing himself to be intimidated, Kesselring assembled his forces with a promptness underestimated by Alexander and Clark. Another reason why he was able to race them to it was because the latter were somewhat short of *matériel* for amphibious operations. The figures speak for themselves: on June 6, 1944 for a first wave of 12 divisions Eisenhower had 3,065 landing craft, whereas Anzio had 237 for four divisions.

Under these conditions, even if Lucas had had the temperament of a Patton, one could hardly have expected him to throw his forces into an attack on the Colli Laziali, over 20 miles from Anzio, with the two divisions of his first echelon and not worry also about his flanks and communications. Finally, Lucas did not have this cavalier temperament, and the day after the landings he noted in his diary: "The tension in a battle like this is terrible. Who the hell would be a general?"

Enter Hitler

The chances lost here, however, were to give rise during the months of February and March to two of the most furious battles of the war. They both ended in defeat for the attacker. On February 29 Mackensen had to abandon his attempt to crush the Anzio beach-head and Clark reported that his repeated attempts to force the Cassino defile had failed.

The battle for the beach-head arose from Hitler's initiative. On January 28 he sent Kesselring the following directive, which is worth quoting in full, so well does it reveal the Führer's state of mind on the day after the disasters suffered by Army Group "South" on the Dniepr at Kanev, and at a time when everyone was expecting an Anglo-American attack across the Channel.

◁ △ *D.U.K.W.s on the beach at Anzio.*
◁ ▽ *A U.S. 155-mm "Long Tom" in action at Anzio.*
◁ *Almost like World War I all over again: a communication trench linking pillboxes in the British sector of the Anzio line.*
▽ *A British patrol pushes forward from the main Allied beach-head on a reconnaissance mission.*
▽ ▽ *War photographers receive their briefing in a wine cellar in Nettuno before moving to their assigned areas.*

"In a few days from now," he wrote, "the 'Battle for Rome' will start: this will decide the defence of Central Italy and the fate of the 10th Army. But it has an even greater significance, for the Nettuno landing is the first step of the invasion of Europe planned for 1944.

"The enemy's aim is to pin down and to wear out major German forces as far as possible from the English base in which the main body of the invasion force is being held in a constant state of readiness, and to gain experience for their future operations.

"The significance of the battle to be fought by the 14th Army must be made clear to each one of its soldiers.

"It will not be enough to give clear and correct tactical orders. The army, the air force, and the navy must be imbued with a fanatical determination to come

out victorious from this battle and to hang on until the last enemy soldier has been exterminated or driven back into the sea. The men will fight with a solemn hatred against an enemy who is waging a relentless war of extermination against the German people, an enemy to whom everything seems a legitimate means to this end, an enemy who, in the absence of any high ethical intention, is plotting the destruction of Germany and, along with her, that of European civilisation. The battle must be hard and without pity, and not only against the enemy but also against any leader of men who, in this decisive hour, shows any sign of weakness.

"As in Sicily, on the Rapido, and at Ortona, the enemy must be shown that the fighting strength of the German Army is still intact and that the great invasion of 1944 will be an invasion which will drown in the blood of the Anglo-Saxon soldiers."

That is why the German 14th Army, whilst it drove off the repeated attempts of the U.S. VI Corps to break out from Aprilia and to cut off the Rome–Gaeta railway at Campoleone, actively prepared to go over to the counter-attack as ordered. On February 10 a counter-attack led by the 3rd *Panzergrenadier* Division (Lieutenant-General Gräser) retook the station at Carroceto. That day the German communiqué announced 4,000 prisoners taken since January 22, whereas the Allies' figure was only 2,800. Rightly alarmed by these setbacks, General Clark sent the British 56th Division (Major-General Templer) into the bridgehead; also, at Alexander's suggestion, he appointed Truscott second-in-command of VI Corps. Meanwhile Colonel-General von Mackensen had been called to O.K.W. to put his plan for a counter-offensive before the Führer. The latter offered no objection when Mackensen explained his idea of driving his attack along the Albano–Anzio line, with diversionary attacks on either side. Hitler did not stop there, however, but took it upon himself to interfere in every detail of the plan, from which he expected wonders. Mackensen thus saw the front on which he was to attack, the troops he was to use, and even the deployment these forces were to adopt, all altered by Hitler.

The operation was entrusted to LXXVI Panzer Corps. It was to attack on a front of less than four miles with two divisions up and the 26th *Panzergrenadier* Division (Lieutenant-General von Lüttwitz) and the 20th *Panzergrenadier* Division (Lieutenant-General Fries) in army reserve. So, Hitler ordered, the infantry could be given supporting fire which would pulverise the enemy's defence. Mackensen tried in vain to point out that such a massive concentration would present a sitting target to the Anglo-American air forces and that *Luftflotte* II, under the command of Field-Marshal von Richthofen, did not have the means to fight them off. It was no good. Hitler also refused to listen to the argument that it was useless lining up the guns wheel to wheel with insufficient ammunition for them to fire at the required rate.

The attack started on February 16 as ordered by Hitler. There was a preliminary softening up by 300 guns, but the 114th and 715th Divisions, which were to advance side by side, were to be denied the support of a creeping barrage. The spongy ground of the Pontine marshes prevented the tanks and the assault guns, which were to support the waves of infantry, from getting off the roads. The 14th Army's offensive might have had the intermittent support of 20 to 30 Luftwaffe fighter-bombers, but the German troops on the ground had to withstand the assault of no less than 1,100 tons of bombs. The Anglo-American tactical air forces boxed in the battlefield and considerably hindered the movement of supplies up towards the 14th Army's front line units.

By nightfall LXXVI Panzer Corps had

▷ *The ruins of Anzio town.*

▽ *An American armoured car moves up towards the line through Anzio.*

advanced some three to four miles into the Allied lines and was about seven to eight miles from its objective of Anzio-Nettuno. Its guns had fired 6,500 shells, but had received ten times as many. For three days Mackensen attempted to regain the upper hand, but in vain: Truscott, who had just relieved Lucas, was too vigilant for him. On February 29, I Parachute Corps took up the attack again in the Cisterna area, but this came to a halt a few hundred yards from its point of departure. The battle around the bridgehead died down and General Clark reinforced the position with the British 5th and the American 34th Divisions. The beaches and the Allies' rear positions continued to be harassed by German heavy artillery with its observation posts up in the Colli Laziali. A huge 11-inch railway gun in particular played havoc among the defenders. The air force was unable to silence it since, as soon as it had fired, "Leopold", as its crew, or "Anzio Annie", as the Allies called it, withdrew into a tunnel near Castel Gandolfo.

At sea, Operation "Shingle" cost Admiral Sir John Cunningham, C.-in-C. Mediterranean, the light cruisers *Spartan* and *Penelope* and three destroyers, all of the Royal Navy. Amongst the weapons used by the Germans were glide bombs and human torpedoes, the latter making their first appearance with the Kriegsmarine.

CHAPTER 105
CASSINO: breaking the stalemate

On the Cassino front General Clark strove to take up the offensive again the day after the Anzio landing. The intention was that the American II Corps, now only one division strong (the 34th, commanded by Major-General Ryder) should cross the Rapido north of Cassino whilst the French Expeditionary Corps, after taking Monte Belvedere, would move down the Liri valley, sweeping past the back of Monte Cassino. This turning movement, to be carried out as it were within rifle range, did not appeal to General Juin, who thought it would have been better to hinge the manoeuvre on Atina. Out of loyalty to General Clark, however, he did not press the point.

After rapidly regrouping at an altitude of 325 feet in the area of San Elia, the 3rd Algerian Division set off to attack its objectives: Belvedere (2,370 feet) and Colle Abate (2,930 feet).

In view of the nature of the terrain, the operation seemed to face insurmountable difficulties. Marshal Juin acknowledges this in his memoirs. Describing an occasion when he was visited by General Giraud he wrote: "The last time I had seen him was during the most critical moment of my Belvedere operation. I took him up to General Monsabert's front line H.Q., from which it was possible to watch the whole action of the Tunisian 4th *Tirailleur* Regiment. He expressed surprise that I had taken upon myself such a hazardous affair and could not refrain

△ *"My God! I'd like to have a word or two with the character who coined 'All roads lead to Rome'." Though German, this cartoon was all too apt a comment on Allied fortunes in Italy.*
▽ *General Clark awards battle streamers to a* Nisei *unit.*

△ *French gunners in action on General Juin's French Expeditionary Corps' sector of the Cassino front.*

and grenade. But none of these three peaks is retaken. And ammunition runs out again; the parsimoniously distributed mouthfuls of food which make up our rations are far away. Hunger comes again and with hunger thirst, the terrible thirst which gnaws at your stomach and drills into your brain. As for sleep, that real sleep which restores, we haven't had any for a long time. Men are falling asleep now under shelling, in the midst of mines and bullets. They're killed almost before they know it. Only wounds wake them up. Some answer back, aiming their rifles and throwing their grenades in a state of half-consciousness." When it was relieved, the Tunisian 4th *Tirailleur* Regiment had lost its colonel, 39 officers, and 1,562 N.C.O.s and men: it was reduced to a third of its strength.

The Germans on their side had lost 1,200 prisoners, and to strengthen the 44th Division, which threatened at any moment to give way under the furious hammer-blows of the 3rd Algerian Division's attack, 10th Army had to send in one regiment of the 90th *Panzergrenadier* Division and another of the 71st Division, both from XIV Panzer Corps. So the French Expeditionary Corps managed to draw onto itself two-thirds of the 44 battalions then fighting opposite the American 5th Army.

The value of this force was well appreciated by General Clark. On the day after the furious fighting on Belvedere he wrote to Juin to express his admiration for the "splendid way" in which the corps had accomplished its mission, adding:

"By a carefully prepared and co-ordinated plan of operations you have launched and sustained a series of attacks which have had remarkable success in attaining their main objective, that is: to pin down by hard fighting the maximum possible number of enemy troops and thus prevent them from intervening against our landing and the establishment of our bridgehead at Anzio. By doing this you have thrown back the enemy along the whole length of your front and inflicted severe losses on troops which were already weary."

Some days later General Alexander associated himself with this praise, and these were no empty words. In his book on the Cassino battle, in which he took part the following February and March as paratroop battalion commander in the famous 1st Parachute Division, Rudolf

from reproaching me, adding: 'I thought I was the only hot-headed fool in our army, but I see today that it's catching'."

The defile was defended by the 44th Division, a famous unit which had been re-formed after Stalingrad and which, recruited in Austria, had taken the name, famous in Prince Eugene's army, of *"Hoch und Deutschmeister"*. The opposing forces were men of equal courage and tenacity. In the afternoon of January 25 the Tunisian 4th *Tirailleur* Regiment (Colonel Roux) raised the tricolour on the two heights it had scaled under withering cross-fire, but one of its battalions was virtually wiped out on the Colle Abate, whilst the other two drove off one counter-attack after another to stay on Belvedere, but only at a heavy price.

René Chambe has left this account of the dramatic combat: "Night passes. This is one of the most critical of all. From right to left the Gandoët, Bacqué, and Péponnet battalions are clinging to the sides of Hills 862, 771, and 700. The enemy is counter-attacking furiously everywhere. He is driven off by bayonet

Böhmler makes the same observation: "The greatest surprise, however, was the fighting spirit shown by the French Expeditionary Corps. The 1940 campaign had cast a sombre shadow over the French Army, and no one believed that it would ever recover from the devastating defeat that had been inflicted on it. But now General Juin's divisions were proving to be the most dangerous customers. Nor was this attributable solely to the Algerians' and Moroccans' experience in mountain warfare. Three factors combined to mould these troops into a dangerously efficient fighting force: the mountain warfare experience of the French colonial troops, the ultra-modern American equipment with which they had been equipped, and the fact that they were led by French officers who were masters of the profession of arms. With these three basic elements Juin had moulded a formidable entity. In the battles that followed, the Corps proved equal to every demand made of it, and Field-Marshal Kesselring himself assured the author that he was always uneasy about any sector of the front on which the French popped up.

"Had Clark given more heed to Juin's views in the Cassino battles and accepted his plan of thrusting via Atina into the Liri valley, the three savage battles of Cassino would probably never have been fought and the venerable House of St. Benedict would have been left unscathed."

With two divisions so hard pressed there was no question of Juin's being able to exploit his costly victory at Belvedere, which now left him in front of the rest of the Allied line. Some time afterwards he was reinforced by General Utili's motorised group, the first Italian formation to move up to the front again (having had its first taste of fighting in December). It operated on the right of the French Expeditionary Corps in the snowy massif of the Abruzzi and acquitted itself well.

In the American II Corps area, the 34th Division did not succeed in breaking out of the bridgehead it had won on the right bank of the Rapido.

The monastery destroyed

Not wishing to leave things in this state of half-failure, General Alexander put at the disposal of the 5th Army the New Zealand Corps (Lieutenant-General Freyberg), consisting of the 2nd New Zealand, the 4th Indian, and the British 78th Divisions.

But before launching his attack, General Freyberg demanded the destruction of the historic Monte Cassino abbey which

▽ *The bombing on March 15. Overleaf: Aftermath of the bombing campaign.*

Above the town, at the top of Monte Cassino, stood the Abbey of St. Benedict, a religious foundation of great importance in which the body of St. Benedict was preserved. Believing quite erroneously that the Germans had turned the abbey into an observation post, the Allies bombed this too. The Germans managed to evacuate the abbot and his monks, together with the treasures, as the bombing started. And when the destruction was complete, the Germans took over the ruins.
▽ Hits on and around the abbey.
▽▽ The bombardment.

overlooked the Liri valley from a height of 1,700 feet. General Clark showed some scepticism when informed by his subordinates that the Germans were using the monastery as an artillery observation post and had heavy weapons stored inside it. He thus wholeheartedly opposed this act of vandalism and it is a fact, proved over and over again, that on the evening before February 15 the only soldiers anywhere near the monastery were three military policemen stationed there to keep the troops out.

Freyberg appealed to Alexander, who finally agreed with him, perhaps on the evidence of a misinterpreted radio message. A German voice had been heard asking:

"'Wo ist der Abt? Ist er noch im Kloster?' (Where is the 'Abt'? Is it still in the monastery?)

"'Abt' is the German military abbreviation for 'abteilung', meaning a section. But unfortunately 'Abt' also means 'Abbot', and since 'Abt' is masculine and 'abteilung' feminine, the conversation referred to the Abbot."

Sir Henry Maitland Wilson, C.-in-C. Mediterranean, made available the necessary air formations. In the morning of February 15, therefore, 142 four-engined and 87 two-engined American bombers flew over Monte Cassino in three waves, dropping 453 tons of high explosive and incendiary bombs, and reduced the monastery of Saint Benedict to a complete and absolute ruin.

"The monks had no idea that the rumble of heavy bombers which they could hear approaching from the north concerned them in any way. Prayers were just being said in the bishop's small room. The monks were praying to the Mother of God to protect them, and when they reached the words *'pro nobis Christum exora'*, a terrific explosion shattered the peace. The first bombs were bursting. It was nine forty-five."

This bombardment, of which he disapproved, aroused two different impressions in General Clark. In his book *Calculated Risk* he says:

"... and when the clock got around to nine-thirty, I immediately heard the first hum of engines coming up from the south. I tried to judge their progress by the steadily increasing volume of sound, a mental chore that was interrupted by a sudden roaring explosion. Sixteen bombs had been released by mistake from the American planes; several of them hit near my command post, sending fragments flying all over the place, but fortunately injuring no one, except the feelings of my police dog, Mike, who at that time was the proud mother of six week-old pups.

"Then the four groups of stately Flying Fortresses passed directly overhead and a few moments later released their bombs on Monastery Hill. I had seen the famous old Abbey, with its priceless and irreplaceable works of art, only from a distance, but with the thundering salvoes that tore apart the hillside that morning, I knew there was no possibility that I ever would see it at any closer range."

The Germans dig in

After the massive Allied air attack on February 15, Monte Cassino lay in ruins. But following this bombardment the German defenders moved into the ruins of the monastery and drove off with heavy losses the 4th Indian Division (Major-General Tuker) coming up to assault the peak. The 2nd New Zealand Division (Major-General Kippenberger) suffered the same fate before Cassino.

The second battle for the Liri valley was a definite success for the defenders, XIV Panzer Corps. The third brought General von Senger und Etterlin the high honour of Oak Leaves to his Iron Cross.

Clark and Freyberg, in spite of Juin's further representations in favour of the Atina manoeuvre, stuck to the narrower

△ German officers help the abbot into the car taking him to safety.

▽ Cassino town after the raid of March 15, when 775 aircraft dropped 1,250 tons of bombs.

pincer, which had just failed, combined with carpet bombing, which was of more use to the defenders than the attacking forces.

On March 15, 775 bombers and fighter-bombers, including 260 B-17 Flying Fortresses, dropped 1,250 tons of bombs on the little town of Cassino and its immediate surroundings. It was then shelled for two hours from 1230 hours by 746 guns. But when the Ghurkas and the New Zealanders moved in to attack they found to their cost that, as Böhmler says:

"The U.S. Air Force had presented the Germans with a first-class obstacle: the towering piles of rubble, the torn and debris-strewn streets, the innumerable deep bomb craters made it quite impossible for the New Zealand 4th Armoured Brigade to penetrate into the town and support the infantry. Its tanks had to halt on the edge and leave the infantry to its own devices as soon as the latter penetrated the zone of ruin and rubble. The most strenuous efforts to clear a way for the tanks with bulldozers made painfully slow progress."

The attackers, whether stumbling over the rubble in the little town of Cassino or trying to scale the heights of the monastery above it, were up against the 1st Parachute Division, an élite German unit with a fine commander, Lieutenant-General Richard Heidrich, and commanding positions. The area was sown with mines, on one of which Major-General Kippenberger, commanding the 2nd New Zealand Division, had both his feet blown off. The defenders, though cruelly decimated, were ably supported by concentrated fire from a regiment of *Nebel-werfers*.

The fighting in the streets of Cassino resembled that in Stalingrad in its ferocity. On the slopes up to the monastery Ghurkas and paratroops fought for a few yards of ground as in the trench warfare of World War I.

On March 23 Freyberg called off his attack, which had already cost him over 2,000 men and had reached none of its objectives.

From January 16 to March 31 the American 5th Army alone suffered casualties amounting to 52,130 killed, wounded and missing (American 22,219, British 22,092, French 7,421, and Italian 398).

This would appear to justify Clausewitz's principle, quoted shortly before by Manstein to Hitler, that defence is the "most powerful form of warfare".

◁ ◁ *The gutted abbey.*
◁ *American infantry advance along a path (marked with white tapes) cleared of mines and booby traps by the engineers.*
▽ *The monastery.*

CHAPTER 106
Drive to Rome

Faced with the setbacks of Anzio and Cassino, Sir Harold Alexander now had to remedy the situation. He did so by bringing the British V Corps directly under his command and allotting to it the Adriatic sector. The British 8th Army, under the command of General Sir Oliver Leese since December 23, was given the sector between the Abruzzi peaks and the Liri valley. The American 5th Army, though still responsible for the Anzio front, was thus restricted to the area between the Liri and the Tyrrhenian Sea. It also had to hand the British X Corps, on the Garigliano, over to the 8th Army.

The decision of the Combined Chiefs-of-Staff Committee not to go on with Operation "Anvil" as the prelude to a landing in Normandy was communicated to General Maitland Wilson on February 26. He was thus able to divert to the 15th Army Group units and *matériel* previously reserved for this operation. On May 11 Alexander had under his command nine corps, of 26 divisions and about ten independent brigades.

His aim was the destruction of the German 10th Army by a double pincer movement: the first would open up the Liri valley to the Allies and the second would begin, once they had passed Frosinone, by VI Corps breaking out of the Anzio beach-head and advancing to meet them.

Juin proposes an entirely new plan

In the French Expeditionary Corps, which had taken over from the British X Corps in the Garigliano bridgehead, General Juin was not satisfied with the objective assigned to him, Monte Majo. It was the same kind of narrow turning movement "within rifle range" that had led to the Belvedere butchery and the setbacks at Cassino. So on April 4 he set out his ideas on the manoeuvre in a memorandum to General Clark. In his opinion, instead of turning right as soon as Monte Majo had been captured, "they should infiltrate under cover of surprise into the massif dominated by the Petrella and seize the

◁ ◁ *A cheerful column of American infantry presses on unopposed in the final swift drive on Rome.*
△ *A Canadian prepares to lob a grenade into a house suspected of containing a German position. Behind him two other Canadians are ready to rush in and mop up.*
◁ *Germans taken prisoner at Cisterna.*

key points . . . and, from there, by an out-flanking movement, open the way to frontal advances mounted concurrently to secure Highway 7 and the road from Esperia up to and including the road running parallel to the front of Arce.

"The aim being to bring to bear on the Arce sector a force of considerable size so as to be able to break out in strength behind the enemy's rear and advance towards Rome."

Clark agrees

After a little hesitation Clark was won over to his subordinate's plan. This had the great advantage of including in the French Expeditionary Corps' out-flanking movement the Hitler Line or "Senger defile", which blocked off the Liri valley at Pontecorvo. On the other hand there was a formidable obstacle in the Monti Aurunci, which reached over 5,000 feet at Monte Petrella. It might be assumed that the enemy had not occupied the heights in strength, and that surprise could be achieved by using the natural features as Guderian had done in the Ardennes in May 1940 and List in the Strumitsa gap on April 6, 1941.

However, everything depended on the speed with which an early success could be exploited. As usual, Kesselring would

◁ *Typical Italian terrain: a constant succession of steep ridges divided by swift-flowing streams and rivers. In the foreground two Americans provide covering machine gun fire for an attack.*
▽ *Lieutenant-General Mark Clark, commander of the American 5th Army. Was he right to push on to the political objective of Rome rather than pursuing the military objective of cutting off major German units just north of Cassino?*

General Juin (centre, with goggles) explains his plans to General de Gaulle.

▽ French troops enter Castelforte

not take long to muster his forces, but General Juin was relying on the legs of his Moroccan mountain troops and of his 4,000 mules.

Though Clark agreed to the French plan, he could not get Sir Oliver Leese to accept its corollary, the Atina plan, and though he used a corps against Cassino where Freyberg had sent in one

division, the pincer was still too short and there were heavy losses.

Kesselring had 23 divisions, but most of them were worn out and short of ammunition, whereas the Allies had an abundance of everything. Here again the Germans were waging "a poor man's war" as General Westphal put it.

Another serious disadvantage for Kesselring was his enemy's overwhelming superiority in the air and at sea. This was so important that it caused him to worry not only about a landing at Civitavecchia or at Leghorn but also about whether Allied air power would cut off XIV Panzer Corps' communications at Frosinone. The uncertainty of his situation compelled Kesselring to write in his memoirs about his main reason for concern at this time: "The great dangerous unknown quantity which lasted until D-day plus 4 was the following: where would the French Expeditionary Corps be engaged, what would be its main line of advance and its composition?"

The military balance

And so the 10th Army and subordinate staffs were ordered to signal back with maximum urgency to Army Group as soon as the French had been identified on the front. The Expeditionary Corps had camouflaged itself so well when it moved into position in the foothills of the Monti Aurunci that Kesselring only realised it was there when the Monte Majo action was over. A clever decoy movement by Alexander made him think that the frontal attack would be combined with a landing in the area of Civitavecchia and would start on May 14, and so two German divisions were held north of Rome, and arrived too late at the battle for the Gustav Line.

At zero on D-day the German 10th Army was deployed as follows:

1. from the Tyrrhenian Sea to the Liri: XIV Panzer Corps (94th and 71st Infantry Divisions);
2. from the Liri to the Meta (7,400 feet): LI Mountain Corps (Gruppe "Baade", 1st Parachute, 44th Infantry, and 5th Gebirgsjäger Divisions);
3. from the Meta to the Adriatic: Gruppe "Hauck" (305th and 334th Infantry Divisions, 114th Jäger Division); and
4. in army reserve: 15th Panzergrenadier Division behind LI Mountain Corps.

The first encounter was thus to be

between the 12 Allied divisions (two Polish, four British, four French, and two American) and six German. The inferiority was not only numerical: at the moment when the attack started both General von Senger und Etterlin, commander of XIV Panzer Corps and Colonel-General von Vietinghoff were on leave, and, in spite of Kesselring's order, 94th Division (Lieutenant-General Steinmetz) had no men on the Petrella massif.

The French go in

At 2300 hours on May 11, 600 Allied batteries (2,400 guns ranging from 25-pounders to 9.4-inch) opened up simultaneously on a front of some 25 miles. At midnight the Allied infantry moved forward. When dawn broke both General Leese and General Clark had to admit that in spite of the surprise effect the night attack had not brought the expected success. The Polish II Corps (General Wladislas Anders: 3rd "Kressowa" and 5th "Carpathian" Divisions) had failed on the slopes of Monte Cassino and, for all the fighting spirit shown by these men, escapees from Russian jails, their losses were very heavy. In the Liri valley the British XIII Corps (Lieutenant-General Kirkman) had got two of its divisions across the Rapido, but without really denting the resistance put up by LI Mountain Corps (General Feuerstein) and here again 1st Parachute Division was particularly successful.

Though the French Expeditionary Corps had been strengthened by the 4th Moroccan Mountain Division (General Sévez) and the 1st Motorised Infantry Division (General Brosset) its task was not made any easier by the fact that the enemy opposite (71st Division: Lieutenant-General Raapke) was ready and expecting to be attacked. During this night operation, which they were ordered to carry out so as to facilitate the British XIII Corps' crossing of the Rapido, the French stumbled on to minefields and were attacked by flame-throwers. By the end of the day on the 12th it was feared that the

△ General Anders, whose Polish troops were responsible for the final success at Cassino.

▽ French troops with their German prisoners at Castelforte

French attack might have run out of steam and that Kesselring would have time to occupy the whole of the Petrella massif. Without losing a minute, General Juin reshaped his artillery attack so as to concentrate everything on the Monte Majo bastion. This bold stroke broke the resistance of the German 71st Division and in the afternoon of May 13 the Moroccan 2nd Division raised an immense tricolour on the top of the 3,000-foot hill. On its right the 1st Moroccan Motorised Infantry Division had cleared out the bend in the Garigliano. On its left the 3rd Algerian Division had captured Castelforte and was moving forward towards Ausonia.

The French push round the east flank

Further over to the left the American II Corps was well on its way to Formia. On that day, as Marshal Juin wrote,

The Liri valley, before Cassino. In the foreground is a knocked-out Sherman tank, and in the background an ambulance, with its crew going to pick up casualties.
▷ *A road on the way to Rome under German shellfire.*
▽▷ *The legs of the swift Allied advance once the obstacle of Cassino had been removed.*

"having toured the fronts in the lower areas from end to end of the bridgehead where the actions were developed, I was able to see with what ardour and enthusiasm the troops drove forward to their objectives. It is true that the commanders were there in the breach in person: Brosset, driving his own jeep, was giving orders through a loud-hailer and Montsabert was conducting his battle by means of a portable radio which never left his side. There were also other reasons for this feverish excitement. Towards mid-day a message was heard in clear from the enemy ordering his troops to withdraw and the prisoners were flowing in."

Without losing a moment General Juin threw his Mountain Corps into the breach. This now included the 4th Moroccan Mountain Division and General Guillaume's Moroccan *Tabors*. Leaving the beaten tracks, with their machine guns and mortars on their backs, they scaled the steep slopes of Monte Petrella like mountain goats, reaching the top on May 15. Without waiting to get their breath back they then hurled themselves at the Revole massif (4,150 feet). Meanwhile, passing behind the Mountain Corps, the 3rd Algerian Division took Ausonia and reached Esperia, thus extending the action of the 1st Moroccan Motorised Infantry Division which had captured San Giorgio on the right bank of the Liri.

Poles, British, and Americans drive forward

What would have happened if at the same time the British 8th Army, in a sweep as wide as General Juin had wanted, had outflanked the Pontecorvo position? In all evidence XIV Panzer Corps would have faced total disaster, a disaster which would then have overtaken the 10th Army. It was only on May 17 that the Polish II Corps, now attacking again, found the monastery on Monte Cassino deserted. It was again only on May 19 that the British 78th Division (XIII Corps) attacked the "Senger defile" in the Aquino area, but unsuccessfully. This lack of liaison between the French and the British naturally held up the French Expeditionary Corps' exploitation towards Pico and the Monti Ausoni.

But Kesselring, throwing in everything he could lay hands on, sent units of the 90th *Panzergrenadier,* the 305th, and the 26th Panzer Divisions to stop them. He also sent the 29th *Panzergrenadier* Division against the American II Corps, which had advanced through Formia and Itri and by May 22 was threatening Terracina. This was trying to pay Paul by robbing Peter, that is to say Colonel-General von Mackensen. Reinforced to the equivalent of eight divisions by the transfer of the American 36th Division to the Anzio bridgehead, the American VI Corps had no particular difficulty in breaking the resistance of the German 14th Army during the day of May 23. Forty-eight hours later II and VI Corps met on the shores of Lake Fogliano. On the same May 23 the French Expeditionary Corps was spreading out over the Monti Ausoni whilst the Canadian I Corps (Lieutenant-General E. L. M. Burns: 1st Infantry and 5th Armoured Divisions), which had just relieved the British XIII Corps, was forcing its way through the Pontecorvo defile.

Kesselring attempts to cover Rome

Kesselring tried once more to protect Rome by establishing a new position on the line Colli Laziali–Monti Lepini to secure Vietinghoff's right, and to achieve this he withdrew from the Leghorn area his last reserve motorised division, the "Hermann Göring" Panzer Division, and sent it immediately to Valmontone. The bombing by the Anglo-American air force, which on one single day (May 26) destroyed 665 vehicles of the 14th Army alone, considerably held up these troop movements. Now Valmontone was, in accordance with General Alexander's instructions, precisely the objective of the American VI Corps. If Truscott, now in Cisterna, therefore advanced with the main body of his forces along the Corti–Artena axis, he had every chance of cutting off the 10th Army's move to cover Rome. The latter's rearguard was still at Ceprano, some 40 miles or more from Valmontone, and the Germans would thus be driven back against the Abruzzi mountains, which were virtually impassable, and entirely cut off.

But, for reasons which Alexander said were inexplicable, Clark ordered VI Corps to attack with its 34th, 45th Infantry, and 1st Armoured Divisions north west to the line Velletri–Colli Laziali, sending only a slightly reinforced 3rd Division along the Valmontone axis (northwards). This decision, taken in the afternoon of May 25, brought only a slight reaction from Alexander, who remarked to General Gruenther, the American 5th Army chief-of-staff, when the latter brought him the news: "I am sure that the army commander will continue to push toward Valmontone, won't he?"

"Rome the great prize" was the title General Mark Clark gave to the 15th chapter of his memoirs. We are thus forced to conclude that this able but impetuous man had lost sight of the fact that a commander's supreme reward is to receive in his tent those who have been sent on behalf of the enemy commander to sue for conditions of surrender. But Alexander was also taken in by the Roman mirage at this time: did he not forbid the French Expeditionary Corps, then coming down from the Monti Lepini,

◁ ◁ *Homeless Italians strive to escape from the war.*
▽ ◁ ◁ *Italian refugees pass through the Allied lines on their way to the safety of rear areas.*
◁ *A village destroyed in the Allied advance from Cassino.*
▽ *Clark (left) enters the suburbs of Rome.*
Overleaf: *Rome was the first Axis capital to fall to the Allies, and in a special ceremony in July, the American flag that had been flying over the White House on December 7, 1941 was raised in front of the Victor Emmanuel II monument. The troops taking part in the retreat ceremony were from the 85th Division.*

to use the Frosinone–Rome highway, which he intended to restrict to the British 8th Army?

Oddly enough, back in London, Churchill tried to put Alexander on his guard against the attractions of this prestige objective. On May 28 he wrote to him: "at this distance it seems much more important to cut their line of retreat than anything else. I am sure you will have carefully considered moving more armour by the Appian Way up to the northernmost spearhead directed against the Valmontone-Frosinone road. A cop is much more important than Rome which would anyhow come as its consequence. The cop is the one thing that matters." Two days later he came back to the point: "But I should feel myself wanting in comradeship if I did not let you know that the glory of this battle, already great, will be measured, not by the capture of Rome or the juncture with the bridgehead, but by the number of German divisions cut off. I am sure you will have revolved all this in your mind, and perhaps you have already acted in this way. Nevertheless I feel I ought to tell you that it is the cop that counts."

Rome declared an "open city"

These were words of wisdom indeed, but
in Italy the die was cast in the shape of
the objective given to the American VI
Corps. On May 31 its 36th Division found
a gap in the German 14th Army defences,
turned the Velletri position and scaled
the Colli Laziali. Furious at this setback,
Kesselring recalled Mackensen and replaced him with General Lemelsen. He now
had to order the evacuation of Rome,
which he proclaimed an "open city".
On June 4 the American 88th Division
(Major-General J. E. Sloan) was the
first unit to enter the Eternal City.

General Clark tells a story worthy of
inclusion in any history of the campaign.
Writing of his first visit to Rome he says:
"Many Romans seemed to be on the

verge of hysteria in their enthusiasm for the American troops. The Americans were enthusiastic too, and kept looking for ancient landmarks that they had read about in their history books. It was on that day that a doughboy made the classic remark of the Italian campaign when he took a long look at the ruins of the old Colosseum, whistled softly, and said, 'Geez, I didn't know our bombers had done *that* much damage in Rome!'"

German and Allied losses

On May 11 Kesselring had 23 divisions. These had been reduced to remnants. The 44th, 71st, 94th, 362nd, and 715th had been virtually wiped out. His Panzer and *Panzergrenadier* divisions had lost most of their equipment. Amongst the reinforcements which Hitler had sent

through the Brenner there were badly trained divisions such as the 162nd, recruited from Turkman contingents, the Luftwaffe 20th Infantry Division, and the 16th *Panzergrenadier* Division of the *Waffen* S.S. These went to pieces at the first onslaught.

During the same period the Americans lost 18,000 killed, missing, and wounded, the British 10,500, the French 7,260, the Canadians 3,742, and the Poles 3,700. Some 25,000 Allied prisoners were taken.

Churchill's hopes of a new offensive

These losses were not enough to hold up the 15th Army Group's advance. Also, in North Africa the 9th Colonial Infantry Division and the 1st and 5th French Armoured Divisions were now ready for combat. It is clear that a bold

▽ *Mark Clark talks to a priest outside St. Peter's on his arrival in the city on June 4.*

action along the Rome–Terni–Ancona axis could have brought to an end all enemy resistance south of the Apennines.

Churchill wrote to Alexander on May 31: "I will support you in obtaining the first priority in everything you need to achieve this glorious victory. I am sure the American Chiefs-of-Staff would now feel this was a bad moment to pull out of the battle or in any way weaken its force for the sake of other operations of an amphibious character, which may very soon take their place in the van of our ideas."

In other words the Prime Minister was flattering himself that he could get General Marshall to abandon Operation "Anvil" and exploit the victories of the 15th Army Group across the Apennines.

On June 7, three days after the fall of Rome, Alexander reported that not even the Alps could daunt his army. He struck a chord in Churchill's mind for the Prime Minister now saw a chance of reaching Yugoslavia or even Vienna (across the

▽ *American troops celebrate the fall of Rome.*

△ Lieutenant Rex Metcalfe of
Flint, Michigan, inspects his
men before setting off to do
guard duty.

iterranean theatre now that "Overlord"
was so close, and all effort had to be
concentrated.

Marshall, it would appear, was merely
obeying the dictates of high strategy. It
was clear to him, in effect, that an Anglo-
American drive towards Vienna, and out
of line with the main thrust, would
contribute less to the success of Operation "Overlord" than would a landing in
Provence, which would open up the ports
of Marseilles and Toulon to Allied men
and *matériel*, whilst a strong Franco-
American force, operating first up the
Rhône, then the Saône, would give a
right wing to Eisenhower when he broke
out into Champagne. To him this reasoning respected the principle of the con-
vergence of effort, so dear to American
military doctrine. It can easily be seen
how Marshall froze at Churchill's
passionate arguments.

In any case, it is highly doubtful on
military grounds whether an advance to
the Alps or into Yugoslavia in 1944 was
practicable, even if Alexander's armies
had not been weakened for the sake of
"Dragoon". The German commanders had
proved themselves masters of defensive
warfare in mountain regions, and they
were to continue giving the Allies immense problems even when operating with
minimal resources and under pressure
from all sides.

Kesselring re-establishes himself in the Apennines

Although Roosevelt could not accept his
colleague's views, he was nevertheless
unable to bring nearer by even a single
day because of questions of transport,
men, and *matériel*, the start of Operation
"Anvil" scheduled for August 15. Between
June 11 and July 22, three American and
five French divisions successively
dropped out and became inactive, though
the 9th Colonial Division did take Elba
between July 17 and 19 in Operation
"Brassard", led by General de Lattre de
Tassigny. This Allied inactivity allowed
Kesselring, who lost no chances, to
re-establish himself in the Apennines
and especially to give Field-Marshal von
Rundstedt his 3rd and 15th *Panzergrenadier* Divisions, whilst the "Hermann
Göring" Panzer Division was sent off
to the Eastern Front.

so-called Ljubljana gap) before
Russians, whose political ambitions he
was beginning to fear. Additionally
Churchill had always favoured an invasion of German-occupied Europe from
the Mediterranean.

The agreed strategy is confirmed

However, not even the British Chiefs-of-
Staff believed that an advance to the Alps
and beyond that year was practical, while
President Roosevelt and the American
Chiefs-of-Staff remained adamant that
Operation "Dragoon" (formerly "Anvil"),
the landing in the south of France, must,
as formally agreed, now take precedence
over any other operations in the Med-